ECE/EB.AIR/44

ECONOMIC COMMISSION FOR EUROPE
Geneva

STRATEGIES AND POLICIES
FOR
AIR POLLUTION
ABATEMENT

1994 major review prepared under
the Convention on Long-range Transboundary Air Pollution

UNITED NATIONS
New York and Geneva, 1995

NOTE

Symbols of United Nations documents are composed of capital letters combined with figures. Mention of such a symbol indicates a reference to a United Nations document.

*

* *

The designations employed and the presentation of the material in this publication do not imply the expression of any opinion whatsoever on the part of the Secretariat of the United Nations concerning the legal status of any country, territory, city or area, or of its authorities, or concerning the delimitation of its frontiers or boundaries.

ECE/EB.AIR/44

UNITED NATIONS PUBLICATION

Sales No. E.95.II.E.15

ISBN 92-1-116628-4

CONTENTS

LIST OF TABLES

LIST OF CHARTS AND MAPS

INTRODUCTION: MANDATE AND AIM OF THE REVIEW

By the terms of the Convention on Long-range Transboundary Air Pollution, the Contracting Parties shall, *inter alia*, "endeavour to limit and, as far as possible, gradually reduce and prevent air pollution including long-range transboundary air pollution" (article 2); "develop... policies and strategies which shall serve as a means of combating the discharge of air pollutants" (article 3); and "exchange information on and review their policies ... aimed at combating... the discharge of air pollutants" (article 4). Furthermore, by the terms of article 8 (*g*), they shall "exchange available information on national, subregional and regional policies and strategies for the control of sulphur compounds and other major air pollutants". The resolution on long-range transboundary air pollution adopted in 1979 at the High-level Meeting within the Framework of the ECE on the Protection of the Environment states that the Signatories to the Convention will seek to bring closer together their policies and strategies for combating air pollution including long-range transboundary air pollution (ECE/HLM.1/2, annex II).

The Helsinki Protocol on the Reduction of Sulphur Emissions or their Transboundary Fluxes by at least 30% calls upon Parties to develop "national programmes, policies and strategies... and report thereon as well as on progress towards achieving the goal to the Executive Body" (article 6). Finally, by the terms of article 8 (Information exchange and annual reporting) of the Sofia Protocol concerning the Control of Emissions of Nitrogen Oxides or their Transboundary Fluxes:

"1. The Parties shall exchange information by notifying the Executive Body of the national programmes, policies and strategies that they develop in accordance with article 7 and by reporting to it annually on progress achieved under, and any changes to, those programmes, policies and strategies, and in particular on:

"(*a*) The levels of national annual emissions of nitrogen oxides and the basis upon which they have been calculated;

"(*b*) Progress in applying national emission standards required...;

"(*c*) Progress in introducing the pollution control measures...;

"(*d*) Progress in making unleaded fuel available;

"(*e*) Measures taken to facilitate the exchange of technology; and

"(*f*) Progress in establishing critical loads.

"2. Such information shall, as far as possible, be submitted in accordance with a uniform reporting framework."

Similar provisions are made in the Geneva Protocol concerning the Control of Emissions of Volatile Organic Compounds or their Transboundary Fluxes, which was adopted and signed in 1991, and in the Oslo Protocol on Further Reduction of Sulphur Emissions, which was adopted and signed in 1994. These two protocols have, however, not yet entered into force.

The overall aim of the major review is to examine and thus further the implementation of the Convention and its related protocols. The analysis of measures to abate emissions of sulphur, nitrogen and volatile organic compounds and of the actual and projected levels of emission of these pollutants will be an important element of the review. Such an analysis should allow conclusions to be drawn about the need for further policy measures to reach the objectives of the Convention and its protocols and provide information for the development of further strategies on the national and international levels. This also includes the support of cooperative efforts in the different bodies working within the framework of the Convention.

In 1994, Parties and Signatories were requested to submit the information required for this major review. To facilitate responses a questionnaire, prepared on the basis of the annotated outline of the major review, was provided. By 16 January 1995, the secretariat had received information from 33 Parties. Twenty-nine Parties (Austria, Belarus, Belgium, Bosnia and Herzegovina, Bulgaria, Canada, Croatia, Cyprus, Czech Republic, Denmark, Finland, France, Germany, Greece, Italy, Netherlands, Norway, Poland, Portugal, Russian Federation, Slovakia, Slovenia, Spain, Sweden, Switzerland, Ukraine, United Kingdom, United States, and the European Community) provided the information on strategies and policies that forms the basis for chapters II, III and IV.

Chapter I

EMISSION LEVELS AND TRENDS IN THE EFFECTS OF AIR POLLUTANTS

A. NATIONAL ANNUAL TOTAL EMISSIONS IN THE ECE REGION, 1980-2010

Country-by-country data on national total emissions and current reduction plans for future years are presented in seven tables: table 1, sulphur dioxide emissions 1980-2010; table 2, nitrogen oxide emissions 1980-2010; table 3, ammonia emissions 1980-2010; table 4, emissions of non-methane volatile organic compounds 1980-2010; table 5, emissions of methane 1980-2010; table 6, carbon monoxide emissions 1980-2010; and table 7, carbon dioxide emissions 1980-2010. The emission data have been received from Parties in official submissions in the context of this major review, or previous reviews. Also data on sulphur emissions for Parties that signed the Protocol on Further Reduction of Sulphur Emission in June 1994 were taken from annex II of that Protocol (ECE/EB.AIR/40). On the basis of tables 1 and 2, a graphical representation of trends (1980-1993) in the levels of sulphur and nitrogen oxide emissions for the ECE region as a whole and selected subregions is given in figures I.1 and I.2.

To estimate emissions, Parties generally employed source statistics and emission factors as defined within the CORINAIR programme for the 1990 inventory. In some cases, such as Italy, the emission data for the years 1985 to 1989 were estimated on the basis of the CORINAIR '85 methodology whereas estimates for subsequent years are based on the CORINAIR'90 methodology. Future recalculations based on the latest methodologies may lead to some adjustments. For the years 1985 to 1992 the emissions data for Belgium were calculated on the basis of the emission inventories of the Brussels, Flanders and Wallonia regions.

Emission projections were reported for the following two scenarios: (1) current reduction plans, reflecting the politically determined intention to reach specific targets; and (2) the baseline scenario, reflecting the state of legal/regulatory provisions in place by 31 December 1993 and, in addition, as an indication of the uncertainty of projections, an upper and a lower limit for emission projections. Data falling under category (1) are included in tables 1 to 7, whereas those falling under category (2) are reported in tables 8.1 to 8.6, projections of emissions of major air pollutants for the years 1995, 2000, 2005 and 2010.

B. NATIONAL ANNUAL EMISSIONS BY SOURCE CATEGORY FOR THE YEARS 1985, 1990-1993 AND 2000

Emission inventories by source categories are presented in tables 9.1-9.6 (national annual emissions of major air pollutants by source category), with a separate table for each pollutant and each Party for which data have been received. The source category split adopted with the guidelines is based on engineering principles consistent with national practice. Definitions of these source categories are taken from the report of the EMEP Workshop on Emission Inventory Techniques, Regensburg (Germany), 2-5 July 1991. Items 1 to 10 comprise anthropogenic emissions, whereas item 11 is foreseen for biogenic and natural emissions uncontrolled by man. Emission inventory data by source category were requested for 1985 and every year from 1990 onwards; projections in this format were requested for the year 2000. A summary of these data for sulphur, nitrogen oxides, VOCs and CO for those Parties that submitted a complete set of data, is given in figures II.1-4 (national annual emissions by source category for the years 1985, 1990-1993 and 2000).

TABLE 1

Emissions of sulphur (1980-2010*) in the ECE region

(Thousands of tonnes of SO₂ per year)

	1980	1981	1982	1983	1984	1985	1986	1987	1988	1989	1990	1991	1992	1993	1995*	2000*	2005*	2010*
Austria	397			242		195		152	122	93	90	84	76	71	80	78		
Belarus	740	730	710	710	690	690	690	811	780	720	710	724	509	433	592	552	490	
Belgium	828	712	694	560	500	400	377	367	354	325	317	324	304			248	232	215
Bosnia and Herzegovina											480							
Bulgaria	2050							2420	2228	2180	2020	1667	1120	1422	1380	1374	1230	1127
Canada	4614	4241	3612	3625	3955	3692	3627	3762	3835	3695	3267	3151	3030	3042	2831	2969	3075	3120
Croatia	150 [a]										180					133	125	117
Cyprus						36	37	41	46	47	51	41	45	43	50	62	62	62
Czech Republic	2257	2341	2387	2338	2305	2277	2177	2164	2066	1998	1876	1776	1538	1419	1128	538		
Denmark	451	362	369	314	296	339	284	251	242	193	180	242	189	157	169	90	90	
Finland	584	534	484	372	366	383	332	328	302	244	260	194	139	121		116	116	116
France	3338	2588	2490	2094	1866	1470	1342	1290	1226	1334	1298	1378	1238	1136		868	770	737
Germany	3166 [b]	3010 [b]	2843 [b]	2666 [b]	2578 [b]	2369 [b]	2230 [b]	1907 [b]	1218 [b]	939 [b]	5633	4430	3896 [c]			1300	990	
Germany, former GDR	4320	4374	4611	4678	5084	5385	5406	5434	5255	5250								
Greece	400					500					510					595	580	570
Hungary	1633					1404	1362	1285	1218	1102	1010	913	827			898	816	653
Iceland	6				6	6												
Ireland	222	192	158	142	142	140	162	174	152	162	178	179	160		155			
Italy	3800 [c]		3150 [c]		2656 [c]	2244 [c]	2257 [c]	2274 [c]	2216 [c]	2001 [c]	2251				1535	1209	1042	
Liechtenstein	0.4				0.1						0.1					0.1		
Luxembourg	24			14		16										10		
Netherlands	489	463	403	323	299	261	263	262	247	205	201 [d]	177	167 [c]	168 [c]		92		56
Norway	142	127	110	103	95	98	91	74	67	59	54	45	37	37		34		
Poland	4100 [e]					4300 [e]	4200 [e]	4200 [e]	4180 [e]	3910 [e]	3210 [f]	2996 [e]	2830 [e]	2725		2583	2173	1397
Portugal	266		306			198	234	218	204		282	290 [c]	346 [c]	290 [c]		304	294	
Romania								1762	2397	1647	1504	1167	559					
Russian Federation	7161 [g]	6949 [g]	7090 [g]	6934 [g]	6503 [g]	6191 [g]	5707 [g]	5622 [g]	5145 [g]	4677 [g]	4460 [g]	4392 [g]	3839 [g]	3456 [g]		4440 [g]	4297 [g]	4297 [g]
Slovakia	780					613	604	614	589	573	543	446	380	325		337	295	240
Slovenia	235	254	256	270	249	240	244	218	210	211	195	180	188	182		92	45	37
Spain	3319			2543		2190	1961	1903	1587	1950	2316					2143		
Sweden	507	431	371	304	296	267	272	226	224	160	130	113	102	103 [c]	100	100		
Switzerland	126				95			80	73	68	62	62	59	58	55 [c]	57 [c]	58 [c]	60 [c]
Turkey	860				276	322	354											
Ukraine	3850	3492	3427	3498	3470	3463	3393	3264	3211	3073	2782	2538	2376	2194	2073	2069	2069	2069
United Kingdom	4898	4438	4213	3682	3721	3726	3897	3900	3813	3721	3780	3574	3500	3069 [c]	2951	2320	1470	980
United States	23779	22512	21211	20618	21467	21218	20391	20520	20948	21042	20701	20659	20621			15000		14220
Yugoslavia	406 [h]	408 [h]	409 [h]	440 [h]	456 [h]	478 [h]	470 [h]	484 [h]	502 [h]	506 [h]	508 [h]	446 [h]	396 [h]	401 [h]	508 [h]	680 [h]	889 [h]	1135 [h]
European Community	25513 [i]					13626 [i]										8860 [j]		

Source : data submitted by the Parties to the Convention on Long-Range Transboundary Air Pollution.

* Projections based on current reduction plans.

Emissions of sulphur : Notes

a Estimate.
b Figures apply to the Federal Republic of Germany as prior to 1989.
c Preliminary data.
d Slightly different from CORINAIR 1990.
e Not based on the EMEP/CORINAIR methodology.
f 3273 kt according to the EMEP/CORINAIR methodology.
g Figures apply to the European part within EMEP.
h Emissions from stationary sources only.
i CORINAIR total of 12 EC member States.
j 5th Community Programme of Policy and Action in Relation to the Environment and Sustainable Development.

TABLE 2

Emissions of nitrogen oxides (1980-2010*) in the ECE region

(Thousands of tonnes of NO_2 per year)

	1980	1981	1982	1983	1984	1985	1986	1987	1988	1989	1990	1991	1992	1993	1995*	2000*	2005*	2010*
Austria	246			241		245		234	226	221	222	216	201	182	171	155		
Belarus	234	235	235	237	240	238	258	263	262	263	285	281	224	206	251	217	184	
Belgium	442					315	307	321	335	347	343	347	350					
Bulgaria								416	415	411	376	273	260	238	300	380	350	290
Canada	1959	1907	1897	1884	1871	1984	1959	2037	2117	2120	1999	1976	1939	1952	1972	2000	2059	2167
Croatia	60[a]										83							
Cyprus						9	9	10	10	11	11	13	13	14	15	18	20	20
Czech Republic	937	819	818	830	844	831	826	816	858	920	742	725	698	574	573	398		
Denmark	274	240	260	254	266	294	312	302	292	272	269	319	274	264	254	203	192	
Finland	264	248	245	236	233	252	256	270	276	284	284	286	257	253		224	224	224
France	1823	1701	1688	1645	1632	1615	1618	1630	1615	1772	1584	1619	1599	1519				
Germany	2926[b]	2842[b]	2817[b]	2862[b]	2923[b]	2908[b]	2939[b]	2861[b]	2777[b]	2617[b]	3033	2934	2904[c]					
Germany, former GDR	514	510	513	514	550	568	572	590	596	604								
Greece	273					306									280	279		
Hungary						262	264	265	258	246	238	203	183					
Iceland	13				12	12												
Ireland	73	86	86	85	84	91	100	115	122	127	115	119	125		130[d]	129[d]	121[d]	
Italy	1480[c]				1568[c]	1741[c]	1804[c]	1904[c]	1982[c]	2035[c]	2053				2128	2098	2060	
Liechtenstein	1					1					1							
Luxembourg	23		21		19													
Netherlands	582	575	561	554	571	573	586	597	599	583	570[e]	561	550[c]	568[c]		249		120
Norway	186	178	183	190	205	216	230	237	229	233	231	220	220	225		161[f]		
Poland	1500[g]					1500[g]	1590[g]	1530[g]	1550[g]	1480[g]	1280[h]	1205[g]	1130[g]	1140		1345		
Portugal	166		192			96	110	116	122	221	221	232[c]	248[c]	245[c]				
Romania								369	253	1753	883	805	443					
Russian Federation	1734[l]	1915[l]	2002[l]	1976[l]	1879[l]	1903[l]	1871[l]	2653[l]	2358[l]	2553[l]	2675[l]	2571[l]	2298[l]	2269[l]				
Slovakia								197		227	227	212	192	184				
Slovenia	48[j]	49[j]	49[j]	48[j]	49[j]	50[j]	54[j]	53[j]	55[j]	54[j]	53[j]	50[j]	51[j]	57[j]				
Spain	950		937	937		839	854	892	892	992	1257					892		
Sweden	424	417	412	401	411	426	432	434	412	404	398	397	391	391	376	312	303	311[a]
Switzerland	196			192	214			200	194	189	184	175	161	150	127[c]	100[c]	98[c]	99[c]
Turkey	1145	1145	1153	1153	1102	1059	1112	1094	1090	1065	1097	989	830	700	700	700	700	700
Ukraine																		
United Kingdom	2392	2328	2312	2332	2321	2438	2533	2644	2749	2842	2860	2835	2750	2752	2460	2000	1842	1860
United States	18672	18609	18048	17488	17952	17785	17614	18028	18677	18512	18599	18535	18217			18180		20070
Yugoslavia	47[k]	50[k]	50[k]	53[k]	58[k]	58[k]	58[k]	60[k]	63[k]	62[k]	66[k]	57[k]	49[k]	54[k]	66[k]	88[k]	115[k]	147[k]
European Community						10428[l]										7300[m]		

Source : data submitted by the Parties to the Convention on Long-Range Transboundary Air Pollution.

* Projections based on current reduction plans.

Emissions of nitrogen oxides : Notes

a   *Estimate.*

b   *Figures apply to the Federal Republic of Germany as prior to 1989.*

c   *Preliminary data.*

d   *Based on current administrative regulations.*

e   *Slightly different from CORINAIR 1990.*

f   *Data for 1998. Target value.*

g   *Not based on the EMEP/CORINAIR methodology.*

h   *1446 kt according to the EMEP/CORINAIR methodology.*

i   *Figures apply to the European part within EMEP.*

j   *New emission factors.*

k   *Emissions from stationary sources only.*

l   *CORINAIR total of 12 EC member States.*

m   *5th Community Programme of Policy and Action in Relation to the Environment and Sustainable Development.*

TABLE 3

Emissions of ammonia (1980-2010*) in the ECE region

(Thousands of tonnes of NH$_3$ per year)

	1980	1981	1982	1983	1984	1985	1986	1987	1988	1989	1990	1991	1992	1993	1995*	2000*	2005*	2010*
Austria											99[a]	99[a]	100[a]	101[a]				
Belarus											4[b]							
Belgium						74					79	78	77					
Bulgaria											323	280	130	220	140	143	140	140
Canada																		
Croatia																		
Cyprus																		
Czech Republic																		
Denmark						152		152		146	140	134		126	121	103		
Finland						43		45			41	41	41			32	23	23
France											645	635	623	625				
Germany	571[d]	558[d]	565[d]	576[d]	586[d]	589[d]	581[d]	572[d]	561[d]	557[d]	759	666	648[c]					
Germany, former GDR	263	264	253	266	268	268	266	266	270	262								
Greece																		
Hungary	170					170	170	150		170	176	150	140					
Iceland																		
Ireland											126							
Italy						508[c]	505[c]	506[c]	501[c]	497[c]	384							
Liechtenstein																		
Luxembourg																		
Netherlands	251						258			234	215[e]	221	170[c]	162[c]		82		50
Norway									38	39	39	39	40	40				
Poland	550[g]					550[g]	550[g]	550[g]	550[g]	550[g]	550[h]	470[g]	447[g]	382		41[f]		
Portugal											93	93[c]	93[c]	93[c]				
Romania																		
Russian Federation	1189[i]	1192[i]	1214[i]	1245[i]	1247[i]	1239[i]	1286[i]	1277[i]	1269[i]	1258[i]	1191[j]	1161[j]	1084[j]	903[j]				
Slovakia											62		61					
Slovenia																		
Spain											324							
Sweden											74	73	72	71[c]	69	68	67	66[k]
Switzerland	62				60						61	61	62	63	62[c]	63[c]	64[c]	65[c]
Turkey																		
Ukraine											23[b]							
United Kingdom											382			382[c]		382		
United States						1685												
Yugoslavia																		
European Community																		

Source : data submitted by the Parties to the Convention on Long-Range Transboundary Air Pollution.

* Projections based on current reduction plans.

Emissions of ammonia : Notes

a   Including nature.
b   Based on the gridded emissions.
c   Preliminary data.
d   Figures apply to the Federal Republic of Germany as prior to 1989.
e   Slightly different from CORINAIR 1990.
f   Based on the emissions by source category.
g   Not based on the EMEP/CORINAIR methodology.
h   581 kt according to the EMEP/CORINAIR methodology.
i   Figures apply to the European part within EMEP. Agricultural sector only.
j   Figures apply to the European part within EMEP. Including industrial sources.
k   Estimate.

TABLE 4

Emissions of NMVOCs (1980-2010*) in the ECE region

(Thousands of tonnes per year)

	1980	1981	1982	1983	1984	1985	1986	1987	1988	1989	1990	1991	1992	1993	1995*	2000*	2005*	2010*
Austria	374			391		412		439	432	434	430	419	403	388	366	305		
Belarus	549	546	543	543	540	516	506	509	535	511	533	545	412	372	442	380	323	
Belgium						688					395	393	399					
Bulgaria											393	380	375	375	357	357	276	265
Canada						2107	2120	2161	2181	2191	2086	2014	1985	1994	1997	2017	2122	2266
Croatia																		
Cyprus																		
Czech Republic						275					574 a	537 a	499 a	478 a				
Denmark	154 b	150 b	151 b	153 b	157 b	159 b	161 b	161 b	162 b	161 b	165 b	168 b	166 b	148		112 b		
Finland								210	215		209					151	108	108
France											2402 b	2361 b	2332 b	2286 b				
Germany	2676 c	2596 c	2600 c	2584 c	2595 c	2569 c	2560 c	2513 c	2439 c	2350 c	3008	2881	2791 a					
Germany, former GDR	667	672	639	652	676	706 (614 d)	717	742	771	769								
Greece	215					232	263	228	205	205								
Hungary											205	144	136					
Iceland																		
Ireland											197 e	105 f	104 f					
Italy						1771 a	1798 a	1865 a	1879 a	1913 a	2554							
Liechtenstein																		
Luxembourg																		
Netherlands	579 g	555 g	543 g	526 g	513 g	500 g	489 g	485 g	479 g	468 g	451 h	429 i	439 j	423 j		196 j		120
Norway	168	179	188	201	212	221	236	241	241	258	251	255	265	270		181 k		
Poland	1431 l					1439 l	1466 l	1471 l	1468 l	1452 l	1221 m	1231 l	1058 l	1058				
Portugal											644	663 a	620 a	624 a				
Romania													109					
Russian Federation	5513 n	5356 n	4886 n	4534 n	4400 n	4585 n	4307 n	4837 n	2790 o	3715 o	3566 o	3259 o	3204 o	2475 o				
Slovakia											146 p		124 p					
Slovenia									39		35							
Spain						1265 b	882 b	922 b	955 b		1112 b							
Sweden						600 q			586		533	516 q	501	489 r	445 b	342 b	287 b	
Switzerland	311			339							297	290	274	262	240 s	243 s	265 s	289 s
Turkey																		
Ukraine						1626	1660	1687	1604	1512	1369	1302	1171	972	972	972	972	972
United Kingdom	2432	2421	2427	2401	2405	2435	2477	2514	2567	2631	2612	2609	2556	2565 a	2100	1519	1340	1276
United States	25719	24044	22556	23053	23712	22691	22997	22430	22698	21690	21477	21232	20617			15930		15750
Yugoslavia																		
European Community																		

Source : data submitted by the Parties to the Convention on Long-Range Transboundary Air Pollution.

* Projections based on current reduction plans.

Emissions of NMVOCs : Notes

a Preliminary data.

b Not including nature.

c Figures apply to the Federal Republic of Germany as prior to 1989.

d Including CH4.

e Based on the emissions by source category.

f Based on the emissions by source category. Not including nature and agriculture.

g Including nature (3 kt), CFC (3 kt in 1992) and CH4 for source category 4 (3.7 kt in 1992).

h Slightly different from CORINAIR 1990. Including nature (3 kt), CFC (3 kt in 1992) and CH4 for source category 4 (3.7 kt in 1992).

i Including nature (3 kt) and excluding CH4 and CFC.

j Preliminary data. Including nature (3 kt), CFC (3 kt in 1992) and CH4 for source category 4 (3.7 kt in 1992).

k Data for 1999. Target value.

l Not based on the EMEP/CORINAIR methodology.

m 1295 kt according to the EMEP/CORINAIR methodology.

n Total emissions of hydrocarbons including CH4 from fuel industries. Figures apply to the European part within EMEP. Stationary and mobile sources.

o Total emissions of hydrocarbons excluding CH4. Figures apply to the European part within EMEP. Stationary and mobile sources.

p Anthropogenic only.

q Estimate. Not including nature.

r Preliminary data. Not including nature.

s Preliminary data. Including CH4 for mobile sources.

TABLE 5

Emissions of methane (1980-2010*) in the ECE region

(Thousands of tonnes of CH$_4$ per year)

	1980	1981	1982	1983	1984	1985	1986	1987	1988	1989	1990	1991	1992	1993	1995*	2000*	2005*	2010*
Austria											810 [a]	814 [a]	815 [a]	815 [a]				
Belarus																		
Belgium											370	387	420					
Bulgaria								646	660	638	589	442	439	664	450	450	420	420
Canada											2905					3300	3400	3500
Croatia																		
Cyprus																		
Czech Republic											1549	1421	1318	1230 [b]				
Denmark	403 [c]	405 [c]	406 [c]	406 [c]	406 [c]	407 [c]	407 [c]	407 [c]	407 [c]	406 [c]	406 [c]	408 [c]	408 [c]	407 [c]	382 [c]	355 [c]	354 [c]	
Finland									520		249 [d]							
France	5551 [f]	5519 [f]	5501 [f]	5394 [f]	5267 [f]	5326 [f]	5299 [f]	5163 [f]	5213 [f]	5056 [f]	3678 [e]	3944 [e]	3861 [e]	3850 [e]				
Germany											6214	6114	6164 [b]					
Germany, former GDR	1185	1205	1205	1235	1259	1301	1286	1291	1302	1282								
Greece											581							
Hungary																		
Iceland																		
Ireland											850 [g]							
Italy						2264 [b]	2331 [b]	2397 [b]	2469 [b]	2543 [b]	3778 [b]							
Liechtenstein																		
Luxembourg																		
Netherlands	1063 [h]					1146 [h]					1178	1200 [h]	1185 [l]	1160 [l]		1091		
Norway	264							280	280	287	289	289	293	294		291 [g]		
Poland											6107		3647 [l]	2990				
Portugal											379	381 [b]	372 [b]	372 [b]				
Romania													1424					
Russian Federation	5462 [k]	5414 [k]	5396 [k]	5423 [k]	5441 [k]	5427 [k]	12900 [l]	5428 [k]	5358 [k]	5312 [k]	5174 [k]	4923 [k]	4649 [k]	3680 [k]				
Slovakia											354 [m]		337 [m]					
Slovenia									90		82							
Spain											2985							
Sweden											340 [c]	339 [c]	337 [c]	336 [e]	335 [c]	300 [c]	296 [c]	
Switzerland	262				239						234	233	231	229	226 [b]	221 [b]	217 [b]	214 [b]
Turkey																		
Ukraine																		
United Kingdom	5185	5146	5117	5095	4399	4854	5008	4961	4911	4877	4828	4825	4736	4652 [b]	4811	4257	3993	3730
United States											27550 [n]							
Yugoslavia																		
European Community																		

Source : data submitted by the Parties to the Convention on Long-Range Transboundary Air Pollution.

* Projections based on current reduction plans.

Emissions of methane : Notes

a   Including nature.

b   Preliminary data.

c   Not including nature.

d   Based on the emissions by source category. Not including nature.

e   Preliminary data. Not including nature.

f   Figures apply to the Federal Republic of Germany as prior to 1989.

g   Based on the emissions by source category.

h   Including nature (121 kt).

i   Preliminary data. Including nature (121 kt).

j   Not based on the EMEP/CORINAIR methodology.

k   Figures apply to the European part within EMEP. Preliminary data including emissions from livestock.

l   Figures apply to the European part within EMEP. Preliminary data including emissions from livestock and mining industries.

m   Anthropogenic only.

n   20400 to 34700 kt.

TABLE 6

Emissions of carbon monoxide (1980-2010*) in the ECE region

(Thousands of tonnes of CO per year)

	1980	1981	1982	1983	1984	1985	1986	1987	1988	1989	1990	1991	1992	1993	1995*	2000*	2005*	2010*
Austria	1636 a			1561 a		1648 a		1684 a	1578 a	1605 a	1573 a	1503 a	1413 a	1326 a				
Belarus											191 b							
Belgium											1124	1131	1177					
Bulgaria								997	995	985	901	654	623	786	820	850	800	750
Canada	10273					10781					9778							
Croatia																		
Cyprus																		
Czech Republic	894		906		895	899	740	738	737	884	888	1102	1045	967				
Denmark	673	675	686	702	727	741	753	754	756	744	770	824	812	715		647	562	
Finland											556 a							
France	9216 c	9146 c	8858 c	8648 c	8529 c	8399 c	8156 c	8036 c	7821 c	7575 c	10736 c	10598 c	10268 c	9758 c				
Germany	12013 d	10772 d	9974 d	9293 d	9347 d	8939 d	8828 d	8471 d	8176 d	7762 d	10909	9604	9135 e					
Germany, former GDR	3487	3475	3339	3308	3505	3742	3786	4036	3964	3833								
Greece											804							
Hungary												915	836					
Iceland																		
Ireland											431 a							
Italy						6919 e	6821 e	6744 e	6668 e	6591 e	10347							
Liechtenstein																		
Luxembourg																		
Netherlands	1530	1418	1374	1354	1357	1307	1252	1192	1179	1131	1027 f	947	863 e	876 e				
Norway	886	872	892	894	923	958	1002	1013	997	954	940	880	851	836		602 a		
Poland											7406 g		7083 h	8655				
Portugal											1086	1109 e	1145 e	1168 e				
Romania								1016	1142	2655	2098	2376	498					
Russian Federation	13512 i	15005 i	13617 i	13696 i	13672 i	14122 i	13142 i	13119 i	12988 i	13054 i	13174 i	12869 i	11574 i	11193 i				
Slovakia											462		343					
Slovenia																		
Spain											4975							
Sweden											1347	1312	1275	1236 e	1164	760	631	
Switzerland	711				621						430	406	379	358	311 e	273 e	280 e	289 e
Turkey																		
Ukraine						9832	9722	9269	9085	8794	8141	7406	5496	4218	4218	4218	4218	4218
United Kingdom	5298	5361	5493	5462	5575	5797	6037	6323	6692	7103	7020	7021	6708	6708 e	5513	3324	1884	1374
United States	117032	111583	105369	105200	102489	97885	95159	90086	89874	84727	83807	82266	79092			64980		66780
Yugoslavia																		
European Community																		

Source : data submitted by the Parties to the Convention on Long-Range Transboundary Air Pollution.

* Projections based on current reduction plans.

Emissions of carbon monoxide : Notes

a Based on the emissions by source category.
b Based on the gridded emissions.
c Not including nature.
d Figures apply to the Federal Republic of Germany as prior to 1989.
e Preliminary data.
f Slightly different from CORINAIR 1990.
g 7389 kt according to the EMEP/CORINAIR methodology.
h Not based on the EMEP/CORINAIR methodology.
i Figures apply to the European part within EMEP.

TABLE 7

Emissions of carbon dioxide (1980-2010*) in the ECE region

(Millions of tonnes of CO_2 per year)

	1980	1981	1982	1983	1984	1985	1986	1987	1988	1989	1990	1991	1992	1993	1995*	2000*	2005*	2010*
Austria	59 [a]			55 [a]		57 [a]		58 [a]	56 [a]	56 [a]	60 [a]	64 [a]	58 [a]	58 [a]	65 [b]	66 [b]		
Belarus																		
Belgium																		
Bulgaria								100	102	98	91	68	68	72	75	80	80	80
Canada	440	442	401	387	404	421	416	434	466	490	461	452	466	470	471	518	546	564
Croatia																		
Cyprus																		
Czech Republic	196					194					171	161	148	144 [a]				
Denmark	63 [c]	53 [c]	55 [c]	53 [c]	54 [c]	62 [c]	62 [c]	60 [c]	56 [c]	50 [c]	52 [c]	63 [c]	57 [c]	59	59	54	52	
Finland											55 [d]					65 [d]	65 [d]	65 [d]
France	503	453	432	413	403	388	374	368	371	384	372	396	386	377				
Germany	797 [e]	762 [e]	728 [e]	728 [e]	739 [e]	731 [e]	736 [e]	724 [e]	716 [e]	701 [e]	1023	985	943 [a]	928 [a]				
Germany, former GDR	317	318	316	314	330	347	348	350	346	339								
Greece	48					59	58	63	67	72								
Hungary	92					89	87	87	84	81	74	72	66					
Iceland																		
Ireland											31	32 [a]						
Italy						408 [a]	414 [a]	434 [a]	443 [a]	458 [a]	441					232		
Liechtenstein																		
Luxembourg																		
Netherlands	167 [f]					150 [f]					174 [f]	174 [f]	177 [f]			175 [g]		
Norway	34	31	30	31	33	32	34	35	35	35	36	34	34	36		35 [h]		
Poland									509 [i]	488 [i]	407 [j]	397 [i]	393 [i]					
Portugal											57	61 [a]	56 [a]	53 [a]	46 [k]	54 [k]		
Romania								134	127	132	130	106	198					
Russian Federation						1560 [l]			1650 [l]		1670 [l]	1630 [l]	1630 [l]		1670 [l]	1760 [l]		1900 [l]
Slovakia											50 [a]		50 [a]					
Slovenia											13	12	13	13				
Spain						205	199	197	185	217	218					272		
Sweden	82 [m]	74 [m]	69 [m]	64 [m]	63 [m]	67 [m]	68 [m]	67 [m]	63 [m]	63 [m]	60 [m]	59 [m]	60 [m]	62 [n]	62	63	67	121 [o]
Switzerland											46 [p]					46 [p]		
Turkey																		
Ukraine																		
United Kingdom	164 [q]	157 [q]	154 [q]	152 [q]	148 [q]	154 [q]	158 [q]	159 [q]	159 [q]	156 [q]	158 [q]	159 [q]	155 [q]	154 [r]	156 [q]	168 [q]	164 [q]	
United States											4400							
Yugoslavia																		
European Community	2850	2715	2620	2575	2605	2660	2660	2700	2600		2765					2765		

Source : unofficial data submitted by the Parties to the Convention on Long-Range Transboundary Air Pollution, for information only.

* Projections based on current reduction plans.

Emissions of carbon dioxide : Notes

a Preliminary data.
b Excluding emissions from biogenic fuels.
c Emissions from biomass not included. Electricity import/export corrected.
d From fuels.
e Figures apply to the Federal Republic of Germany as prior to 1989.
f According to the national communication on climate change policies.
g 173-177 kt. According to the national communication on climate change policies.
h Target value.
i Not based on the EMEP/CORINAIR methodology.
j 415 kt according to the EMEP/CORINAIR methodology.
k Emissions from combustion only.
l Figures apply to the European part within EMEP.
m Excluding biomass fuels and biomass-related wastes.
n Preliminary data. Excluding biomass fuels and biomass-related wastes.
o Estimate.
p As reported under the Framework Convention on Climate Change.
q The United Kingdom does not endorse point estimates for future years.
r Preliminary data. The United Kingdom does not endorse point estimates for future years.

C.   THE SPATIAL RESOLUTION OF EMISSIONS FOR THE YEAR 1990

Parties within the geographical scope of EMEP were requested to report on emissions of sulphur, nitrogen oxides, ammonia and non-methane volatile organic compounds originating from their territory, at the level of 50 km x 50 km grid elements for the year 1990. Maps of the EMEP area giving absolute values of the emission level for each pollutant are presented in figures IV.1-4. The sulphur and nitrogen oxide data for Belgium, Denmark, France, Germany, Hungary, Luxembourg and Spain were not officially submitted, but calculated by EMEP-MSC-W on the basis of previously transmitted spatial distribution and current national emission levels.

D.   TRENDS IN THE ENVIRONMENTAL EFFECTS OF SULPHUR, NITROGEN OXIDES, AMMONIA AND VOLATILE ORGANIC COMPOUNDS

Within the framework of the Convention all effect-related International Cooperative Programmes (ICPs) (see chap. IV, sect. A) assess trends in the environmental effects of major air pollutants. Several reports (in particular on fresh waters, materials and integrated monitoring) with some preliminary interpretation of results have already been presented at the 1994 session of the Working Group on Effects. In their plans for future work, the ICPs pay special attention to the assessment of the long-term trends in effects. To stimulate and coordinate activities in this field, a workshop will be organized jointly by all ICPs in 1995.

Many Parties have national programmes for the evaluation of trends in environmental effects. Several Parties, especially in central and eastern Europe, stress the importance of adverse effects on human health. In general, Parties in western Europe report on improvements concerning levels of concentrations of SO_2, whereas NO_2 concentrations and related health problems in urban areas have not been reduced significantly. An area of increasing concern is the formation of photochemical smog during the summer months in urban areas. Many Parties emphasize the effects of acid deposition on ecosystems and materials, and state that there have been improvements, though limited, during the 1980s.

In *Belgium* air quality improved markedly with important reductions in urban SO_2 concentrations (to 30 $\mu g/m^3$ as a yearly average in 1992 in Brussels) and, since 1985, a stabilization of SO_2 levels in the ambient air, though the short-term air quality standards are still occasionally exceeded in some areas. The reduction in NO_2 concentrations has not been as significant and the short-term health guidelines (190 $\mu g/m^3$ hourly max.) are not met. In *Bulgaria* emissions of sulphur, nitrogen and volatile organic compounds lead to harmful effects in 17 areas covering only a small part of the national territory, but areas inhabited by over 40% of the population. In *Finland* significant reductions in sulphur depositions from domestic sources (to less than 0.5 g/m^2 per year) have been noted. In *Germany* annual mean SO_2 concentrations in ambient air have decreased considerably in conurbations, so that in the western part they are currently in the range of 20-40 $\mu g/m^3$ and in the eastern part they have decreased from above 300 to 100 $\mu g/m^3$. In rural areas measurements show a decrease in SO_2 from 11 $\mu g/m^3$ in 1973 to 6 $\mu g/m^3$ in 1993, whereas NO_2 concentrations remained stable at about 9 $\mu g/m^3$. In the *Netherlands* acidifying depositions have decreased from nearly 7000 eq./ha/yr in the early eighties to just above 4000 eq./ha/yr ten years later. In *Norway* sulphur concentrations in air and precipitation have been reduced by 30-40% since 1979, but critical loads are still exceeded in more than 30% of the country. Nitrate concentrations in lakes in southern Norway have almost doubled in the 1974-86 period and the high levels have since been maintained.

Chapter II

NATIONAL STRATEGIES

A. GENERAL OBJECTIVES AND TARGETS OF AIR POLLUTION ABATEMENT POLICY

1. Basic principles

A number of basic principles guide national policies for air pollution abatement in the ECE region:

(*a*) Sustainable development or *sustainability* is a long-term objective for the policies of many Parties. It was particularly stressed in the reports submitted by Austria, the Czech Republic, the Netherlands, Portugal, Slovenia, and the Russian Federation;

(*b*) The *precautionary principle* in some form or other is applied as a guiding principle in Austria, Croatia, the Czech Republic, Germany, Slovenia, Sweden, and Switzerland;

(*c*) The application of the *polluter-pays principle* at the national level is guiding national policy developments in Croatia, Cyprus, the Czech Republic, Germany, the Netherlands, Slovenia, Sweden, Switzerland, and the United Kingdom;

(*d*) A number of Parties (Cyprus, the Czech Republic, the Netherlands) set the objective for air pollution abatement policies to reduce emissions at their source, following a *pollution prevention* approach;

(*e*) In addition, Sweden applies a *substitution principle* in environmental legislation which stipulates that substances harmful to health and the environment should be replaced by less harmful ones.

2. General objectives and strategies

The following paragraphs give an overview of the basis for national strategies and their main objectives. Many Parties have developed action plans or long-term programmes to implement their strategies. Some Parties have specified objectives for air pollution abatement policies on the basis of the effects of those pollutants. Many Parties base their air pollution abatement policy on some notion of best available technology (BAT) or best available techniques not entailing excessive cost (BATNEEC). Most Parties, however, apply a combination of both, source- and effect-oriented principles.

(a) *Bosnia and Herzegovina*: At this moment, a detailed account of a strategy regarding air pollution is not feasible. National production of power plants and the industrial sector is, though slightly increasing, just over 10 per cent of what it was in the pre-war period. Only some minor monitoring and data work can be undertaken, thus not allowing any well-founded planning.

(b) *Bulgaria*: The National Environment Strategy for 1991-2000 was adopted in January 1992. It had been drawn up with the help of the United States Environmental Protection Agency, the World Bank and the Agency for International Development. The Strategy's action plan covers nine major areas, including legislation, standards, monitoring and economic instruments. In March 1994 the Strategy was updated. Two long-term programmes—on the reduction of sulphur and nitrogen oxide emissions and on the reduction of emissions of greenhouse gases by 2010—are being developed. They are expected to be completed in 1996.

(c) *Canada*: The basis for national air pollution abatement strategies can be divided into three categories: (i) programmes to meet international commitments aimed at solving global problems including the achievement of targets for greenhouse gas emissions and the phasing-out of ozone-depleting substances; (ii) national and sub-national emission management strategies to resolve and prevent regional air pollution problems, such as acidification, smog, air toxics and visibility deterioration; (iii) the use of bilateral and multilateral forums to reduce the impact of air pollutants that contribute to such air pollution problems.

(d) *Croatia*: With a view towards implementing a systematic policy on environmental protection in general and air pollution problems in particular, a national strategy is being drawn up to serve as the principal basis for coordinating economic interests and overall development efforts on the one hand and the need for environmental protection on the other.

(e) *Cyprus*: The Environmental Action Plan, approved by the Council of Ministers in 1991, is being implemented. It deals with those industrial units which need special and urgent attention because of the problems they create for the environment.

(f) *Denmark*: Environmental objectives are integrated into sectoral policies, in particular concerning energy, transport and agriculture (see sect. C below). In 1990 Parliament adopted two action plans related to energy and transport that set targets for greenhouse gas emissions. The targets for carbon dioxide emission reductions are expected to contribute to a 60% reduction in sulphur emissions and a 50% reduction in nitrogen oxide emissions by the year 2005 based on 1988 levels.

(g) *Finland*: The introduction of air pollution control measures was prepared with the broad participation of different groups in society. This work took place in committees such as the 1976 Committee on Air Pollution Control in Industrial Sectors, the 1985 Sulphur Committee and the 1988 Nitrogen Oxides Committee. By making use of structural adjustments and taking into account the timetable for process retrofitting, the cost of the resulting programmes was kept down.

(h) *Germany*: The main objective of the basic law on air quality control (see sect. B below) is to protect human beings, animals and plants, soil, water, the atmosphere, as well as cultural assets and other material goods against harmful environmental impacts. For this purpose a precautionary approach is followed to minimize environmental risks. This requires, in particular, that emission standards are continually updated to reflect the state of the art in emission reduction.

(i) *Greece*: The national strategy to reduce air pollution is based on a number of energy-related measures, such as fuel substitution, energy efficiency improvements and the use of cleaner fuels, and encouraging the fitting of pollution control devices to private vehicles.

(j) *Netherlands*: Environmental policy can be characterized by a number of general principles, in addition to those mentioned above there is the stand-still approach and the abatement at the source. A two-track policy is followed that bases source-oriented measures on both the precautionary principle and effect-oriented air quality standards. Thus source-based regulation is preferred as it permits better control and is generally less costly than effect-oriented measures. Regarding acidification and ozone formation, the goal of the Netherlands policy is to reduce effects to negligible levels in the long run. However, it is recognized that these levels cannot be reached at present and less ambitious long-term targets have been set (see chap. III, sects. A.1 and A.2). A framework for risk management has been developed for a number of substances that pose hazards to humans and their environment. Priority substances falling into this category are cadmium, lead, polyaromatic hydrocarbons (PAHs), dioxins, asbestos, fluorides, carbon monoxide ozone, particulates, hydrogen sulphide, ammonia, nitrogen oxides and sulphur dioxide. Criteria documents are drafted for each of these substances as a basis for abatement programmes. Guidelines have been drawn up for industrial air emissions, to be used by the licensing authorities for setting limit values in the permits. Under the National Environmental Policy Plan (NEPP), industrial sectors are in addition requested to come up with proposals on how to reach the emission reduction targets set in that plan. The first National Environmental Policy Plan (NEPP-1) appeared in 1989, NEPP-2 in 1993. NEPP-2 covers the main aspects of environmental policy and sets the framework for decisions to be taken during the following four years. It also includes an indication for policy directions in the longer term.

(k) *Poland*: The State Environmental Policy was adopted in 1991 by Parliament. It sets a number of goals to be met by the year 2000. The Programme for the implementation of the State Environmental Policy was approved by the Government in 1994. Apart from the emission targets for sulphur dioxide and nitrogen oxides, mentioned in section 3 below, the State Environmental Policy sets a target of a 50% cut in particulate emissions based on 1990 levels. Although no figures are given, limitations are also to be achieved by the year 2000 for volatile and persistent organic compounds, heavy metals, benzo(a)pyrene, CO_2 and other gases. It also calls for the elimination of domestic coal-fired boilers in conurbations and health resorts and the introduction of catalytic converters in all cars being produced or used.

(l) *Portugal*: The main objectives of air pollution abatement policy are: the protection of public health, the well-being of the population and the conservation of nature; the preservation of harmony between nature, industrial activities, transport and human life, through the establishment of conditions for integrated, harmonious and sustainable development; the establishment of obligatory preventive and corrective measures for ensuring that the levels of atmospheric pollutants do not exceed the maximum limits imposed by air quality standards; the fostering of public or private initiatives for promoting improvements in the quality of the air through the use of clean technologies and fuels; and the development of an integrated policy for the preservation of environmental components with the objective of avoiding the transfer of pollution from one medium to another.

(m) *Russian Federation*: In order to attain acceptable targets for air quality in the cities and industrial centres, emissions of the main pollutants should be reduced by 20-40%, and emissions of certain precursors by even more. This, judging from the existing trends and the steady increase in the number of motor vehicles, will not be possible before the years 2005-2010. The targets for air pollution abatement and the time-limits for their attainment should be laid down in the federal programme entitled "Clean Air for Russia" and in the federal targeted programme for reducing the adverse effects of road transport on the environment. These programmes are to be drawn up in 1994-1995 in the light of figures from an official forecast for the development of the country's economy, which has hitherto been lacking. The system for attaining targets for ambient air quality is based to a significant extent on the setting of maximum permissible emissions (MPEs) and their attainment by stationary sources. The MPE is that quantity of emissions from an individual source which, taking into account the effects of surrounding sources, does not cause the maximum permissible concentrations (MPCs) of the substances concerned to be exceeded. Over the past 10 to 15 years, work on setting standards for emissions has covered some 13,000 enterprises, which together account for more than 80% of all emissions from stationary sources. An action plan of the Government of the Russian Federation on environmental protection for 1994-1995 has been drawn up. It is to be confirmed during 1994.

(n) *Slovenia*: Environmental objectives are focused on sectoral policies, in particular those concerning energy, transport and agriculture (see sect. C below). The Environment Project, supported by World Bank funds, was set up in 1992 to establish priorities for investments into the environmental sector. In this project the need for the desulphurization of the exhaust gases from thermal power plants, supplied with indigenous coal, was set as the highest priority. As a result of 1992 investments the desulphurization of one of the three thermal units in Sostanj is almost finished. The second unit will not be adequately equipped until 2000, while the third one will operate only as the power reserve for the Slovene power system. The second priority for environmental investments was given to gasification in the populated areas in Slovenia. This project is also financially supported by the European Community.

(o) *Spain*: A number of environmental objectives are set out in the national energy plan which establishes the main guidelines for the period from 1991 to the year 2000 (see sect. C below).

(p) *Sweden*: The overall objective of air pollution policies is to reduce emissions to levels at which neither the environment nor human health is harmed. Concerning urban air pollution, the goals are to bring concentrations of carbon monoxide, sulphur dioxide, soot and particulates down below the levels specified in guidelines by the year 2000 and to cut emissions of carcinogens by half by 2005. Compared to the 1980 levels, deposition of sulphur has to be reduced by 75% in the south of Sweden and by 50% in central Sweden, and nitrogen deposition has to be reduced in the order of 50% in large areas of Sweden to avoid exceedances of critical loads for acidifying compounds.

(q) *Switzerland*: The principles of the air pollution control policy are set out in the 1985 Law on the Protection of the Environment. Its objective is to protect human beings, animals and plants, their biological communities and habitats against harmful effects or nuisances and to maintain the fertility of the soil. Both a source-oriented (through emission standards) and an effect-oriented (through ambient air quality standards) approach are followed. Irrespective of existing environmental pollution, as a precautionary measure, emissions are to be limited as much as technology and operating conditions allow, provided this is economically feasible. Emissions shall be limited more stringently if harmful effects are found or expected, taking into consideration the existing level of environmental pollution. In 1986 the Government adopted an overall Air Pollution Control Strategy covering sulphur dioxide, nitrogen oxides and volatile organic compounds.

(r) *United Kingdom*: The two main bases for air pollution abatement policy are the scientific evaluation of causes, transport and effects on the one hand and the use of BATNEEC to reduce emissions from industrial activities on the other. The principal objective of the 1990 Environmental Protection Act, which introduced a system of integrated pollution control, is to ensure that licensing authorities enforce the application of BATNEEC. Also in 1990 a programme and a national plan for the implementation of the European Community's Large Combustion Plants Directive were published. In 1993 the Government adopted a strategy for

the 30% reduction target of VOCs. This strategy was the first in the country to consider all sources of a pollutant and will provide a model for future action on sulphur and nitrogen.

(s) *United States*: The major goals of air pollution abatement policy are: to ensure the entire nation has healthy air; to play a leading role in reducing and eliminating all substances that harm the stratospheric ozone layer; to reduce greenhouse gas emissions to 1990 levels; and to protect the physical, chemical and biological components and processes of ecosystems from damage from air pollution deposition.

(t) *European Community*: In 1993 the Council of Ministers for the Environment endorsed the 5th Community Programme of Policy and Action in Relation to the Environment and Sustainable Development. This programme also sets emission reduction targets to be achieved before the year 2000. The protection of human health and the environment will be ensured by measures that enforce air quality standards and emission limitations. The measures cover all sectors, in particular transport and industry. For the latter, an integrated approach will replace the present one dealing separately with the three environmental media (air, water, soil). Emission standards will be set on the basis of best available technology, taking into account environmental quality standards.

3. Emission reduction targets

Most Parties specify abatement targets for sulphur, nitrogen oxides and volatile organic compounds. These are often more stringent than the emission reduction targets specified under the protocols. The emission figures for the years 1995 and onwards given in tables 1 to 7 provide an overview of current national reduction plans, i.e. politically determined emission reduction targets. The following subparagraphs present the targets as they follow from the protocols to the Convention and as they are specified in national legislation:

(*a*) The Parties to the 1985 Protocol on the Reduction of Sulphur Emissions or their Transboundary Fluxes by at least 30%, listed in table 13, undertook to reduce sulphur emissions by at least 30% below 1980 levels by the end of 1993 and, as decided by the Executive Body, these levels should not be surpassed thereafter. The 1994 Protocol on Further Reduction of Sulphur Emissions specifies in its annex II a set of differentiated abatement targets for Parties. These have been included as current reduction plans in table 1 except for those Parties that reported stricter targets. Furthermore, *Cyprus* intends to stabilize emissions and gradually reduce them from the year 2000 onwards. The *Netherlands* plans to reduce sulphur emissions to 92,000 tonnes by the year 2000 and to 56,000 tonnes by 2010. In *Poland* a programme to limit sulphur dioxide emissions was adopted in 1988. Its targets are to stabilize emissions at 1980 levels by 1995, to reduce them by 30% by the year 2000 and by 50% by 2010. These targets were confirmed in 1991 and supplemented by a long-term target of an 80% reduction to be achieved possibly around 2020. The stricter emission ceilings (up to 2010) of the Oslo Protocol, which Poland has signed, will replace the earlier targets. The target in *Switzerland* is to bring sulphur dioxide emissions down to 1950 levels (i.e. a 57% reduction compared to 1980 levels). The *United States* aims at cutting annual emissions of sulphur dioxide by 10 million tonnes below 1980 levels.

(*b*)   The Parties to the 1988 Protocol concerning the Control of Emissions of Nitrogen Oxides or their Transboundary Fluxes, listed in table 13, have the obligation to stabilize nitrogen oxide emissions by the end of 1994 at 1987 levels (or 1978 for the United States). In addition, twelve Parties (Austria, Belgium, Denmark, Finland, France, Germany, Italy, Liechtenstein, Netherlands, Norway, Sweden and Switzerland) made a declaration to the effect that they will aim for a reduction of nitrogen oxide emissions in the order of 30% based on emission levels of any year between 1980 and 1986 as soon as possible and at the latest by 1998. Furthermore, *Austria* aims at reducing its NO_x emissions by 40% by the end of 1996, 60% by the end of 2001 and 70% by the end of 2006 below its 1985 levels. *Cyprus* intends to stabilize its emissions and gradually reduce them from the year 2005 onwards. In *Denmark*, based on an action plan, a 50% reduction in nitrogen emission from the agricultural sector into the aquatic environment and to the air is envisaged by the year 2000 based on 1985 levels, while NO_x emissions from the transport sector are to be reduced by 40% before 2000 and 60% before 2010, based on 1988 levels; total NO_x emissions are to be reduced by 35% by the year 2000. The *Netherlands* plans to reduce nitrogen oxide emissions to 249,000 tonnes by 2000 and to 120,000 tonnes by 2010; it targets a maximum emission level for ammonia of 82,000 tonnes for the year 2000 and 50,000 tonnes for 2010. In *Poland* a programme to limit nitrogen oxide emissions was adopted in 1989 and confirmed in 1991; it calls for the stabilization of emissions at 1987 levels by 1994, a 10% reduction by 2000 and a 50% reduction by 2010. In *Sweden* the Board of Agriculture has proposed a reduction in ammonia emissions that would lead approximately to a 10% decrease in national emission levels. The target in *Switzerland* is to reduce nitrogen oxide emissions to 1960 levels (i.e. a 69% reduction compared to 1984 levels).

(*c*)   The 1991 Protocol concerning the Control of Emissions of Volatile Organic Compounds or their Transboundary Fluxes specifies three options for emission reduction targets that have to be chosen upon signature:

(i)   30% reduction in emissions of volatile organic compounds (VOCs) by 1999 using a year between 1984 and 1990 as a basis (this option has been chosen by Austria, Belgium, Finland, France, Germany, Netherlands, Portugal, Spain, Sweden and the United Kingdom with 1988 as base year, by Denmark with 1985, by Italy and Luxembourg with 1990 and by Liechtenstein, Switzerland and the United States with 1984 as base year);

(ii)   The same reduction as for (i) within a Tropospheric Ozone Management Area (TOMA) specified in annex I to the Protocol and ensuring that by 1999 total national emissions do not ex-

ceed 1988 levels (annex I specifies TOMAs in Norway (base year 1989) and Canada (base year 1988));

(iii)   Finally, where emissions in 1988 did not exceed certain specified levels, Parties may opt for a stabilization at that level of emission by 1999 (this has been chosen by Bulgaria, Greece, and Hungary).

In addition, *Austria* aims at reducing its VOC emissions by 40% by the end of 1996, 60% by the end of 2001 and 70% by the end of 2006 below its 1988 levels. In *Denmark* the target is to cut hydrocarbon emissions from the transport sector by 40% before 2000 and by 60% before 2010; total non-methane volatile organic compound (NMVOC) emissions are to be reduced by 30% before the year 2000 with 1985 as the reference year. The *Netherlands* plans to bring VOC emissions down to 193,000 tonnes by the year 2000 and to 117,000 tonnes by 2010. *Sweden* has laid down a national target to cut VOC emissions to 50% by the year 2000 based on 1988 levels. The target in *Switzerland* is to reduce emissions to 1960 levels (i.e. a 57% reduction compared to 1984 levels).

B.   LEGISLATIVE AND REGULATORY FRAMEWORK, INCLUDING NATIONAL PLANS AND PROGRAMMES

This section gives an overview of the legislative and regulatory framework, while the contents of regulatory provisions are summarized in chapter III. Many Parties have framework legislation setting the basis for all environmental regulations or all those related to air pollution abatement. In other cases this legislation is scattered over a larger number of laws, sometimes even extending to the provincial level.

(a) *Austria*: Environmental protection as a general objective is embedded in the Federal Constitutional Law. The main legislative and regulatory provisions concerning air pollution abatement can be found in some 12 laws at the federal level and some additional regulations at the provincial level. A law on ambient air quality has been drafted. It will provide effect-oriented concentration limit values for a number of pollutants, including sulphur dioxide combined with particulates, carbon monoxide, nitrogen dioxide, ozone, lead, benzene, particulates of cadmium, zinc and lead, and deposition and concentration limits for certain ecosystems, particularly forests. In areas where limits are exceeded, measures are foreseen to reduce emissions in all relevant sectors: power plants, transport and heating installations. The law will also provide the basis for a comprehensive monitoring and data network. For the coming years, the preparation of a uniform national law with homogenous regulations for all installations is being considered.

(b) *Belarus*: For 1995, there are plans for a new air pollution prevention and air use act. New normative instruments are to replace the present ones, which were inherited from the former Soviet Union. They will include the amendment of air quality standards, the preparation and application of emission regulations for specific industrial processes, the improvement of legislation on environmental taxes and atmospheric emission penalties, and support for the State programme on energy conservation and the development of non-conventional energy sources.

(c) *Belgium*: The original principle of air pollution control legislation of the 1946 Royal Decree was to reduce nuisance and health risks to the neighbourhood from dangerous, unhealthy and polluting activities, by making such activities subject to prior licensing. This source-oriented approach is still applied, with the special conditions attached to the licence as the main tool to control air pollution from industrial activities. The air quality standards approach was introduced by the 1964 Air Pollution Prevention Act but an effective royal decree on air quality standards for sulphur dioxide and particles did not appear before 1983. From 1971, fuel quality standards, emissions limits and a chimney height formula for combustion sources have been introduced as a way of improving air quality, especially in the five metropolitan areas, where special protection zones were established. At present the European Community Directives on air quality are the basis for air quality legislation. The development of the federal system has enabled divergencies of environmental standards in the regions, but the European standards provide minimum standards.

(d) *Bulgaria*: The Environmental Protection Act was passed in 1991 and amended in 1992. This Act partly replaces the 1975 Act on the Protection of Air, Water and Soil from Pollution. A Clean Ambient Air Bill with provisions concerning ambient air quality indicators and standards, emission standards, licensing procedures, air quality monitoring and administrative structures has been drafted. The Bill has been supplemented on the basis of recommendations by the United States Environmental Protection Agency and the United States Institute for Environmental Legislation. It is envisaged that the Bill will also include some subordinate legislation setting emission reductions for large combustion plants, and warning levels. This is still in preparation.

(e) *Canada*: There is no single federal legislation for air pollution abatement. Air quality is regulated through several pieces of environmental legislation, including the Environmental Protection Act. Federal and provincial Governments work in cooperation within a new federal/provincial system for air quality management established under the Comprehensive Air Quality Management Framework for Canada.

(f) *Croatia*: The Environmental Protection Act was passed in November 1994. It aims at ensuring integral environmental quality, the protection of ecosystems, and the rational and environmentally friendly use of natural resources and energy, thus establishing basic conditions for a healthy and sustainable development. The basic Air Protection Act was passed at the federal level in 1965, and in 1971 a law for the Republic took over which is still in force. This law, however, is completely outdated and the subordinate legislation was never passed. A new Air Protection Act has been prepared and is expected to be passed together with other regulations such as those concerning ambient air quality, and emission limit values for all sources. The Act is based on the Environmental Protection Act, European Community directives

and other international provisions, as well as the experience of industrialized countries.

(g) *Cyprus*: The Control of Atmospheric Pollution Law and its regulations provide the basis for measures to control air pollution.

(h) *Czech Republic*: The basis for air pollution control is the 1991 Clean Air Act, amended in 1992, and the 1991 Czech National Council Act on the national administration of air protection and air pollution charges.

(i) *Denmark*: The Environmental Protection Act provides the basis for regulations to safeguard the environment. The regulatory instruments established by this Act are: (i) the power of environmental authorities to assess polluting activities with a view to giving or refusing approval, or setting certain requirements; and (ii) the power of the Minister of the Environment to lay down emission limitations and production standards. With the 1991 amendments the Act has been strengthened through the introduction of a principle of cleaner technology underlying a holistic and preventive environmental policy.

(j) *Finland*: The Air Pollution Control Act and the Air Pollution Control Decree entered into force in October 1982. Before air pollution had been treated mainly within the framework of the Public Health Act. The Act and the Decree set a general obligation to take measures to prevent air pollution. They define the duties of the air pollution control authorities, empower the State Council to establish regulations for air pollution control and require a licensing procedure for potentially polluting industrial activities. Recently, new air quality guidelines have been drafted which shall be presented for adoption in 1995 to replace the 1984 guidelines that are considered to be insufficient.

(k) *Germany*: The basis for air pollution control measures is given by the 1974 Federal Immission Control Act. It provides the basis for regulations that can be grouped into three categories:

(i) Plant-related regulations, such as licensing requirements of installations particularly liable to cause harmful effects on the environment (the Technical Instructions on Air Quality Control, the Ordinance on Large Combustion Plants, the Hazardous Incidence Ordinance and the Ordinance on Incinerators for Waste and Similar Combustible Materials), regulations dealing with installations not subject to licensing (Ordinance on Small Combustion Plants, Ordinance on Surface Treatment and Dry Cleaning, Ordinance on Limiting Wood Dust Emissions, Ordinance on Filling and Storage of Otto Engine Fuels and Ordinance on Refuelling of Motor Vehicles) and obligations for firms relating to plant safety and the designation of officers to deal with immission control and hazardous incidents (Ordinance on Immission Control and Hazardous Incidents Officers and Hazardous Incidents Ordinance);

(ii) Area-related provisions to control local problems by the preparation of ''clean air plans'', the first of which has now been prepared for the new *Länder*, the designation of ''areas subject to investigation" and of "smog areas", leading to the preparation of emission, immission and effect inventories and a plan of action;

(iii) Product-related regulations, specifying quality standards for substances and products, in most cases established on the basis of European Community regulations (Ordinance on the Sulphur Content of Fuel Oil and Diesel Engine Fuels, Ordinance on Fuel Labelling and Fuel Quality and Ordinance on the Use of Chlorine and Bromine as Fuel Additives).

(l) *Italy*: The basic framework for air pollution control is given by the 1966 Clean Air Law. This Law and its implementing regulations allocate responsibilities to regional and local authorities for licensing, monitoring emissions and setting standards for different types of installations. In addition, there are a number of decrees concerning maximum permissible standards of air pollutant concentrations, emission limits for industrial plants, criteria for regional abatement and air quality protection plans and rules for warning levels in urban areas. The directives of the European Community have provided an important basis for regulations for the control of air pollution.

(m) *Netherlands*: Originally air pollution was dealt with in the Nuisance Act for small stationary sources and in the 1970 Air Pollution Act for medium and large stationary sources, mobile sources, fuels and products, measures in special circumstances such as smog, administrative procedures and financial issues. Environmental pollution legislation for air pollution and other sectors has gradually been integrated into the Environmental Management Act. This process was completed in March 1993. The Environmental Management Act now deals with licensing procedures, emission standards for stationary sources, air quality standards, financial issues and planning. The Air Pollution Act remains in force for emission standards for mobile sources, fuels and products and for special circumstances. Under the new Act, central Government and provinces are required to produce an environmental policy plan every four years and an environmental programme to monitor progress in implementing these plans annually. There has been a shift of emphasis from the imposition of regulations to self-regulation. Government sets a framework in the form of broad policy objectives. The target for each group, an essential component within this framework, is fixed in an open planning process in consultation with the group, so that the overall objectives are achieved. It is the responsibility of each group to indicate how it will achieve its own target and regulate its own conduct. The balance between regulation and initiatives from a group depends on the character of the target group and its level of organization.

(n) *Poland*: All actions for the protection of the atmosphere are regulated by the 1980 Statute on the Protection and Management of the Environment, along with its numerous amendments. An updated text of this statute was published in 1994. A new set of amendments to be decided upon in 1995 is under preparation. Detailed regulations based on the Statute are contained in the ministerial regulation of February 1990 concerning the protection of the air from pollution. They contain norms

for emission and ambient air quality. Matters relating to the enforcement of regulations in this field are dealt with in the 1991 Statute on the State Environmental Protection Inspectorate.

(o) *Portugal*: Air pollution control policy is regulated by a Decree-Law of November 1990 and by a Ministerial Order of March 1993. The Decree sets the framework for air pollution control by defining: the main policy measures for air pollution abatement; the competent authorities; air quality standards and emission limitations; the most important industrial sources of air pollution; the height of chimneys; "critical areas" for air pollution control and the "air quality management commissions" for those areas; the national air quality monitoring network; and the framework for the national emissions inventory. The Ministerial Order sets the air quality standards and measuring methods for SO_2, particulates, NO_2, lead, CO and O_3. It also sets general emission limits for all stationary sources and specific, more stringent, emission limits for certain source categories.

(p) *Russian Federation*: The principles of nature-protection legislation are laid down in the Constitution of the Russian Federation adopted by referendum on 12 December 1993. Constitutional rights and guarantees are of decisive importance in protecting the ambient air inasmuch as, on the one hand, they set constitutional limits on the actions of the federal authority and the constituent territorial entities of the Federation and, on the other, protect man in his environment from damage inflicted by atmospheric pollution. More detailed requirements with regard to the protection of the ambient air are laid down in the Act concerning the protection of the natural environment (1991) and the Act concerning the protection of the ambient air (1992). These laws, however, are not fully appropriate to the present political system nor to the new economic conditions. Consequently, it is the intention to renew in 1994-1995 the nature-protection legislation in force; a draft federal act concerning the protection of the natural environment has already been prepared and a new version of the Act concerning the protection of the ambient air is in preparation. Regulations, rules and standards approved by organs of the former Soviet Union concerning nature protection and governing the utilization of natural resources are in operation in the territory of the Russian Federation today where they do not conflict with the Act of the Russian Federation concerning the protection of the natural environment. These instruments continue in force until such time as the corresponding normative texts of the Russian Federation are adopted.

(q) *Slovakia*: The basic legislation concerning air pollution abatement policy is contained in the Clean Air Act and the Act of State Administration of Air Protection, both of which were amended in 1994. Specific regulations are given by ministerial decrees, such as those on the definition of areas demanding special air protection and the operation of smog warning. An amendment to a code dealing with, *inter alia*, emission standards and the classification of pollution sources is under preparation.

(r) *Slovenia*: Originally air pollution was dealt with in the 1976 Air Protection Act. Now the 1993 Environmental Protection Act is the main legislative instrument for the enforcement of air pollution control. Its implementing ordinances on air pollution control set the legal framework for a comprehensive air pollution programme. The ordinances on air pollution control, amended in 1994, regulate emissions from stationary sources. They contain emission standards for more than 100 individual organic and inorganic pollutants, which correspond to a large extent to those contained in the German Technical Instructions on Air Quality Control and WHO Air Quality Guidelines. One of the ordinances passed in 1994 contains fuel and petrol requirements and regulates the import, the production and the supply of fuels in the transport and energy sector.

(s) *Spain*: Work is under way to amend the 1972 Law on the Protection of the Atmospheric Environment. This follows three major developments: the entry into force of the new constitution in 1978, the joining of the European Community and the adhesion to international conventions and protocols.

(t) *Sweden*: The main legislative instruments are the Environment Protection Act and Ordinance, the Waste Collection and Disposal Act and Ordinance, the Environmental Charges on Emissions of Nitrogen Oxides Act, the Vehicle Emissions Act and Ordinance, the Sulphur Fuels Act, the Taxes on Emissions of Carbon Dioxide Act and the Energy and Liquid Fuels Act. Work is under way to extensively revise the environmental legislation. It is expected that a bill for this will be presented to Parliament later in 1994 in the form of a code.

(u) *Switzerland*: The 1985 Law on the Protection of the Environment and its implementing ordinances, in particular the Ordinance on Air Pollution Control and the Ordinance relating to Environmentally Hazardous Substances set the legal framework of a comprehensive air pollution control programme. The 1986 Ordinance on Air Pollution Control, amended in 1992, regulates emissions from stationary sources. It contains emission standards for about 150 individual inorganic and organic pollutants (corresponding to a large extent to those contained in the German Technical Instructions on Air Quality Control). Moreover, the Ordinance contains fuel and petrol requirements as well as effect-oriented ambient air quality standards. As regards pollution caused by motor vehicles, emission standards are laid down in the Ordinances relating to the Laws on Road Transport, Navigation and Aviation. The 1986 Ordinance relating to Environmentally Hazardous Substances regulates the import, the production, the supply, the use and the export of substances that may present a hazard to the environment. It comprises instructions for the environmental impact assessment of new and existing substances and products. In addition to the general regulations, annexes to this Ordinance contain special regulations for particular groups of chemicals, including chlorofluorocarbons, halogenated organic compounds, and heavy metals. A proposed revision of the Federal Law on the Protection of the Environment is under discussion in the Parliament. It contains a proposal to introduce an incentive tax on gas oil with a sulphur content higher than 0.1%. It is a mere incentive and not a fiscal measure, since the revenue from the tax will be uniformly redistributed to the population. In addition, the revised law contains a proposal to reduce VOC emissions from VOC-containing products by gradually introducing a charge on imported or produced and traded products. As a first step, a charge of Sw F 1 per kg of VOC is foreseen, this should rise two years later to Sw F 2 per kg of VOC and another two years later, if necessary, to Sw F 5 per kg of VOC. A per capita reimbursement as mentioned above is proposed.

(v) *United Kingdom*: The 1990 Environmental Protection Act, supplemented by various regulations, is the main legislative instrument for the enforcement of pollution control. It prescribes industrial processes for which authorization is required as well as substances, such as sulphur dioxide and nitrogen oxides, for the release of which authorization is required (see chap. III, sect. A.5). In addition the 1956 and 1968 Clean Air Acts that deal with smoke, grit and dust from domestic and certain industrial sources are of importance. Furthermore, there are the 1972 and 1974 Road Traffic Acts and the 1974 Control of Pollution Act regulating emissions from road vehicles and the composition of motor fuels and fuel oil respectively. The 1990 Town and Country Planning Act controls the development of land and location of potentially polluting development, as well as other development activities in the proximity of air pollution sources. In addition, a number of European Community directives provide a basis for air pollution control regulations.

(w) *United States*: The Clean Air Act (CAA), as amended in 1990, created a comprehensive plan to reduce the emissions of air pollutants over the next 15 years. It establishes a framework for addressing health and environmental effects associated with criteria pollutants (i.e. carbon monoxide, lead, nitrogen oxides, ozone, particulates (PM10) and sulphur dioxide), health and environmental effects from hazardous air pollutants, visibility, acid deposition, and stratospheric ozone depletion. In October 1993, the President issued the Climate Change Action Plan, which establishes a strategy for reducing greenhouse gas emissions to their 1990 levels by the year 2000.

(x) *European Community*: A number of changes in air pollution legislation are expected. A draft framework directive on ambient air quality assessment and management was approved by the European Commission in July 1994. A revision of the limit values in the Large Combustion Plant Directive are to be discussed in the first half of 1995. The finalization of a directive dealing with organic solvents from certain industrial sectors is also expected in 1995. A draft directive aimed at reducing VOC emissions from filling-stations is in preparation. Also, a directive aimed at reducing emissions from non-road mobile sources is being prepared. A draft directive dealing with light-duty vehicles, setting emission standards for new vehicles from 1996 or 1997, depending on the type of vehicle, is expected to be finalized in 1995. A draft directive dealing with the sulphur content of heavy fuel oil, bunker fuel, domestic fuel and kerosene is approaching finalization. Finally, a directive setting emission standards for aircraft that go beyond those applied by the International Civil Aviation Organization (ICAO) is in preparation.

C. INTEGRATING AIR POLLUTION POLICY AND ENERGY, TRANSPORT AND OTHER POLICY AREAS

An increased integration of decision-making in some key policy areas that determine the level of pollution, such as transport, energy, agriculture, trade and economics, can be considered as a means of strengthening preventive measures and as complementing end-of-pipe control measures. The following paragraphs summarize the most important measures in these policy areas that follow such an approach. As background, table 10, energy consumption patterns and trends, shows the level of energy consumption by Party for the years 1980, 1985, 1990 and projections for 2000 and 2005.

(a) *Austria*: The 1992 Transit Treaty provides a first step towards a comprehensive transport policy. Besides the prevention of noise, the main objectives are to promote the use of railways instead of roads and to reduce emissions of nitrogen oxides. The aim is to bring down by 60% emissions caused by heavy-duty vehicles in transit traffic by the end of the year 2003.

(b) *Belgium*: A number of measures to reduce energy consumption or to substitute energy sources are pursued in the context of the carbon dioxide reduction target. This includes measures in the framework of the European Community and its energy-related programmes. The regions have developed a joint plan for the transport sector. Also, a number of fiscal measures have been introduced to stimulate the use of public transport and to reduce the fuel consumption of vehicles and to promote the switch to unleaded petrol.

(c) *Bulgaria*: In 1993 an Energy Charter containing a long-term programme until 2010 was drawn up. It targets heat and electricity generation to reduce their environmental impacts. Key elements are: an increase in the share of hydroelectric power and renewable energy sources (solar and geothermal); replacing solid fuels by gas and lignite coal by local low-sulphur or imported coal in some power stations; launching a new nuclear power facility after 2005; and replacing steam generators with fluidized bed boilers or installing desulphurization equipment in some thermal power plants.

(d) *Canada*: The new federal/provincial air issues management mechanism is a joint environment-energy structure. There has also been close cooperation between environment and transport with the application of the Motor Vehicle Safety Act to control vehicle emissions. In developing national air pollution management policies, strategies to deal with the transport sector, energy efficiency and energy supply options are generally considered first before other measures are tailored to the remaining problems.

(e) *Czech Republic*: Environmental requirements are part of the energy policy. Flue gas desulphurization facilities are under construction at all large thermal power plants which will be in operation after 1998. In addition, fluidized-bed combustion boilers are under construction or being prepared and will include pressure and co-generation units for the production of electricity and heat based on the combined cycle. Similarly, completion of construction work at the Temelin nuclear power plant will facilitate the reduction of emissions through a decrease in the combustion of coal for power production.

(f) *Denmark*: Environmental targets are drafted by the Ministry of the Environment in consultation with the sector ministries. Within the established framework these are accountable for integrating environmental concerns into their policies. In 1990 two action plans, relating to energy and transport, were presented to Parliament. In a follow-up this has led in the energy sector to *inter alia*: the introduction of efficiency standards for electrical appliances and other equipment; an amendment to the Electricity Supply Act prescribing integrated resource planning in utility capacity planning; negotiations of agreements on specific efficiency improvement targets with industrial branches; the extension of the ban on electricity heating in areas supplied with district heating or natural gas; and negotiations of financial and other support from suppliers of electricity, district heat and natural gas to consumers converting from electric heating to district heating or natural gas. Furthermore it is the intention to increase the use of "green taxes" (see chap. III, sect. B.1) in all sectors. The Transport Action Plan for Environment and Development describes a series of initiatives and specific measures to limit the environmental impact of the transport sector. In 1992 Parliament adopted an agenda, "Traffic 2005", requiring the Government to prepare a nationwide traffic plan based on five strategies: influencing the volume of traffic and transport and the distribution between modes of transport; promoting alternatives to car transport (especially public transport); curbing environmental problems; setting new priorities for investments; and upgrading traffic planning and research. The Action Plan for a Sustainable Development in Agriculture covers all areas of interaction between agriculture and the environment, in particular the emissions of nitrogen and the use of pesticides. Regulations have been introduced in order to improve the utilization of livestock manure and thus to reduce the leakage of nitrate into the aquatic environment.

(g) *Germany*: Controlling emissions by improving energy efficiencies is an integral part of the air pollution control policy. In 1985 the requirement of "heat utilization" was added to the list of obligations to be fulfilled under the Federal Immission Control Act. This means that certain installations are established and operated in such a way that, to the extent possible and reasonable, any heat generated is utilized for internal purposes or made available to third parties. Furthermore, a fundamental requirement incorporated in the Technical Instructions on Air Quality Control in 1986 is the optimization of processes aiming at the most efficient use of materials and energy. The Government aims for a reduction in energy-related carbon dioxide emissions by 25 to 30% by the year 2005 based on 1987 levels.

(h) *Italy*: Large conservation potentials exist in various sectors. To promote energy saving in power generation and use, and the diffusion of renewable energy, regulations have entered into force or are being prepared: an investment promotion law; an instrument for identifying final energy use (ecolabelling, ratings); and an instrument to influence consumer behaviour and promote new products. Transport emissions are dealt with by a number of measures, including fuel quality regulations and financial assistance to convert public transport vehicles to methane and other less polluting fuels. In addition, new traffic management techniques have been introduced in some urban areas. Energy-related measures are intended to also contribute to the European Community target to stabilize carbon dioxide emissions by the end of the year 2000 at 1990 levels.

(i) *Netherlands*: The National Environmental Policy Plans provide for the integration of air pollution policy into such sectors as energy, transport, and agriculture. In general, the integration of environmental issues has touched all relevant sectors, as manifested by policy documents, such as the 1990 part of the decision-making process regarding the Structure Scheme for Traffic and Transport II; the 1990 Policy Document on Energy Conservation; the 1992 Land Use Plan, VINEX; the 1993 Second Structure Scheme for Electricity Supply; and the 1993 Third Phase Manure and Ammonia Policy. To reduce inner-city air pollution caused by private cars, municipalities have already intervened or will intervene to influence the transport choice by establishing traffic-protected areas and parking restrictions, expanding public transport, creating free traffic lanes for public transport, road pricing, encouraging collective business transport, kilometre reduction plans, stimulating cooperation among transport regions. The speed limit on motorways is 120 km/h, on motorways and highways in populated areas 100 km/h and on other (non-urban) roads 80 km/h.

(j) *Poland*: The general outline of the long-term integration of ecological policy into certain sectors is set out in the State Environmental Policy (in the chapter on eco-development as a basis for the environmental policy of the State), adopted by the Government in 1990 and by Parliament in 1991. This is now taken into consideration in the preparation by the Government of sectoral programmes, and these programmes must be agreed upon by the Minister of Environmental Protection, Natural Resources and Forestry. By the end of 1994 such programmes had been established for the power supply and industrial policy. Work and negotiations on transport policy are under way. In the coming years the issue of the integration of ecological and sectoral policies will be included in the ''Strategy for Poland'', adopted by the Government in 1994. Ten sectoral teams are currently working on a plan to implement this strategy.

(k) *Russian Federation*: Comprehensive programmes are being prepared for introducing ambient air pollution abatement measures in industrial sectors. A plan for an energy strategy that has been approved by the Government provides the basis for a programme entitled ''Fuel and Energy''. In the fuel and power complex this plan prescribes *inter alia*: intensifying the degree of oil refining from 60% to 73-75% within the next five years; the replacement of oil fuels by natural gas and an increase in its share in primary energy production from 39% in 1990 to 52% in 2010; and reconstruction and modernization of thermal power stations with obsolete equipment. For mechanical engineering, the defence industry will be converted in order to secure substantial energy savings by reducing the material-intensity of the industry. In transport measures include: the conversion of road transport to diesel engines, making it possible to reduce fuel con-

sumption by one third of the amount consumed by petrol engines; an increase in the proportion of vehicles of low carrying capacity (0.3-1.0 ton); retirement of vehicles which have completed their working life; priority for the use of unleaded petrol, catalysts and more ecological engines. On the basis of these measures it is expected that, despite an increase in the consumption of energy resources by approximately 10% from the 1990 level, emissions of sulphur dioxide from fuel and power industry establishments will drop 6-13% below the 1990 level by the year 2000 and 14-18% below it by the year 2010 and that nitrogen oxide emissions will diminish by 4-15% and 20-30% respectively.

(l) *Slovenia*: An increased integration of decision-making in some key policy areas that determine the level of pollution will be completed in 1995 by the National Programme for Environment. In this document various sectors, such as transport, energy, agriculture, trade and economics, will be considered in order to strengthen preventive measures to diminish the level of air pollution. The first and most important input to the National Programme for Environment is the Strategy for Energy Use, a document amended by Parliament in 1994, containing a long-term programme for the rehabilitation of large thermal units in the energy sector. It is foreseen by the strategy that their annual emissions of SO_2 will be diminished from 140,000 tonnes in 1994 to 26,000 tonnes in 2005.

(m) *Spain*: The National Energy Plan establishes the main guidelines for energy policy for the ten-year period from 1991 to the year 2000. One of the priority objectives of the National Energy Plan is to make the preservation of environmental quality compatible with the principles of efficiency, security and diversification of energy production, transformation, transport and use. For the first time, the Plan establishes a series of energy policy environmental objectives and sets out measures to achieve those objectives by the year 2000. The environmental objectives of energy policy take into account the projected requirements for economic growth during the ten-year period and Spain's starting-point in comparison with geographically and economically comparable countries, as well as the international aspects of environmental policies. Certain objectives have been established in quantitative terms so that they will be readily verifiable. Others, because of their nature, have been established only in qualitative terms. The most important objectives for the existing large combustion plants in the electricity and oil refining sectors are as follows: to reduce SO_2 emissions from such plants by the year 2000 to around 42% of the 1980 level and to reduce NO_X emissions from such plants by the year 2000 to 263 kt. Both of these targets go beyond the overall requirements under the corresponding European Community Directive. The proposed objective for CO_2 is to limit the total growth of emissions by the energy transformation sector to 36% between 1990 and the year 2000. Other objectives include enhancing oil product quality by reducing the lead content of petrol and the sulphur content of distillate and fuel oils, and minimizing the number of new sites for facilities emitting pollutant gases. The main measures to achieve these objectives are the following: the energy conservation and efficiency plan; utilizing combined cycle generating plants fired by natural gas;

converting certain existing oil-fired power stations to use natural gas; increasing the share of imported low-sulphur coal used in domestic coal-burning power stations, particularly lignite-burning plants, gradually reducing the sulphur content of fuels used by generating plants; considerably increasing cogeneration; introducing cleaner combustion technologies; and employing low-NO_x burners and multistage combustion.

(n) *Sweden*: Through the use of economic instruments, environmental concerns have been integrated into the sectors with the most important emission sources. Details of the sulphur tax, the nitrogen charge and the carbon dioxide tax are given in chapter III, section B.1.

(o) *Switzerland*: The national programme "Energy 2000" aims at stabilizing the emissions of CO_2 at the 1990 level by the year 2000. Energy savings and the promotion of renewable energy are key elements of the programme. The implementation of the programme is based on a government decision which came into force in May 1991. The decision will remain in force as long as there is no federal law on energy. Such a law is now in preparation. In addition, a law relating to the introduction of a CO_2 tax on all fossil fuels (coal, heavy fuel oil, gas oil, gas, petrol, diesel) has been drafted. In 1992, the Swiss population accepted by referendum the construction of new railway lines through the Alps. The new railway system called NEAT ("Neue Alpentransversale") will substantially increase the capacity for the transport of goods and heavy-duty vehicles by train. The realization of the project will make it possible to move most of the long-distance transport of goods from road to rail. A popular initiative (Alpeninitiative), accepted in early 1994, has demanded the mandatory transfer of long-distance transport from road to rail. At the same time, the Swiss population accepted the introduction of a mileage- or consumption-dependent tax on heavy-duty vehicles. This permits Government to replace the existing flat-rate tax by a tax in line with the polluter-pays principle.

(p) *United Kingdom*: The Government is firmly committed to the integration of environmental concerns into other policy areas. This was the main motivation behind the 1990 White Paper "This Common Inheritance", which sets out goals for environmental policy across all aspects of government activity. As part of the process of integration for each government department a minister was nominated to be responsible for that department's environmental performance. Air pollution concerns are integrated into the transport sector on the one hand through technological improvements to vehicles, mainly through the implementation of the relevant European Community directives, and on the other hand through the town and country planning system. A Planning Policy Guidance note was issued to local authorities and others, providing advice on using the planning of land use and transport together to reduce the need to travel. The aim is to contribute significantly to environmental goals in the national Sustainable Development Strategy. There is increasing concern about the impact of air pollution on health and close cooperation between the relevant government departments is under way. This is expected to be an area of continuing concern.

(q) *United States*: In February 1991, the National Energy Strategy, which laid the foundation for a more efficient, less vulnerable, and environmentally sustainable energy future, was published. A key component of the Strategy is the integration of energy and environmental policy. In addition, the 1992 Energy Policy Act puts a strong emphasis on environmental protection in the areas of alternative fuels, clean coal technologies, renewable energy and climate change. As a result of these actions, the Environmental Protection Agency and the Department of Energy have worked together to better integrate energy and environmental policy.

(r) *European Community*: The integration of environmental requirements into other policy areas is required under article 130R (2) of the Treaty of Rome. It applies particularly to air pollution abatement. An evaluation of environmental consequences shall be undertaken in the preparation of all policy measures and legal acts, particularly as regards energy and transport.

D. ADMINISTRATIVE STRUCTURES: NATIONAL AND LOCAL AUTHORITIES

In order to be effective, national air pollution abatement policies must be implemented by administrative institutions. The institutional structures and mechanisms for enforcement and support in each country depend on national systems and traditions of public administration, including the division of competences between central, regional and local authorities. Most Parties to the Convention ensure central policy formulation and coordination for air pollution abatement at the national level by a combination of executive and operational bodies with consultative or advisory ones. Decentralization has led to an increasing role for local authorities to deal with problems of a more localized character.

(a) *Austria*: The division of legislative and executive competences between federal and provincial authorities is embedded in the Constitution. As a cross-sectoral issue, regulatory aspects of environmental protection are distributed among the federal level and the provinces (*Länder*). With the 1988 amendment to the Constitution the competence for air and waste management at the federal level has been extended. The provinces are entitled to deal independently with matters pertaining to the protection of nature and landscape and the regulation of agricultural land use and productions.

(b) *Belarus*: The Environment Act confers authority for coordinating the State monitoring activities at all levels on the organs of the Ministry of Natural Resources and Environmental Conservation. Those organs are structured as follows: the Ministry; 6 regional committees and the Minsk city committee; 121 urban and district inspectorates. The bodies responsible for implementing air pollution control policy are the local authorities at the regional and municipal levels.

(c) *Belgium*: Since 1993, the country has been transformed from a unitary State into a federation with three autonomous regions: Flanders, Wallonia and Brussels. In environmental matters, the regions have taken over most of the responsibilities. The national State Secretary of the Environment continues to coordinate national policy by a monthly meeting with the regional ministers in the Interministerial Conference on the Environment. Only international relations, general standards—such as on car emissions or the sulphur content of fuels—and radioactivity remain within national jurisdiction. The creation of three federal administrations, each with their department for the environment and different institutes and societies involved in the environmental matters, has resulted in a complicated structure, where problems of cooperation remain to be solved.

(d) *Bulgaria*: The Environmental Protection Act lists the competent national authorities: the Ministry of the Environment and its authorities, the regional environmental inspectorates, the Ministries of Health Care, of Transport and of the Interior, the Hygiene and Epidemiology Institute and the National Institute for Meteorology and Hydrology, and the municipalities as local authorities. The national monitoring system and the 16 regional environmental inspectorates are under the guidance of the Laboratory Information Centre within the Ministry of the Environment.

(e) *Canada*: In general, the role of the federal Government is to deal with transboundary issues and cases where federal resources are implicated and to lead the development of national emission standards for new emission sources. The provincial governments have a primary role in overseeing the exploitation of resources within their boundaries, remedial programmes for existing sources, the development of specific regulations, the permitting of sources and the detailed enforcement of requirements. As a result, the federal and provincial authorities must cooperate to implement national air pollution policies.

(f) *Cyprus*: The formulation and coordination of environmental policy rests mainly with the central Government. Local authorities are also included since they are responsible for the development of their region. This cooperation covers both the formulation and the implementation phases of policy. Local authorities also express their views to the central Government within the framework of the licensing procedure.

(g) *Czech Republic*: The following four authorities deal with atmospheric protection policy: the Ministry of the Environment deals with policy issues, strategy development, the setting of pollution limits and issuing of permits for projects introducing new technologies, technical standards and prototypes; the Czech Environment Inspection Agency is responsible for the control of existing sources, in particular large and medium-sized installations which include major combustion facilities; the district offices are responsible for national administration at the district level and prepare local strategies; municipal offices deal with small installations, collect fees from these air pollution sources and monitor emissions from all sources within their area.

(h) *Denmark*: Overall responsibility for the environment, including legislation, rests with the Ministry of Environment and its agencies. It also contains the Spatial Planning Department. The Danish Environmental Protection Agency ensures the administration of a large number of laws and regulations. It also administers a

number of environmental subsidy schemes, grants to certain developing countries, the Arctic region and projects in central and eastern Europe. The National Environmental Research Institute carries out research, monitoring, and data collection as an independent body. Other institutions include the National Forest and Nature Agency and the Geological Survey of Denmark. Decentralization is a principle of the Environmental Protection Act. Thus counties and municipalities have an important role in administering centrally issued guidelines. Municipalities are also responsible for the agricultural sector and it is intended that they also take over the inspection and approval procedure for some industries. Counties are the environmental authority for some large polluters, such as iron and steel works, cement plants, refineries, fish farms and landfills.

(i) *Finland*: General guidelines and regulations concerning air quality and deposition, emission levels, composition of fuels and other products, production, import transfer and use as well as labelling of products, and idle use of motor vehicles are issued by the Council of State. The Ministry of the Environment is the highest authority responsible for development and planning, including the preparations of State Council decisions. Environmental licensing is issued by either provincial governments or local authorities, depending on the geographical impact of the activities.

(j) *Germany*: The legislative powers for air quality control rest with the federal Government. Federal States (*Länder*) may enact laws only in cases where the federal Government has not taken regulatory action. Most fields of environmental protection are covered by federal law. The Federal Ministry for the Environment, Nature Conservation and Nuclear Safety is responsible for air quality control. The Federal Environmental Agency (UBA) is subordinate to it and provides scientific support, notably in preparation of statutory and administrative ordinances and in research and development activities. Its tasks also include public education and awareness raising. Compliance with the provisions of the Federal Immission Control Act and its ordinances is subject to official supervision. Supervisory authorities are provided by the federal States. The relevant bodies differ from State to State. Licensing, for instance, can either be the responsibility of a ministry or of authorities such as municipalities, depending on the importance of the project.

(k) *Greece*: As a result of decentralization, local authorities have received certain competences in air pollution control. District offices, for instance, are responsible for the authorization of small installations. Stationary sources of air pollution can also be controlled by district offices or municipalities.

(l) *Italy*: Based on a law of January 1994 the National Environmental Protection Agency (ANPA) will be responsible for environmental research, data collection and handling, technical support for the preparation of standards, supervision and cooperation with the European Environment Agency. The process of setting up ANPA is still going on. The same law also provides for the creation of regional environmental protection agencies. Administrative functions are still entrusted to regional authorities. They include, in particular: the formulation of schemes for the surveying, protection, conservation and cleaning-up of their territory to ensure compliance with national air quality limits; the setting of air quality standards in special areas; the setting of emission limits based on best available technology; the issuing of authorizations or permits for installations except for some large emission sources (in some regions this has been delegated to the provinces); the establishment of monitoring arrangements and regional emission surveys; and the preparation of annual reports on air quality for the Ministry of Environment and Health.

(m) *Netherlands*: On the national level, the Minister for Housing, Spatial Planning and Environment formulates the overall strategies and policies with respect to air pollution abatement. The Minister for Agriculture, Nature Management and Fisheries is responsible for measures to abate ammonia emissions from livestock, although the 1993 policy document on ammonia is being implemented jointly by the two ministries. The portfolio of the Minister for Economic Affairs includes energy conservation and the Minister for Transport and Public Works is responsible for measures to reduce the emissions from traffic and the deposition on water surfaces. The Crown has the power to set environmental quality standards, emissions standards for industrial plants under the Environmental Protection Act and standards for fuels and motor vehicles under the Air Pollution Act. These decisions are taken upon recommendation by the Minister for the Environment, who can also independently translate international legislation, such as European Community directives, into national law. The provincial and municipal authorities are responsible for the air quality in their regions. The provincial authorities have the power to set air quality standards where central Government has not set any or has set less stringent standards. Also licensing is in the hands of provincial and municipal authorities, although national emission standards that are more stringent remain binding. The monitoring and enforcement of compliance with licensing requirements and national emission standards for plants are decentralized to local authorities, while for fuels and motor vehicles they rest with the central Government.

(n) *Norway*: The Ministry of Environment is responsible for coordinating policy formulation. Sectoral authorities have specific competences to achieve the national objectives. The responsibilities of the State Pollution Control Authority, a directorate of the Ministry, include the administration of the Pollution Control Act, especially the issuing of permits, the Product Control Act and monitoring programmes for air pollution and their effects. For mobile sources, emission standards are set by the Ministry of Transport. For ships, emission standards are set by the Maritime Directorate, which is subordinate to the Ministry of Environment in these matters.

(o) *Poland*: The Ministry of Environmental Protection, Natural Resources and Forestry coordinates the implementation strategies and policies for environmental protection. Its major responsibilities are the preparation of draft legislation, standard setting (together with other concerned ministries) and dealing with appeals against decisions at the provincial (*Voivodeship*) level. The State Environmental Protection Inspectorate, under the super-

vision of the Ministry, deals with the enforcement and monitoring of compliance with laws and regulations. Subordinate to it, in each of the 49 provinces, are the Voivodeship Environmental Protection Inspectorates equipped with their own laboratories. Also at the provincial level, but within the structure of the Voivodeship Offices, are the Departments of Environmental Protection, which deal with the issuing of administrative decisions regarding allowed emissions from stationary sources and the calculation of emission fees. At the lowest level, regional governments are responsible for decisions regarding the location of potentially polluting sources and the supervision of public investment projects. The State activities in the field of air pollution are supported by: advisory bodies, in particular the Council for the Protection of the Environment and the Commission for Environmental Impact Assessment; research institutes; and financial institutions, notably the National Fund for Environmental Protection and Water Management, the Voivodeship Funds and the Environmental Protection Bank.

(p) *Portugal*: The national authority for air pollution control is the Institute of Meteorology, which is part of the Ministry of Environment and Natural Resources. At regional level there are five Regional Directorates for Environment and Natural Resources and an Air Quality Management Commission is in place in each of the five designated "critical areas" of Oporto, Estarreja, Lisbon, Barreiro/Seixal and Sines.

(q) *Russian Federation*: The Ministry of Protection of the Environment and Natural Resources is the central organ of executive power providing management in environmental protection. One of the Ministry's essential tasks is to organize and carry out, jointly with other specially authorized organs, environmental monitoring and supervise the observance of the rules of ecological security. The Ministry and its territorial organs thus also coordinate the activities of the Federal Hydrometeorological and Environmental Monitoring Service and those of other ministries, departments and territorial organs in the area of its responsibilities. The territorial and regional administration assists in monitoring the protection of the environment and organizes the preparation of nature protection programmes, the application of protection measures and the carrying-out of a comprehensive independent ecological evaluation of facilities and plants under construction in the territory or region. The powers of the area and municipal administration in the field of nature protection include the application of environmental protection measures in the territory of the area and the observance of rules and standards concerning sanitation and of regulations concerning hygiene. They also organize the ecological evaluation of projects; inform the public concerning the ecological situation; report on the activities of enterprises, institutions and organizations which present a threat to the environment or which violate the legislation on natural resource utilization; and take decisions in accordance with the legislation to levy fines for damage done to the natural environment.

(r) *Slovakia*: There are four levels of environmental administration. The responsibilities of the Ministry of Environment include: the formulation and implementation of policy and programmes; the preparation of legislation, regulations and standards; the imposition of fines; and the maintenance of monitoring and information systems. It directly supervises the district and sub-district offices of the environment, the Slovak Environmental Inspectorate and the State Environmental Fund. Seven of the 38 district offices have an air protection department. These offices deal with appeals from the sub-district level, allow the public to access information, and issue permits in special circumstances or stop certain activities. In 38 of the 121 sub-district offices, i.e. one for each district, air management issues are administered. This includes licensing and the imposition of fines and fees.

(s) *Slovenia*: The Environmental Protection Act defines the competent national authorities: the Ministry of the Environment and its authorities, including the environmental inspectorate and the Hydrometeorological Institute. The local authorities (provincial and municipal) are obliged to provide mandatory local public services concerning air pollution, like the examination, control and cleaning of fire equipment and installation, smoke flues and vents.

(t) *Spain*: The Secretary of State of Environment and Housing, under the Ministry of Public Works, Transport and Environment, has the responsibility for coordinating, at government level, the policies for the rational use of natural resources. The Ministry was renamed in July 1993, making environmental competences explicit. Autonomous Statutes of 17 communities give those administrations competences in the management of the environment.

(u) *Sweden*: The governmental administrative organization consists of the Ministry of the Environment and Natural Resources, the Environmental Protection Agency and 24 County Administrative Boards. In addition there are 286 municipality-operated Environmental and Health Boards. The Agency's main task is to provide the Government with ideas or background data on national policy on environmental issues. Decisions on policy are taken by the Government. The task of implementing a policy, in particular for issues of national interests, e.g. major industrial plants and national parks, is also entrusted to the Agency. The Agency is also responsible for the national monitoring of environmental status, emissions and discharges. Furthermore, the Agency has the task of providing the 24 County Administrative Boards with information, directives, guidelines and advice concerning the measures necessary to comply with the policy. Parts of this information is reworked and adapted from data originally obtained from the Boards. Several issues are taken care of by the County Administrative Boards themselves, but the Boards also frequently commission municipalities to carry out the necessary work, e.g. to supervise industrial plants to comply with inspection programmes or local environmental monitoring of the effects of air pollutants.

(v) *Switzerland*: The Federal Government has only those competencies which are granted in the Federal Constitution. Competencies which have not been assigned to the Federal Government are attributed to the cantons. The specialized federal authority responsible for air pollution control policy is the Federal Office of Environment, Forests and Landscape, an office in the Department of the Interior. Its responsibilities include the preparation and partial implementation of decrees, ordinances and international treaties. The implementation of federal laws and ordinances is largely the responsibility of the cantons and municipalities. In addition, cantonal law covers supplementary regulations on environmental protection.

(w) *Ukraine*: The State authorities responsible by law for the protection of the ambient air are the Cabinet of Ministers, the Councils of People's Deputies and their executive and regulatory bodies, as well as the specially authorized body—the Ministry of Environmental Protection and its local organs. The Environment Ministry's functions include: overall administration, implementation of a harmonized scientific and technical policy, coordination of the activities of ministries, departments, enterprises and organizations, establishment of environmental standards, issuance of permits for the release of pollutants into the atmosphere and establishment of limits for emissions.

(x) *United Kingdom*: National air pollution policy is formulated centrally. Responsibilities for the administration and enforcement of policies lies with Her Majesty's Inspectorate of Pollution (HMIP) in England and Wales and Her Majesty's Industrial Pollution Inspectorate (HMIPI) in Scotland or local authorities, depending on the size of the process in question. Larger processes, or those potentially polluting several environmental media, fall under the Integrated Pollution Control system and are regulated by HMIP and HMIPI. The plan is to establish an environmental agency in England and Wales to bring together the functions of several authorities, including HMIP. Smaller processes come under Local Authority Air Pollution Control, but authorization is guided by centrally prepared process guidance notes. At present Government is liaising with local authorities to develop improved local air quality management systems to be able to focus on local problems that cannot be handled by national prescriptions. Local authorities have been able to make control orders to reduce air pollution from smoke and sulphur dioxide since the 1956 Clean Air Act. These orders make it an offence for smoke to be emitted in smoke control areas, which now cover about two-thirds of urban areas.

(y) *United States*: State and local air pollution agencies have the primary role of implementing and enforcing the requirements of the CAA and issuing permits to stationary sources regulated under the Act. States develop and implement plans to achieve compliance with the national air quality standards, and apply such plans through the permit review process.

Chapter III

NATIONAL POLICY MEASURES

Policy measures have been grouped into four categories: regulatory measures, economic instruments, measures related to technology, and the monitoring and assessment of effects. As such a categorization may be difficult in some cases, cross-references should be indicated where appropriate. In practice a mix of instruments will prevail and the different types of measures should be considered complementary. For instance, whereas regulations tend to allow a more direct control of polluting sources and hence reduce the uncertainty of the policy result, economic instruments generally bring about emission reductions in a more cost-effective manner.

A. REGULATORY PROVISIONS

1. Ambient air quality standards

Ambient air quality standards or target levels frequently serve as a reference base for other standards (emissions, fuel quality, control technology) designed to achieve a given desirable level of air quality. Ambient air quality is usually defined in terms of maximum yearly, daily and hourly average concentrations of specified pollutants, sometimes also as maximum concentrations for shorter-term episodes. The legally binding force of standards may be differentiated, for instance, as between stringent, health-related standards and indicative nuisance standards. Standards related to health effects for sulphur dioxide, nitrogen dioxide, ozone, particulates and lead are listed in table 11.1. Standards related to ecological effects for sulphur dioxide and ozone are given in table 11.2. Several Parties have, in addition, established standards for other pollutants considered potentially harmful to health and the environment.

(a) *Austria*: The 1987 Treaty on Ambient Air Quality between the federal Government and the provinces define standards for sulphur dioxide, carbon monoxide and nitrogen dioxide and commitments to take measures to achieve these targets. A framework to combat tropospheric ozone formation is given by the 1992 Ozone Act (amended 1994) with its five ordinances. This law sets warning levels for ozone and defines measures to be taken if they are exceeded. It also stipulates measures to reduce emissions of the precursor substances. The 1989 Emergency Air Pollution Control Act regulates ambient air quality monitoring, sets warning levels for sulphur

dioxide, sulphur dioxide together with particulates, carbon monoxide and nitrogen dioxide and lists steps that have to be taken if one of the levels is exceeded. Finally, the 1984 Second Ordinance to the Forestry Act defines ambient air quality standards (sulphur dioxide, hydrogen fluoride, chlorine hydrogen and ammonia) in order to protect forests.

(b) *Belarus*: The Ministry of Health has defined limits (maximum permissible concentrations, MPCs, and indicative safe exposure levels) for 1,733 pollutants.

(c) *Bulgaria*: 171 standards for maximum permissible concentrations of pollutants in ambient air are in force. Ambient air quality is defined in terms of maximum 30-minute concentrations, maximum permissible concentrations and average daily concentrations. The pollutants subject to mandatory control in determining ambient air quality are sulphur dioxide, nitrogen dioxide, particulates, ozone, carbon monoxide, lead (aerosols), as well as pollutants specific to individual regions (including hydrogen sulphide, ammonia, benzene, hydrocarbons). Standards for these pollutants were harmonized with the International Organization for Standardization (ISO) and the World Health Organization (WHO) standards in 1993-1994. Standards for nine other pollutants are being harmonized in 1994. Short-term (30 min.), medium-term (24 hours) and long-term (annual) standards, harmonized with the WHO, indicated in table 11.1, were introduced as of July 1994.

(d) *Canada*: A three-tiered system of national air quality objectives is followed. It takes into account the need for varying objectives across the large country. The levels listed in table 11.1 are the maximum acceptable levels, which are intended to provide adequate protection against effects on soil, water, vegetation, materials, animals, visibility and personal comfort or well-being. In addition to these objectives, levels for carbon monoxide have been established. A federal provincial advisory committee is presently reviewing the need for objectives for fine particulates, hydrogen fluoride and a number of other pollutants.

(e) *Czech Republic*: The standards for air quality outside urban areas are given by the set of ambient air limits in the Measure to the Clean Air Act. In addition, regulations have been prepared in connection with this Act through a decree of the Ministry of the Environment to regulate air pollution sources during smog hazard conditions.

(f) *Finland*: Proposals for new air quality standards have been circulated for hearings by the Ministry of the Environment.

(g) *Germany*: Ambient air quality standards in the form of air quality criteria have been set in the European Community air quality control directives and have been incorporated into national legislation. In addition, immission standards required in the licensing of plants are laid down in the Technical Instructions on Air Quality Control. They do not include a standard for ozone, but standards for additional substances. Health-related standards which may not be exceeded are differentiated from values for protection against considerable disadvantages and substantial impairments which have been defined as guide values and which allow a weighing against other interests. A harmful environmental effect is assumed if the pollutant concerned exceeds one of the health-related standards, either the long-term or the short-term ambient air quality standards; in such a case, the permit is denied.

(h) *Netherlands*: Since 1986, when the first general administrative order in this area appeared, four different Decrees on Air Quality have entered into force: on sulphur dioxide and suspended particulates (black smoke), on nitrogen dioxide, on carbon monoxide and lead, and on benzene. With the Environmental Protection Act all general administrative orders containing quality standards, including the decrees on air quality, were deemed equivalent to orders under that Act. The Act distinguishes two levels of environmental protection: limit values and guide values. Limit values are minimum values which must be met and may not be exceeded. Guide values indicate the environmental quality to be achieved in the near future and/or to be maintained. The level of environmental quality at which no adverse effects at all occur is designated as the target value. This is the value that should be achieved in the longer term. The target value is not set down in legislation or in regulations, but is published in policy documents. These no-effect levels have, for example, been set for ozone at 120 μg O_3/m^3 as a maximum hourly average and at 50 μg O_3/m^3 as an eight-hourly average during the growing season.

(i) *Norway*: For a number of pollutants the environmental and health authorities have worked out guiding air quality limit values. These are rather strict values, based exclusively on environment and health considerations. An intergovernmental working group has proposed regulations pursuant to the Pollution Control Act, with mandatory limit values for noise and nitrogen dioxide, sulphur dioxide, particulates (PM10) and lead. The regulations are expected to enter into force in 1995. These regulations will conform with the European Community directives on air quality. Some limit values may be more stringent.

(j) *Poland*: A 1990 ministerial regulation establishes maximum permissible concentrations for 44 polluting substances, differentiating between regular and specially protected areas.

(k) *Russian Federation*: The standards of sanitation and hygiene established by the State Committee on Sanitary and Epidemiological Supervision are at present used as criteria for ambient air quality. These are maximum permissible concentrations (MPCs) of, and approximate safe levels of exposure (ASLEs) to, pollutants in the air of inhabited localities. By April 1994 such regulations had been established for 1,925 substances and mixtures. ASLEs are subject to revision or replacement by MPCs in the light of toxicological and hygiene information. The period of validity of an ASLE is three years from the time of its introduction. The scientific methodological principles for fixing the MPC of pollutants, which were introduced some 50 years ago, rest on certain basic assumptions. A concentration is recognized as permissible only if it has no direct or indirect harmful or unpleasant effect on man and does not affect his working capacity, the way he feels or his frame of mind. The requirement for the use of concentrations harmless to plants or animals, which are frequently more sensitive, was introduced into the regulatory instruments more than 10 years ago. In practice this approach is just beginning to be applied. The Environment Ministry is at present examining the question of giving effect to the regulations on maximum permissible concentrations of air pollutants for the main species of conifers.

(l) *Slovenia*: Ambient air quality standards in the form of air quality criteria have been incorporated in view of the forthcoming European Community air quality control directives and the first priority list of substances given in the WHO air quality guidelines. Ambient air quality standards are all health-related. Besides health-oriented limits for ozone, the maximum level to protect the terrestrial vegetation is set as an eight-hourly average during the growing season of 60 μg/m^3.

(m) *Switzerland*: Based upon the Federal Law on the Protection of the Environment, the Government must lay down, by means of ordinances, ambient air quality standards allowing the assessment of the air pollution levels. These ambient air quality standards are set as impact thresholds, taking into account solely man's and the environment's needs for protection. The criteria to be taken into account in setting these standards are that, in the light of current scientific knowledge and experience, air pollution below these levels does not: endanger human beings, animals and plants, their biological communities and habitats; seriously disturb the well-being of the population; damage buildings; harm soil fertility, vegetation or waters. The effects of air pollutants shall be assessed for each pollutant separately, collectively, and also according to the combined action of the resulting mixtures. The effects on particularly sensitive groups such as children, sick and elderly people as well as pregnant women have to be taken into account.

(n) *United Kingdom*: The Government is committed to providing information to the public on ambient air quality levels. Since October 1990, the levels of air pollution have been available on television information systems, where they are updated hourly, and on a Freephone telephone number (currently updated twice a day but to change to hourly updates). Air quality forecasts for the following 24 hours are given twice a day. Information is currently provided on the levels of nitrogen dioxide, sulphur dioxide, ozone and benzene as measured at the sites in the national monitoring networks. Air quality data are supplied daily to 20 organizations, including the media, for their use and 70 other groups have on-line access to the air quality databases. As well as giving numerical data, air quality is classified in descriptive bands in the public information systems which are either similar to or more stringent than the WHO guidelines. The Department of the Environment has established an Expert Panel on Air Quality Standards to make recommendations on air quality standards for particular pollutants derived from human health effects. To date, the Panel has made recommendations for ozone and benzene, and will shortly recommend air quality standards for carbon monoxide and 1,3 butadiene. The Panel is currently working on recommended standards for sulphur dioxide and particulate matter.

(o) *United States*: A fundamental requirement of the Clean Air Act is for the Environmental Protection Agency to identify pollutants and set ambient standards for those pollutants that must be attained by each State for all the air quality regions within it. Regions that achieve the standards are considered "attainment areas"; those that do not meet the standards are considered "non-attainment areas".

2. Target loads or deposition standards

Target loads play a similar role to that of ambient air quality standards in determining the basis for other policy measures. They are often established on the basis of scientifically determined critical loads (see sect. D.2).

(a) *Austria*: With respect to acid deposition there has not been any specification of target loads in legislation, but the second Ordinance on Air Pollutants to Protect Forests includes limit values for depositions of heavy metals, as a maximum yearly average, in kg per hectare per year: lead—2.5; zinc—10.0; copper—2.5 and cadmium—0.05.

(b) *Belgium*: In the Flemish environmental legislation, guide values are specified for the deposition of total non-hazardous dust ($350 mg/m^2$, monthly average), lead ($250 \mu g/m^2$, yearly average), cadmium ($5 \mu g/m^2$, yearly average) and thallium ($10 \mu g/m^2$, yearly average). For non-hazardous dust a limit value of $650 mg/m^2$ per day has been set.

(c) *Canada*: The objective for wet deposition of sulphur is $0.65 g/m^2$ per year.

(d) *Czech Republic*: The concept of the deposition limit is contained in the Clean Air Act; however, these limits have not yet been announced.

(e) *Finland*: The 1984 air quality standards include a long-term target for sulphur deposition of $0.5 g/m^2$ per year. A target of $0.3 g/m^2$ per year has now been proposed.

(f) *Germany*: Deposition standards have been laid down in the Technical Instructions on Air Quality Control for some heavy metals.

(g) *Netherlands*: The objectives for the abatement of emissions of acidifying air pollutants are based on critical loads and levels. These no-effect levels have been set at 400 eq. H^+/ha/yr. for acid deposition. As the available abatement technology is basically inadequate to attain the emission reduction required, a set of deposition objectives has been developed. To prevent ecosystems against the most serious damage, a target for the year 2010 has been set: 1400 eq. H^+/ha/yr. as an average for forests, (with a 30-40% uncertainty margin), including, for nitrogen deposition, a maximum of 1000 eq. N/ha/yr. For the year 2000 the acid deposition target is 2400 eq. H^+/ha/yr. as an average for the whole country, including a maximum of 1600 eq. N/ha/yr.

(h) *Poland*: Maximum permissible deposition levels have been established for cadmium ($0.01 g/m^2$), lead ($0.1 g/m^2$) and total particulates ($200 g/m^2$ in regular and $40 g/m^2$ in specially protected areas).

(i) *Russian Federation*: Target loads for sulphur are determined as for the scenario of a 60% reduction in the gap between critical loads and actual deposition of sulphur, i.e. in accordance with the scenario adopted for the 1994 Protocol on Further Reduction of Sulphur Emissions.

(j) *Slovenia*: In 1994, in implementing ordinances of the Environmental Protection Act, deposition limits have been set as a daily average for: dust—$350 \mu g/m^3$; lead—$100 \mu g/m^3$; zinc—$400 \mu g/m^3$; and cadmium—$2 \mu g/m^3$.

(k) *Switzerland*: In the Ordinance on Air Pollution Control deposition limits have been set as a yearly average (arithmetic mean), for: dust—$200 mg/m^2$ per day; lead—$100 \mu g/m^2$ per day; cadmium—$2 \mu g/m^2$ per day; zinc—$400 \mu g/m^2$ per day; and thallium—$2 \mu g/m^2$ per day.

(l) *United Kingdom*: There are no target loads or deposition standards specified on a statutory basis. However, authorities will take account of relevant information on critical loads in individual plant authorizations.

(m) *United States*: A study is under way to determine the feasibility and effectiveness of an acid deposition standard or standards to protect sensitive and critically sensitive aquatic and terrestrial resources.

3. Fuel quality standards

The regulation of sulphur content in fuels is a major element in emission control policies in the ECE region. At present, most Contracting Parties regulate the sulphur content of fossil fuels. The maximum permissible content is generally specified separately for heavy, medium, light and extra-light fuel oil, as well as for gas oil, coke and coal. In a few countries, fuel quality standards are uniformly applied nationwide. Another approach is for them to be more stringent in large urban areas and specially sensitive zones than in rural areas. In addition, in some cases, special attention is given to standards for the lead content of petrol. National standards for the different fuel types are summarized in table 12, fuel quality standards.

(a) *Bulgaria*: Over the next eight to ten years a reduction of the sulphur content of diesel oils to 0.05% and of other industrial diesel oils to 0.02% in accordance with European Community directives is envisaged. A programme to this end is being drafted by the Ministries of the Environment, Health Care and Industry.

(b) *Canada*: The fuel oil standards given in table 12 are not universally mandated and stricter standards are imposed regionally and locally. In 1990, new regulations eliminating lead from petrol used in all vehicles except farm machinery, marine engines and heavy-duty truck engines were enacted. The permissible levels for the exempted categories is 26 mg Pb per litre. In October 1994, the diesel sulphur content standard for road vehicles was lowered from 0.3% to 0.05%. This standard was arrived at through voluntary agreement with diesel suppliers in Canada.

(c) *Cyprus*: The maximum concentration of sulphur in the various types of fuel is regulated by the Petroleum Law and its Regulations. In practice the sulphur content in fuels is much lower than the maximum level provided in the Law. This also applies to the medium and heavy fuel oil, whose concentration of sulphur is usually 2%, whereas the maximum provided by the Law is 4%.

(d) *Czech Republic*: The limits given by decree of the Ministry of the Environment are expressed for domestic coal in terms of a specific sulphur content, i.e. after recalculation on the basis of the heat capacity of the fuel. The contents in imported coal are set as a percentage of sulphur in the dry fuel. The declared limitations in sulphur content in fuels may be exceeded only when emission limits are met using combustion product sulphur-removal equipment. An amendment to this decree is being prepared in an attempt to limit the combustion of black-coal sludges in heating facilities with a thermal output of up to 0.2 MW. The aim of this amendment is also to implement requirements for the sulphur content of diesel fuel and heating oil, pursuant to the 1994 Protocol on Further Reduction of Sulphur Emissions.

(e) *Germany*: As a general principle, high-sulphur fuels may only be used in plants equipped with desulphurization technology. In January 1994, a new Fuel Quality Ordinance came into effect. In the future, all fuels (Otto- and diesel-engine fuels and liquefied petroleum gas) will have to meet quality requirements corresponding to the standards set by the European Community in 1993, limiting the sulphur content of diesel fuel to 0.05%. By providing suppliers with the possibility, as of October 1994, of labelling diesel fuels accordingly, the Ordinance is expected to lead to an early introduction of low-sulphur diesel fuel.

(f) *Netherlands*: Since the introduction of the 1974 general administrative order on the sulphur content of fuels, standards have been tightened step by step. Fuel standards currently in force are presented in table 12. They are not applicable in cases where standards for combustion plants have to be complied with.

(g) *Norway*: Current regulations issued by the Ministry of Environment in 1985 in pursuance of the 1981 Pollution Control Act state that the maximum sulphur content shall be 2.5%. In the 13 southern and southwestern counties the maximum sulphur content is 1.0%. In the cities of Oslo and Drammen, only distillates with a maximum content of 0.8% are allowed and use of residual oil is forbidden. In the northern parts of Norway the 2.5% sulphur oil is rarely used because sulphur taxes on oil products make the 2.5% more expensive than the 1.0%. New regulations to reduce the sulphur content in gas oils to 0.2% are under preparation.

(h) *Russian Federation*: Work is in progress to obtain new petrols with a maximum lead content of 0.01 g/l, a maximum sulphur content of 0.05%, a maximum sulphur mercaptide content of 0.001% and a maximum content of aromatic hydrocarbons of 40%, including not more than 5% benzene, and not more than 20% unsaturated hydrocarbons. The sulphur content of diesel fuel should be restricted to 0.3% by 1995 and 0.005% by the year 2000.

(i) *Slovenia*: In October 1995, the diesel sulphur content standard for road vehicles will be lowered to 0.2%. In the future, all fuels will have to meet quality requirements corresponding to the standards set by the European Community in 1993, limiting the sulphur content of diesel fuel to 0.05% by the year 2000.

(j) *Sweden*: The maximum concentrations of sulphur in fuels are set out in a special law. A system of environmental classification of petrol and diesel fuels is specified in legislation and forms the basis for tax differentiation.

(k) *Switzerland*: The 1992 Ordinance on Air Pollution Control requires a maximum sulphur content for diesel of 0.05%. The maximum sulphur content for gas oil is still set at 0.2%, but an incentive tax on gas oil with a sulphur content above 0.1% is planned (see sect. B below).

(l) *United Kingdom*: Regulations to implement the most recent European Community Directive on the sulphur content of gas oil were introduced in October 1994. There are no statutory requirements for the quality of fuel used in various industrial processes. However, the enforcement authorities will specify fuel quality standards in individual plant authorizations, on the basis of guidelines and taking account of local environmental quality and ambient air quality standards.

(m) *United States*: Regulations have been issued to ban petrol lead additive at the end of 1995, to require reformulated petrol in the most severe ozone non-attainment areas, to require oxygenated petrol in carbon monoxide non-attainment areas, and to reduce the sulphur content of diesel fuel.

4. Emission standards

Standards for the control of air pollutants either set maximum permissible quantities, for specific sources and for specified pollutants such as sulphur dioxide and nitrogen oxides, or require specific technological controls to be applied. Emission standards can be set industry by industry or plant by plant or on the basis of national emission standards for specific pollutants.

Quantitative emission standards may be expressed in various forms: e.g. mass of pollutant per unit volume of flue gas; parts of pollutant per million or billion parts of flue gas; mass of pollutant emitted per unit energy output or fuel input. Table 13 (Emission standards) summarizes national standards for SO_2, NO_x and VOCs for the different source categories.

(a) *Austria*: In addition to those limit values given in table 13, a large number of regulations in the provinces exist setting emission limit values for private heating.

(b) *Belarus*: Emission limits in tonnes of pollutant per year have been set for all stationary sources of air pollution. The limits have been set using an air pollutant dispersion model and taking into account the existing background pollution. For monitoring compliance, measurements are made in grams per second. Pollution standards for hydrocarbons, carbon monoxide and smoke have also been set for mobile sources.

(c) *Bulgaria*: Emission standards were introduced in Bulgaria in 1991 by the Ordinance on Standards for Permissible Emissions of Pollutants in the Atmosphere. They apply to stationary sources in power generation, metallurgy, the chemical and petrochemical industries, the production of building materials and incinerators for solid household waste. Transitional regulations, valid until the end of 1995, were adopted for plants put into operation before the end of 1992. Standards for carbon monoxide and smoke emissions are in force for road transport. Standards for nitrogen oxides and hydrocarbons are being developed.

(d) *Canada*: Several new emission standards have been introduced. The emission standards for light-duty vehicles were tightened beginning with the 1994 model year. They are being implemented through voluntary agreements with vehicle manufacturers. The NO_x emission standard for thermal power plants has been tightened and a further review is scheduled for 1995. NO_x and SO_2 emission limits which incorporate overall plant thermal efficiency considerations have also been prepared for new stationary gas turbine engines. Standards for new NO_x and VOC sources are being established in the light of the best available control technologies economically achievable (see also sect. C.2).

(e) *Croatia*: Until the relevant national legislation is passed, standards adopted in European Community directives are applied.

(f) *Cyprus*: Emission standards for each registrable process are prescribed on the licence granted to the industrial source operator. For non-registrable processes sulphur dioxide emission standards are directly proportional to the sulphur content of the fuel used.

(g) *Czech Republic*: Emission limits for stationary air pollution sources were issued in 1992. They are classified according to the types of technology and have been established for fuel and energy production industries, metallurgical industry, the production of non-metallic mineral products, the chemical industry, waste combustion and other branches of industry. Where limits were not established for a given technology, the general

limits are valid; these limits are established for individual pollutants or compounds.

(h) *Germany*: The emission limits listed in table 13 are only the most important. With respect to SO_2, fluidized-bed furnaces are generally subject to a limit of 0.4 g SO_2/m^3. This standard is also generally used as a guide value in the licensing of smaller new plants. This ensures that these plants use fuels low in sulphur whilst fuels with a higher sulphur content are used in plants equipped with desulphurization systems. In addition to the limit values provided in table 13, there are plant-specific limits for VOCs which may be more stringent. A requirement stipulating that emissions be reduced to the technically feasible limit applies to substances with a high accumulation potential as well as to not readily bio-degradable and highly toxic substances. With regard to NO_x emissions, the values required since 1992 in the licensing of new small combustion plants are 0.4 g NO_x/m^3 in the case of solid and 0.3 g NO_x/m^3 in the case of liquid fuels.

(i) *Italy*: Emission limit values for both small and large existing combustion plants were adopted in July 1990 by a Ministry of Environment decree. Emission limit values for new small combustion plants (<50 MW_{th}) are in preparation; regional authorities are charged with setting emission limit values for new small combustion plants when licences are issued.

(j) *Netherlands*: Specific limits, given in table 13, have been established by general administrative order under the Environmental Protection Act for SO_2 and NO_x emissions from combustion plants (including gas-turbine plants and stationary piston engines) and for NO_x emissions from nitric acid plants. Specific limits have also been established for emissions from waste incineration plants. Refineries have to comply with a standard of 2000 mg/m^3, as an average of all SO_2 emissions from combustion plants and processes in the refinery. From January 1996 on, the standard will be 1500 mg/m^3 and from January 2000 it will be 1000 mg/m^3.

(k) *Poland*: Emission limits for stationary combustion installations are set out in the 1990 regulation on the protection of the atmosphere from pollution. Three categories of installations are distinguished: those in operation before March 1990, those under construction in March 1990 and put into operation before the end of 1994; and those that went into operation after 1994 or whose construction was started after March 1990. For mobile sources, emission limits for carbon monoxide and fumes are set out in a regulation issued by the Transport Ministry in February 1993.

(l) *Slovakia*: Emission limit values for new stationary sources were stipulated in 1992. Emission limit values are established for SO_2, NO_x, CO and dust from stationary combustion sources with a thermal output above 0.2 MW. In addition, emission standards for waste incineration plants and a number of different technologies are applied. Sources authorized before October 1991 (i.e. existing sources) have to meet emission standards for new sources individually by January 1999.

(m) *Switzerland*: General emission standards for non-carcinogenic VOCs are set according to the classes of risk (20-150 mg/m^3, depending on the mass flow). In addition to these standards, provided in table 13, tighter standards are set for 25 carcinogenic VOCs (0.1-5 mg/m^3, depending on the mass flow). For some VOCs plant-specific requirements exist.

(n) *United Kingdom*: Recommended emission standards for a wide range of industrial processes are included in guidance notes used by Her Majesty's Inspectorate of Pollution or local authorities in granting authorizations for individual sites. Where necessary to give effect to European Community Directives (e.g. the Large Combustion Plants Directive), these standards are given binding statutory effect (see also sect. 5, below).

(o) *United States*: There are different types of federal standards for stationary and mobile sources. Stationary source emission standards for ambient pollutants and some standards for hazardous air pollutants are based on best available technology (BAT), although often expressed in terms of performance standards that allow an emission source to meet the standard any way it can. This type of standard is discussed below in section C.2. Mobile source standards are typically emission standards (e.g. tailpipe emission standards for cars) or product standards (e.g. quality standards for fuels).

5. Licensing of potentially polluting activities

A common regulatory procedure in ECE member countries is for the Government to authorize (by certification or licensing) the initial operation of potential sources of air pollution and to impose specific environmental requirements (such as quantitative emission standards or a specific technology for pollution abatement) for the continued operation of such sources. Licences may also prescribe a time schedule for progressively more stringent requirements, thus forcing industries to develop more advanced technology. In the case of mobile sources, certification may additionally specify regular in-service controls and inspections—including pollution control tests—as a prerequisite for continued operation (e.g. of vehicles). With regard to stationary sources, most ECE countries require operating permits either for all major sources of pollution or for specified categories of activities or establishments.

(a) *Austria*: Under the 1975 Forestry Act an additional approval is required if a plant endangers one of the forest functions and a licence may be refused. For industrial processes, the 1994 Industrial Code requires licensing of potentially polluting activities. Requirements include that plants have to apply best available technologies to limit emissions.

(b) *Belarus*: A licensing scheme has been in place since 1993.

(c) *Belgium*: A special law of 1980 assigns responsibility for policing dangerous, unhealthy and polluting activities. The regions control the regulation of industrial air pollution sources, from the issuing of licences to the inspection. They now apply the European Community Environmental Impact Assessment Directive and consequently a more systematic approach to air pollution control is to be expected. The Flemish administration applies the German Technical Instructions on Air Quality standards in licences for those sectors where no regulations are available. The provinces have a mainly administrative and advisory task in the issuing of licences for "class I" industrial activities. They have limited authority to make police regulations to ensure public health and safety, and some operate environmental services or laboratories. The provincial governor has a coordinating role in the event of disasters. The municipalities have the authority to give "class II" licences, and issue directives on the environmental conditions to be met. They also have the possibility to regulate environmental matters which were not regulated by higher ranking authorities. Additionally they can impose special conditions for enterprises that rent or buy their land.

(d) *Bulgaria*: A licensing procedure was introduced in Bulgaria in 1993 by Ordinance No. 1 on Environmental Impact Assessment. Licences for activities of national significance are issued by the Ministry of the Environment. Activities of local and regional significance are licensed by the regional inspectorates with the Ministry of the Environment. The Environmental Protection Act describes the procedure in detail. Licences are valid for one year. Mobile sources of pollution are subject to annual technical inspections by the Ministry of the Interior, including checks of exhaust gases.

(e) *Canada*: Stationary emission sources and major mobile sources require emission permits from the province in which the source operates. Certificates of approval are required prior to construction and are renewable. Conditions required to receive a certificate of approval vary between provinces. New cars are required to meet the federal motor vehicle standards. In addition, provincial annual automobile inspection and maintenance programmes are mandatory in some provinces, and are being considered in others.

(f) *Cyprus*: For industry, the licensing procedure prescribed by Air Pollution Control Regulations is applicable to the registrable processes. The operating conditions, time schedules and emission limits are prescribed in the licence. The regular inspection of vehicles falls within the scope of the arrangements implemented for the control of car emissions.

(g) *Denmark*: The main instruments for licensing are provided for in the Environmental Protection Act, supplemented by different environmental protection directives and guidelines. Licensing of polluting activities takes place at three different administrative levels, depending on the potential risk of the activities. There are about 10,000 enterprises in Denmark that fall within the scope of licensing legislation. All procedures in the licensing operation are fully public. The licence represents an unreserved right to operate and, in accordance with given restrictions, to discharge pollutants to water and emit pollutants into the air. The conditions are valid for at least eight years, but the permit itself is not restricted in time.

(h) *Finland*: The activities of a large number of facilities or substantial changes in their operation is subject to notification, which forms part of the environmental licensing system. The processes include: chemical pulp mills, iron and steel works, cement factories, hazardous waste treatment facilities, power stations, certain refineries and certain chemical plants.

(i) *Germany*: The establishment and operation of installations which, on account of their nature or their operation, are particularly liable to cause harmful effects on the environment or otherwise endanger or cause considerable disadvantages or considerable nuisance to the general public or the neighbourhood are subject to licensing. Relevant installations are listed in the Ordinance on Installations Subject to Licensing. The licensing procedure provides for the participation of the affected public, and it mainly serves to ensure that immission and emission standards are complied with, that the generation of residuals is avoided and that waste heat is utilized. A special inspection and maintenance test prescribed by law was introduced in 1985 for ottoengine passenger cars not equipped with catalytic converters in order to regularly monitor the pollutant emissions of vehicles in traffic. As of December 1993, the test is also mandatory for all diesel-engine and catalyst-equipped vehicles, including heavy-duty vehicles and buses.

(j) *Greece*: Licensing is required for all polluting activities. The application for an operating permit has to be accompanied by an evaluation of environmental impacts. Depending on the size of the installation this will be examined by the prefectural council. The permit will include the required emission control equipment.

(k) *Italy*: Emission authorizations are a crucial part of the legislation. The regional administrations have received some 300,000 applications for authorization, which they have not been able to examine in the envisaged period (120 days for existing plants and 60 days for new ones). The extension of the authorization system to all plants has paralysed the public administrations. It does not allow the selection of projects on the basis of their urgency. Experience suggests that the authorization procedure should be simplified by identifying a scale of severity for the pollution problem and by introducing a system of self-certification. To this end the Ministry of the Environment has drawn up two provisions which identify the industrial and craft activities associated with emissions which result in little or no air pollution. In the first instance, a generalized authorization is envisaged, in the second no authorization would be required.

(l) *Netherlands*: Under the Environmental Protection Act, permits are required for all plants. The permitting authorities (provinces and municipalities) determine the maximum permissible emissions. When national emission standards have been established by general administrative order, the power of the permitting authorities is limited. They are allowed only to impose stricter requirements in the permits to the extent stipulated by the general administrative orders. These are issued only when large numbers of identical emission sources can be identified. The provincial authorities have agreed to use the emissions allowed by the Netherlands Emission Guidelines, which are derived from the German Technical Instructions on Air Quality Control, as maximum emission levels in permits. In some cases small plants are exempted from the permit requirement by virtue of general administrative orders. The permitting authorities are now

also empowered to set requirements relating to the rational use of energy and raw materials, as well as to traffic to and from the facility in the environmental permits. Central Government may issue general administrative orders setting such requirements for certain categories of establishments. An environmental impact assessment (EIA) is required prior to the start of permitting procedures for major projects, such as power plants, highways, industrial sites. The EIA must devote attention to alternatives for the projects in question. To guarantee that "clean" cars remain clean throughout their road life, passenger cars must regularly undergo a mandatory emission test.

(m) *Norway*: Emissions from industrial plants are controlled mainly by emission permits issued for each single plant. For instance, all enterprises having furnaces with a capacity exceeding 150 kg of fuel oil per hour must apply for a permit. SO_2 emissions from all industrial processes are also controlled in a similar way. If the SO_2 emissions from the process correspond to or are greater than the emissions from burning 150 kg of fuel oil per hour a permit must be applied for. The permits comprise all types of discharges and emissions. When conditions in the individual permit are determined, the more stringent standards practised in Europe (such as the German Technical Instructions on Air Quality Control) and the United States are taken into account. In addition, guiding limit values for polluting substances determined on the basis of the type and quality of the receptor are used. The number of new emission permits for emissions to the air was 54 in 1990 and 51 in 1991. To ensure that the permits are complied with, the Pollution Control Authority may impose a pollution fine payable to the State for transgressions.

(n) *Poland*: Economic activities that may affect the environment require a set of decisions concerning the location and the specific conditions, including the permissible emission of pollutants. The permissible emission levels are defined for the installation as a whole and for separate sources within the enterprise. The permits issued for a limited period are based on documentation, *inter alia*, on the technologies and the control measures applied, emission sources and the kind of pollutants emitted, the conditions of discharge, local air pollution and the diffusion of the emissions and plans for emission reductions. Emission levels are so that permissible concentrations are not exceeded. Until economic units obtain a permit they are charged a double rate for the pollution discharge. If the requirements of a permit are not met, a fine ten times the unit rate of emission fees is imposed and/or certain activities have to be ceased.

(o) *Russian Federation*: Under the Act on the protection of the natural environment, regulations concerning the procedure for the issue of licences have been drawn up and were confirmed by the Nature Ministry of the Russian Federation in December 1993. These regulations lay down the conditions and procedure for the utilization of natural resources, the rights and duties of those utilizing natural resources, the ecological conditions in which activities are permitted, and the consequences of non-compliance with those conditions. Under these regulations, the existing procedure for obtaining a permit for the emission of pollutants into the atmosphere remains in force.

(p) *Slovenia*: Operating permits for all sources of pollution are required and for specified categories of activities, like chemical pulp mills, iron and steel works, cement factories, hazardous waste treatment facilities, power stations, refineries and chemical plants, an environmental impact assessment is needed. The corresponding procedure is prescribed by the Environmental Protection Act. All licensing procedures are fully public.

(q) *Sweden*: The main instruments for licensing are the Environment Protection Act and Environment Protection Ordinance. They are supplemented by different environmental protection directives and guidelines. The licensing of the polluting activities takes place at three different administrative levels, depending on the potential risk of the activity. It covers both applications concerning new activities and those for changes at existing installations. The Environment Protection Ordinance lists those activities for which a licence is required. There are about 28,000 enterprises that fall within the framework of the licensing legislation. All procedures in the licensing are fully public. Applicants must advertise their plans in the local press. The applicants also have to present an environmental impact assessment. Licences represent an unreserved right to operate and, in accordance with given restrictions, discharge pollutants to water and emit pollutants into the air. The conditions are valid for at least ten years, but the permit itself is not restricted in time. For all potentially polluting activities the supervisory authorities issue monitoring programmes for emissions that have to be carried out and paid for by the owners of the polluting installations. Reporting to the supervisory authority is usually done monthly or quarterly.

(r) *Switzerland*: All new plants need a construction permit. According to the Ordinance on Air Pollution Control the owner of a plant has to submit an emission declaration to the local authority. If the emissions are expected to lead to exceedances of ambient air quality standards or in general terms to excess pollution, the local authority is allowed to require emission standards below the general standards set in the Ordinance on Air Pollution Control. Central heating systems up to a thermal capacity of 350 kW need type approval and have to be certificated before they are brought on the market. A mandatory two-yearly inspection and maintenance programme for petrol and diesel-fuelled passenger cars and light-duty vehicles as well as for heavy-duty vehicles is in force.

(s) *Ukraine*: In 1992, a regulation concerning the issuance of permits was adopted. Without a permit an enterprise is not entitled to emit polluting substances into the air. The procedure usually includes the establishment of maximum permissible emissions for the installation. Systematic inspections of compliance with the requirements are conducted and for about 200 enterprises such checks are carried out at least once a year.

(t) *United Kingdom*: Part 1 of the 1990 Environmental Protection Act requires operators of prescribed industrial processes to obtain an authorization from their local authority or Her Majesty's Inspectorate of Pollution (HMIP) in England and Wales and Her Majesty's Industrial Pollution Inspectorate (HMIPI) in Scotland. Best available techniques not entailing excessive cost (BATNEEC) are required to be used to prevent, or where not practicable, to minimize polluting releases and render them harmless. Conditions set out in the authorizations will be reviewed at least once every four years, in line with developing technology and awareness of risk. Processes coming under Local Authority Air Pollution Control are authorized in line with operating conditions set out in various Process Guidance (PG) notes which give the Secretary of State's view on what constitutes BATNEEC for different categories of processes. Most PG notes contain guidance on emission limits, operational controls, monitoring and recording of emissions, chimney height determination and good housekeeping measures such as training, dealing with breakdowns and keeping spare parts. For processes subject to HMIP/HMIPI control, authorizations are given in line with Integrated Pollution Regulation Process Guidance Notes (IPR Notes). In addition to giving guidance on what constitutes BATNEEC for each process, IPR Notes include emission limits and timetables for bringing existing plants up to the standard required for new plants. They also include details of any environmental quality standards, European Community and international obligations and advice on techniques for pollution abatement and compliance monitoring.

(u) *United States*: Final regulations have been issued related to the establishment of State operating permit programmes for sources of air pollution. States are now in the process of developing legislation and the other necessary components to establish such programmes.

6.   Product-oriented requirements and labelling

A product-oriented approach is followed, in particular to control VOC emissions, for instance in the case of solvents. In such cases product reformulation will be required in order to replace polluting substances by less harmful substitutes. Alternatively, the labelling of potentially polluting products may be required.

(a) *Austria*: The 1987 Chemicals Act and its amendments follow the system used by the European Community (EC) in regulating chemical substances. New substances must be tested and registered before being put on the market; existing substances are listed and classified into special hazard categories which have to be reflected in packaging and labelling. Most of the regulations correspond to EC directives while some are stricter. Several ordinances to the Act deal with bans or restrictions of chemicals. Concerning organic solvents, a broad field of applications, including paints, coating materials, wood preservatives, adhesives, and removers, is covered. Benzene in all preparations and almost all uses of halogenated solvents have been banned. As of January 1996 the maximum content of aromatic hydrocarbons will be limited to 5% and the total organic solvent rate in paints and coating materials to 10%. Other chemicals banned or limited in use include asbestos, formaldehyde, pentachlorophenol, polychlorobiphenyls (PCBs), 1,1,1-trichloroethane and tetrachloromethane.

(b) *Bulgaria*: Paint producers have adopted a strategy of replacing organic thinners with water-soluble ones. This step has reduced emissions of volatile organic compounds. There is a plan to mark environment-friendly products with a green dot or other similar labels.

(c) *Germany*: Environmentally compatible products can be awarded an environmental label. The label has been awarded, for example, to low-emission oil- and gas-fired burners and paints low in (with less than 10 to 15%) or free of solvents.

(d) *Netherlands*: A product-oriented approach is followed to control VOC emissions. The abatement policy is aimed mainly at preventing emissions by lowering the VOC content of products and/or switching to low-emission (production) techniques. Government and industry have agreed to measures on a sector-by-sector basis. For VOC sources that cannot be eliminated by emission prevention, add-on technology will have to be installed.

(e) *Switzerland*: A voluntary agreement between the federal authorities and the paint and lacquer producer association on the reduction of the content of organic solvents in paints and lacquers exists. Paints and lacquers with a solvent content up to 2% are defined as solvent-free, those with a content between 2-15% are described as low-solvent products. The labelling is done on a voluntary basis.

(f) *United States*: As of May 1993 products containing or manufactured with class I substances (CFCs, halons, carbon tetrachloride and methylchloroform) and products whose constituents include class I and class II substances (hydrochlorofluorocarbons (HCFCs)) must be labelled with a warning that the product contains or was manufactured with a substance which harms public health and the environment by destroying ozone in the upper atmosphere.

7. Other regulatory measures

Some Parties apply regulatory measures other than those listed under subsections 1 to 6 above. They are mainly measures geared to special national circumstances.

(a) *Germany*: As a result of the unification of the two German States in 1990, the environmental legislation in place in the Federal Republic of Germany has become applicable in all of Germany. For the new federal States, the transitional grace periods, which commenced on 1 January 1990, are one year longer than for the western part of the country. In addition to priority measures designed to avert immediate hazards, the introduction of the state of the art in technology has been a basis for industrial development and modernization. Energy- and heat-generation plants are now subject to the provisions of the Ordinance on Large Combustion Plants. Other combustion plants subject to licensing (with a capacity of 1 to 5 MW_{th}) have applied such measures as the conversion to low-emission materials, optimization of production processes, retrofitting with flue gas treatment systems, conversion to low-emission fuels in the case of combustion plants burning lignite rich in sulphur, use of energy-generation plants with high thermal efficiencies, utilization of residual heat as well as modernization of storage tanks to reduce hydrocarbon emissions. The period within which plants subject to the provisions of the Technical Instructions on Air Quality Control must be retrofitted, extends to June 1996 as a rule. By June 1999, at the latest, all plants must either be retrofitted, shut down or replaced by new plants. The implementation of the Ordinance on Small Combustion Plants, particularly regular inspections of the plants by chimney sweeps, is another priority measure. In addition, the use of lignite briquettes in homes and of raw lignite in commercial enterprises has been restricted to low-sulphur lignite. Alternatively, these sectors have to convert to low-emission fuels. Also insulation measures have to initiated. The conversion to low-sulphur fuels has to be completed by January 1995. The development of the rates of implementation of the three-way catalyst, distribution of unleaded petrol and low-sulphur diesel fuel, as well as the introduction of vapour balance systems at petrol stations corresponds to that in the old federal States.

(b) *Netherlands*: Physical planning makes it possible to mitigate the effects of air pollution by maintaining sufficient physical space between the pollution source and the area affected. Special consideration is given to the location of industrial sites. General indicative zoning standards have been developed to protect certain (urban and natural) areas from pollution. More and more attention is being paid to special natural areas with regard to their sensitivity towards pollution. Measures in the framework of the Decree on Manure Use under the Soil Protection Act include a minimization of the amount and annual period when manure may be spread on the land and the requirement that manure be ploughed under immediately after or during spreading. A Decree on Manure Basins requires the covering of slurry pits to reduce ammonia emissions. Furthermore, a guideline to prevent an increase in NH_3 emissions near sensitive objects has been in force since 1987. A revision of this guideline was published in 1991. This guideline will be replaced by the Interim Act on Ammonia and Livestock, which entered into force early in August 1994. The Note on Manure and Ammonia Policy (Third Phase) describes the strategy of the Netherlands Government up to the year 2000. For land-using livestock production, a target environment for ammonia is to be introduced as from 1996. At the same time, an ammonia levy will be introduced as a penalty. Entrepreneurs may decide what measures to take in order to meet the target. This may include manure treatment on the holding, modifying the stocking rate per hectare, spreading the nature with a special technique designed to minimize emissions, or storing the manure and sealing the storage facility.

(c) *Russian Federation*: The existing legislation prescribes liability for ecological offences. The Act concerning the protection of the natural environment provides that any official or citizen found guilty of unlawful acts which violate the legislation on nature protection and cause damage to the natural environment and to human health shall bear disciplinary, administrative, criminal, civil or material liability and that an enterprise, institution or organization shall bear administrative and civil liability. Fines imposed under this Act are described in section B.1. Criminal liability for ecological crimes, i.e.

socially dangerous acts which undermine ecological law or the ecological safety of society, and cause damage to the natural environment and to human health is prescribed by the Criminal Code. Pollution of the air by wastes from industrial production which are harmful to human health shall be punishable by hard labour for a term of not more than one year or by a fine of not less than three minimum monthly wages; the same acts, if they have caused substantial damage to human health or to agricultural production, are punishable by a prison term of maximum five years.

B. ECONOMIC INSTRUMENTS

Economic instruments refer to any measures that aim to reduce the pollution burden through financial incentives and hence will lead to a transfer of resources from the owner of a polluting source to the community or will directly change relative prices.

1. Emission charges and taxes

Emission charges or taxes require payment in relation to the amount of a given pollutant or the characteristics of the pollutant. In some countries a system of fines is used in cases where standards are exceeded or licence requirements are not met. If rates are high enough to internalize the full social costs of a polluting activity at its source, they are in line with the polluter-pays principle: they compel the polluter to absorb those costs as part of his production costs. The rates charged should therefore be proportionate to the estimated cost of the environmental damage caused by the emissions. Charges or taxes are often linked to energy consumption, as emissions in many cases can be directly related to energy use; in those cases where they are applied to the price of products, such as fuels, they have been included under subsection 2.

(a) *Austria*: As a result of increasing environmental damage and its costs, it has become broadly accepted that market-oriented instruments, used as a complement to existing regulations, will be necessary for a more effective and cost-efficient environmental policy. At present, however, environmental taxes still play a subordinate role in comparison to other taxes. In 1992 environmental taxes amounted to S 41 billion and constituted around 8% of the central Government's gross tax revenue. In the discussion on further tax reform, the introduction of a tax on energy or a CO_2 tax will remain a central topic.

(b) *Belarus*: An environmental tax has been in operation since 1992. Air pollution taxes are levied within specified limits at rates depending on the hazard rating (four classes) of the substance. When emission limits for these substances are exceeded, the tax is multiplied by five. When permitted emission rates of other substances or those concerning vehicle emissions are exceeded, the offending enterprises are fined according to established scales.

(c) *Bulgaria*: In 1978 charges on stationary sources of emissions exceeding permitted levels were introduced

for 16 pollutants, including particulates, sulphur dioxide, nitrogen dioxide, ammonia and lead aerosols. Charges were revised in 1993. They are determined in accordance with the Ordinance on Determining and Imposing Sanctions for Damage and Pollution of the Environment. The list of pollutants was expanded to include 100 substances. Charges are proportional to the expected losses from the impact of pollutants on the environment. Natural persons polluting the environment are fined under the Environmental Protection Act.

(d) *Canada*: The provinces of Ontario and British Columbia have introduced emission/effluent fees as part of their facilities permit systems.

(e) *Czech Republic*: Fees are paid for the emission of most pollutants. Every operator of a large source (0.2-5 MW_{th}) pays a fee calculated on the amount of a substance emitted and the fee rate for this substance. If the operator emits more than one pollutant, the overall fee is the sum of the fees for the individual pollutants. The rates are per tonne for: solid emissions—US$ 100; sulphur dioxide—US$ 33; nitrogen oxides—US$ 27; carbon monoxide—US$ 20; and hydrocarbons—US$ 67. Other substances subject to the payment of such fees are divided into three classes. Class I (US$ 670 per tonne) includes asbestos, beryllium, cadmium, mercury, thallium, and benzene; class II (US$ 335 per tonne) arsenic, antimony, tin, chromium, cobalt, nickel, lead, aniline, pyridine, phenol, tetrachloromethane; and class III (US$ 33.5 per tonne) ammonia, acetone, alkenes, furfural, hydrazine and styrene.

(f) *Denmark*: A tax on CO_2 emissions was introduced in 1992, motivated by international concern about the greenhouse effect. The tax rate is DKr 100 per tonne of CO_2. Aviation, shipping, biofuels and oil, and gas consumption in refineries are exempt.

(g) *Finland*: In 1990 carbon taxes were introduced. As of January 1994 energy taxes are based on the carbon content (60%) and the energy component (40%). The estimated total revenue from this tax in 1994 is Fmk 1500 million.

(h) *Italy*: There are no charges on air pollution; however, the Ministry of Environment has proposed that environmental taxes be levied on: emissions of sulphur dioxide, nitrogen oxides, suspended particles, volatile organic compounds produced by certain categories of large-scale industrial plants; the production of chlorofluorocarbons and halons; and emissions of carbon dioxide from large-scale combustion plants.

(i) *Netherlands*: There is no system of emission charges or taxes. Possibilities for an ammonia tax are being studied at present. Non-compliance with permit requirements may be fined. The revenues acquired from fines are not earmarked for pollution abatement. Preparations have been started for the introduction of a regulatory tax on energy. A national variant is being prepared should the European Community not reach a timely decision.

(j) *Poland*: In a ministerial regulation of December 1993 the levels of fees for the emission of 62 different substances or groups of substances are defined. Three groups are distinguished and rates per kilogram emitted are in group I from Zl 1,000,000 for propenenitrile, arsenic, asbestos, benzene, benzo(a)pyrene, chloroethene, chromium and nickel; Zl 500,000 for bismuth, cerium, halogen derivations of hydrocarbons, tetrachloromethane, dioxins, certain halons, cadmium, cobalt, manganese, molybdenum, lead, polychlorinated biphenyls, mercury and 1,1,1-trichloroethane; to Zl 100,000 for tin and zinc. Group II includes ammonia (Zl 1,400 per kg), sulphur dioxide (Zl 1,500 per kg) and carbon dioxide (Zl 1 per kg). If an operating permit is violated, a fine of ten times the fee rate is imposed and this may be doubled if the violation continues.

(k) *Russian Federation*: A fee for pollution of the natural environment is levied on enterprises, institutions and other legal persons irrespective of their organizational and legal form or form of ownership, including joint ventures with the participation of foreign legal persons and citizens. The fee comprises payments for every substance contained in the emissions. It depends on the quantity of the emissions and takes into account the regional ecological heterogeneity of the territories. Payments for emissions within the limits of the permissible standards are made as part of production costs. Payments for exceeding the permissible standards are made out of the profits remaining at the disposal of the natural resource utilizers. The sums levied for pollution of the natural environment are transferred by natural resource utilizers, in accordance with a percentage system not subject to appeal to the account of the extrabudgetary State Ecological Funds after 10% has been assigned as income to the budget of the Federation in order to finance the activity of territorial organs of State administration for the protection of the natural environment. The following ecological offences are liable to a fine: failure to observe environmental quality standards; non-fulfilment of the duty to carry out a State ecological evaluation and of the requirements set forth in the conclusions of an ecological evaluation; violation of ecological requirements in the planning, construction, reconstruction or operation; non-compliance with the instructions of the organs performing State ecological monitoring; production and use of prohibited chemical substances and substances which have a harmful effect on the ozone layer; and refusal to supply up-to-date, complete and reliable information concerning the state of the natural environment. These acts are punishable by a fine levied by the administrative procedure on: citizens—between 1 and 10 times the amount of the minimum wage; officials—between 3 and 20 times the minimum wage; and enterprises, institutions and organizations—between 50,000 and 500,000 roubles. The specific level of the fine is determined by the organ imposing the fine according to the nature and type of the offence committed, the degree of guilt of the offender and the damage caused.

(l) *Slovakia*: Polluters have to pay a fee depending on the quantity and type of substance they emit. Tariffs per ton of emissions are for: particulates—SK 3,000; sulphur dioxide—SK 1,000; nitrogen oxides—SK 800 and carbon monoxide—SK 600. Other substances are classed in four groups with fees per ton ranging from SK 20,000 for carcinogens to 1,000. Polluters do not have to pay the full amount at once, as the fee was phased in starting with 20% in 1992 and reaching 100% in 1998.

(m) *Slovenia*: The 1994 Environmental Protection Law stipulates that the environmental damage caused by the emissions should be charged, but at present environmental taxes still play a subordinate role in comparison to other taxes. The only fees which are paid are related to water pollution.

(n) *Sweden*: The tax on the sulphur content in coal, oil and peat fuels was introduced in 1991. It corresponds to SKr 30,000 (about ECU 3,300) per ton of sulphur emitted. The sulphur tax has not replaced administrative regulations but is complementary to them. The nitrogen oxide charge came into force in 1992. It is levied on large and medium-sized combustion plants. The charge is SKr 40,000 (about ECU 4,300) per ton emitted and is refunded to the group of plants that have to pay it in proportion to the amount of useful energy produced. Total emissions from plants liable to the charge decreased from 25 kilotonnes in the late 1980s to less than 15 kilotonnes in 1993. In addition, there is a tax on domestic flights based on emissions of NO_x and VOCs. Since 1991 Sweden has had a tax on carbon dioxide emitted when burning fossil fuels. The tax has improved the competitiveness of biomass fuels, for example wood chips for energy production in district heating plants. However, it is still difficult to assess the effects of the CO_2 tax.

(o) *Ukraine*: The first step in applying an economic instrument relating to the use of natural resources was taken in 1992 with the introduction of charges for environmental pollution. The air pollution charge is applied to the total quantity of emissions, including those within the maximum permissible emissions. Basic standard charges have been set for emissions of pollutants from stationary sources. Those for emissions from mobile sources are determined according to the quantity and type of fuel, the rate being highest for leaded petrol, medium for diesel fuel and lowest for unleaded petrol.

2. Product charges, taxes, and tax differentiation, including fuel taxes

Product charges and taxes are often a substitute for emission charges and taxes, where the level of pollution resulting from a particular activity can better be quantified by the amount of a product that is used in or results from the activity. Thus these charges or taxes are applied to the price of the product that causes pollution as it is manufactured, used as a factor of production or consumed. In general a classification system will be required distinguishing products according to the pollution that they may cause. Tax differentiation is especially used in relation to fuel taxes in order to set an incentive for the consumption of low-pollution fuels. Differentiation of fuel and car taxes have, for instance, been widely applied to stimulate the introduction of unleaded petrol.

(a) *Austria*: A new car registration tax was introduced in January 1992. While the tax base is the sales price, the tax rate depends on the standard fuel consumption of the car. At the same time, the value added tax (VAT) rate for new vehicles was reduced from 32% to the standard rate of 20%. In 1993 the excise duty on different fuels was as follows: leaded petrol—S 6.43 per kg; unleaded petrol—S 5.35 per kg; diesel—S 3.61 per kg; and other motor fuels—S 3.61 per kg. In January 1994 the mineral oil tax was raised by S 0.60 per litre. Heavy transport is charged a road traffic contribution, which is differentiated with respect to the payload of trucks and trailers.

(b) *Bulgaria*: Tax differentiation according to the age of imported motor vehicles, and a tax reduction on cars fitted with catalysts were introduced in 1993. Tolls are charged for road use and transit passage across the country.

(c) *Canada*: At the federal level there is a progressive tax on automobile weight, beginning at Can$ 30 for vehicles weighing 2007 kg. There is also an excise tax on automobile air conditioners of Can$ 100. Fuel taxation differs between the provinces. At the federal level alternative fuels are exempt from excise tax. In some provinces there are tax incentives on cars with low fuel consumption and disincentives on those with a high fuel consumption. Some provinces use tax differentiation also to stimulate the use of natural gas, propane, ethanol and methanol as or in vehicle fuel.

(d) *Croatia*: Taxation of equipment for the use of solar energy and photovoltaics is reduced. Also fuel taxes are differentiated. Import duty is reduced for equipment to be used for environmental protection.

(e) *Denmark*: The green tax burden has for most of the 1977-1993 period been between 3% and 4% of gross domestic product (GDP). Duties on oil products and electricity were introduced in 1977. In 1982 duties on coal and lignite were introduced. The following are the rates of environmental taxes on fossil fuels, 1993-1998, including 25% VAT.

Product	Unit	1993	1994	1995	1996	1997	1998
Petrol, leaded	DKr/litre	3.63	3.88	4.44	4.66	4.73	4.79
Petrol, unleaded	DKr/litre	2.81	3.06	3.63	3.85	3.91	3.98
Diesel, ordinary	DKr/litre	2.55	2.55	2.84	3.13	3.25	3.25
Diesel, light	DKr/litre	2.43	2.43	2.71	3.00	3.13	3.13
LPG	DKr/litre	1.68	1.68	1.88	2.08	2.16	2.16
Electricity	DKr/kWh	0.46	0.51	0.54	0.58	0.63	0.71
Coal	DKr/ton	1.165	1.165	1.265	1.378	1.490	1.603
Waste, incineration	DKr/ton	200	200	200	200	263	263
Light fuel oil	DKr/litre	2.20	2.20	2.20	2.20	2.20	2.20
Heavy fuel oil	DKr/kg	2.48	2.48	2.48	2.48	2.48	2.48

In 1988 a charge on CFCs was imposed as part of an action plan to reduce their consumption. The charge rate is DKr 30/kg. A charge on waste (ex VAT) was introduced in 1986 (DKr 40/tonne), and raised considerably in 1990 (DKr 130/tonne). The charge was raised again in 1993 and differentiated between disposal (DKr 195/tonne) and incineration (DKr 160/tonne)). Since 1990 anyone engaged in activities covered by the Raw Material Act is obliged to pay a raw material charge (DKr 5/m^3). The charge is paid in conjunction with the extraction and import of natural resources such as sand, gravel, clay, chalk. The charge on nickel-cadmium batteries is part of a voluntary agreement between the Government and the battery trade organizations.

(f) *Finland*: The tax for leaded petrol is Fmk 2.36, while that for unleaded petrol is 45 penniä and that for reformulated petrol 5 penniä lower. The tax for sulphur-free diesel oil is 15 penniä (9%) lower than the basic tax.

(g) *Germany*: A tax difference of DM 0.10 per litre exists at present to promote the use of unleaded petrol. After having been raised in January 1994, the rates levied are DM 0.98 for unleaded petrol, DM 1.08 for leaded petrol and DM 0.61 for diesel fuel. There are plans to change the motor vehicle tax. It is envisaged that pollutant and noise emissions will serve as the basis for assessment for both passenger cars and heavy-duty vehicles.

(h) *Greece*: The revenues from a tax of Dr 5 per litre levied on petrol is used for pollution reduction measures.

(i) *Italy*: The only important existing economic measure having a significant environmental aspect is the price differentiation in favour of unleaded petrol, introduced in November 1989. According to a law of November 1993, a reduced excise duty is applied to fuel oils having a sulphur content of less than 1%. Diesel vehicles registered for the first time between February 1992 and 31 December 1994 and having emissions not exceeding the limits of the relevant European Community Directive are exempt from the first payment of the vehicle property tax. As of January 1994, an amount of 250,000 tonnes of a product named "bio-diesel", obtained through the esterification of vegetable oils and their derivatives, and used as fuel or as additive in diesel engines, has been exempt from existing excises on fuels. Concerning electricity, the introduction of a binomial and progressive tariff system for domestic electricity consumption has been a decisive factor in discouraging the use of electricity for heating purposes (cooking, hot water, home heating, etc.).

(j) *Netherlands*: An environmental tax on fuels has existed since 1988. The funds raised by the tax are part of the general revenues. The tax is collected on energy sources which are used as fuels. Use as raw material or feedstock is not subject to this tax. Electricity is not taxed directly, but electricity generated from any of the fields subject to tax is taxed indirectly via the tax paid on the fuel input. The fuels which are taxed are: petrol, light fuel, diesel/gas oil, heavy fuel oil and other mineral oils, liquefied petroleum gas (LPG), coal, blast furnace gas, coke oven gas, refinery gas, coal gas, natural gas, and residuals which are used in the chemicals and petroleum industries. The basis for rate assessment is derived from the energy content (50%) and the CO_2 emissions (50%) of the fuels taxed. The sale of lead-free petrol is promoted by means of fiscal measures. A surcharge on the petrol excise duties is more than twice as high for leaded than for lead-free petrol. The sale of "clean" cars was promoted by means of fiscal measures between 1986 and 1993. During those years it was possible to pay a lower special user's tax on new cars satisfying more stringent emission standards than those then in force.

(k) *Norway*: A carbon tax on oil and natural gas was introduced in 1991. The carbon tax is levied on the amount of fuel consumed. It now starts at NKr 352 per ton of CO_2 for petrol and NKr 350 per tonne of CO_2 for natural gas combustion in the North Sea. For distilled fuel oil it starts at NKr 157 per tonne of CO_2 and for residual oil NKr 137 per tonne of CO_2. A carbon tax equivalent to NKr 169 per tonne of CO_2 is levied on coal and coke used in combustion processes. The tax difference between lead-free petrol and leaded petrol was increased in 1992 and is now NKr 0.66 (ECU 0.08) per litre. In 1992 the structure of the sulphur taxes on oil products was revised. There is no tax if the sulphur content is below 0.05%. In the 0.05-0.25% sulphur range the tax is NKr 0.07 per litre. For a sulphur content greater than 0.25% there is an additional tax of NKr 0.07 per litre per 0.25%. For instance the sulphur tax for residual oil with 0.95% sulphur is NKr 0.28 per litre.

(l) *Poland*: Since January 1992 fees for environmental pollution have been set to cover all operations involving the loading and refuelling of petrol. Rates (Zl/Mg) differ according to the type of tank: 15,500 for tanks with fixed roofs; 10,000 for tanks with floating roofs; 8,500 for underground tanks and surface tanks at fuel depots; 6,500 for railway tanks; 4,500 for tanker trucks and 9,500 for vehicle tanks. Where steps have been taken to reduce emissions by more than 85% only 15% of the rate is charged. There is also a tax differentiation to enhance the use of unleaded petrol, which is Zl 500 per litre cheaper than leaded petrol. Also, local tax rates on vehicles equipped with catalytic converters are reduced.

(m) *Portugal*: Lower taxes are applied to unleaded petrol and low-sulphur fuel oil ($\leq 1\%$).

(n) *Russian Federation*: Virtually no charges or taxes are currently levied on fuel with a view to environmental protection. A decision has already been taken at government level, however, to introduce payments for emissions of carbon dioxide in the very near future and to channel the proceeds into the extrabudgetary ecological fund. Another proposal for a carbon tax institutes a procedure for the transfer by enterprises and organizations in industry, construction and transport of 0.5% of the cost of the energy resources they consume to the account of regional (70%) and federal (30%) energy-saving funds. Such a tax is already being levied in several constituent territorial entities of the Federation.

(o) *Slovakia*: A classification system has been introduced to support the introduction of some environmentally friendly products, such as electric cars, thermal pumps, solar energy, and low-VOC paints. The value added tax on such products will be reduced. The tax on unleaded petrol has been reduced by 13%. Also the use of gas for vehicles is encouraged by a tax reduction. Income from the operation of small hydro-power stations, plants for geothermal energy, wind power plants and thermal pumps is not subject to income taxation for the first five years. Finally, no road tax has to be paid for electric cars, vehicles using solar energy and cars for municipal waste transport.

(p) *Slovenia*: The tax for unleaded petrol is nearly 5% lower than the tax for leaded petrol.

(q) *Sweden*: There are some important traditional excise taxes on petrol, diesel oil, energy and on the sale of new cars. The annual revenue from these taxes is approximately SKr 30 billion. Several product taxes have been introduced with a specific environmental objective (taxes on fertilizers, pesticides and batteries). These charges/taxes are generally too low to affect the supply or demand significantly. Two important tax differentiation schemes for car fuels (and air emissions) are in operation: (1) the tax differentiation (environmental classes) of diesel fuels came into force in 1991 and strongly affected the market. Sulphur emissions from diesel vehicles have dropped by approximately 75%; (2) as in many other European countries there is also a difference in the taxation of leaded and unleaded petrol. The tax difference has gradually been increased from SKr 0.16 per litre to SKr 0.51. The latter amount by far exceeds the extra cost for replacing lead in high octane petrol qualities with other additives.

(r) *Switzerland*: There is a tax differentiation (8 centimes, approximately 7% of the market price) between unleaded and leaded petrol. The basic tax for diesel is between the tax for unleaded and leaded petrol, so the retail price of diesel is higher than that of unleaded petrol.

(s) *United Kingdom*: In March 1993, the Chancellor of the Exchequer announced his intention to introduce VAT on domestic fuel and power, starting at a rate of 8% in April 1994, rising to 17.5% in April 1995. This is expected to reduce domestic energy consumption by about 3.5% by the end of the decade. For motor fuels the Government introduced a tax differential in 1986, which now stands at approximately 21 pence per gallon (about 9% lower for unleaded than leaded). The Government has made a commitment to raise duty on road fuel by at least 5% per annum in real terms up to the year 2000. It has been estimated that this will result in a 7% reduction in national fuel consumption.

3. User and administrative charges

User and administrative charges constitute payments for specific services supplied by public authorities. User charges are, for instance, applied to cover the cost of waste collection or sewerage treatment and hence are less frequently found in the field of air pollution. Administrative charges are usually applied to cover the cost of licensing and monitoring activities by authorities.

(a) *Bulgaria*: In 1993 administrative charges were introduced to cover the cost of licensing. Also those granted tariff concessions, such as importers of exhaust gas treatment installations, have to pay administrative charges.

(b) *Finland*: Charges on the processing of environmental licence applications have been introduced. A medium-sized power station, for instance, must pay Fmk 35,000 and a pulp mill or an oil refinery 140,000.

(c) *France*: There is a single charge of FF 1,000 to cover the administrative costs of licensing procedures. For classified installations this varies depending on the level of pollution, the average amounting to some FF 10,000.

(d) *Germany*: Administrative acts performed under pollution control legislation are subject to the payment of fees.

(e) *Netherlands*: Applicants for a permit are charged by the competent authorities for the administrative costs of licensing.

(f) *Norway*: Depending on the potential size of the emissions of a plant and the vulnerability of the surrounding environment, industrial activities subject to licensing are classified into one of four surveillance classes (class 1 having the greatest emission potential and class 4 the lowest). This *inter alia* governs the frequency of inspections and audits carried out by the Pollution Control Authority. The industrial plants have to pay a charge to obtain or to apply for changes to an existing permit. The charges are differentiated, but the aim is to finance the costs of the permit system, not to control pollution. The industry also has to pay a charge when the authority monitors whether the emission permit conditions are complied with (inspections/audits). The charges almost fully finance the authority's costs related to the licensing system.

(g) *Sweden*: There are some 30-40 administrative charges related to the protection of the environment. Most of them cover only part of the costs involved. Some central authorities like the Chemical Inspectorate and the Nuclear Power Inspectorate are entirely financed by charges. All point sources of any importance pay an annual fee for licensing, supervision and enforcement (totalling more than SKr 100 million per year).

(h) *United Kingdom*: The 1990 Environmental Protection Act allows the establishment of a charging scheme for the recovery of costs incurred by the enforcement authorities in regulating processes. Charges on processes with a large emission potential are levied according to the number of components a process contains and is reviewed each year. There are three categories of charges: an application fee; a subsistence charge payable annually for the holding of each authorization, to cover the ongoing costs of inspection, monitoring and enforcement; and a charge for the substantial variation of an authorization. By way of example, the fees charged in 1993-94 were generally £2,500 per component in the application charge (or £3,750 per component for new processes); £1,540 per component for the subsistence charge; and £1,250 per component for the substantial variation charge. The charge for smaller processes covers compliance monitoring and enforcement costs, including sampling and analysis of emissions. The current fees in operation here are broadly £965 for the initial application; £620 as an application fee for substantial changes; and £585 annual subsistence charge. Non-payment may result in the revocation of an operator's authorization.

4. Emission trading

Emission trading requires a definition and distribution of property rights to environmental media such as the air, or parts thereof ("bubble concept"). Instead of determining the emission limits for a specific plant, a sum of emissions for a specific area or source category is defined and transferable rights to emit (permits) are distributed among enterprises. These can then decide whether to reduce emissions and sell permits or whether to buy additional permits. Consequently, emission reductions will occur where they are the cheapest to accomplish.

(a) *Germany*: Since 1985, the application of a compensation provision (bubble concept) is possible under the Federal Immission Control Act. Details concerning this possibility were specified in 1986 in the Technical Instructions on Air Quality Control with respect to the retrofitting of existing plants.

(b) *Italy*: Emission trading as such is not applied in Italy. The so-called bubble concept, which considers a plant to be a single complex from the point of view of atmospheric emissions, is applied to the licensing of existing refineries. Regional authorities may apply the same concept to the licensing of existing plants, but only within a single plant.

(c) *Netherlands*: There is no system of credits or quotas. Sector-specific emission targets (not quotas), functioning as in the bubble concept, have been laid down in various voluntary agreements between the Government and branches of industry. There are also voluntary agreements regarding the efficient use of energy, with quantitative targets and monitoring schemes.

(d) *Poland*: No emission trading scheme has yet been introduced, but work is under way to establish the legal prerequisites for the introduction of such a system. Studies on possible schemes are under preparation in a project sponsored by the PHARE programme.

(e) *Switzerland*: In some cantons the application of a limited form of the bubble concept is being examined at the local level (through emission certificates). The application will in any case only be possible for the remaining emissions after the implementation of the emission standards set in the Ordinance on Air Pollution Control.

(f) *United Kingdom*: There is currently no system of emissions trading in operation, although the structure of the National Plan for the implementation of the European Community Large Combustion Plants Directive in effect allows a form of trading for the largest power generators. Each generator is given an absolute quantity of emissions of SO_2 and NO_x which it can allocate between its plants subject to the approval of Her Majesty's Inspectorate of Pollution and to not breaching the BATNEEC requirements in individual plant authorizations. This flexibility is not available to the refineries sector or other companies operating large combustion plants under current provisions. The Government is at present considering the possibility of a sulphur permit quota switching scheme for the large combustion plants sector.

(g) *United States*: The programme for SO_2 emission reduction is built on a market-based system of tradable allowances. Each regulated entity is allocated a set of allowances that it may use to cover actual SO_2 emissions, bank for later use, or sell to others. With this mechanism, the allowances should end up in the hands of those entities that value them the most because their control costs are greatest, resulting in large savings nationwide. In the first auctions held by the Chicago Board of Trade environmental groups purchased allowances to retire them. Enforcement is provided by an automated system to track trading and continuous emission monitors. Many local governments are adopting trading schemes to add flexibility to their attainment programmes. The most extensive programme is in Los Angeles, where a comprehensive emission trading system is being used to reduce the emissions of nitrogen oxides and volatile organic compounds. The programme gradually reduces allowable levels of industrial sources emissions, which is necessary if the area is to attain the ozone ambient air quality standards.

5.   Subsidies and other forms of financial assistance

Subsidies are another form of economic instrument although they usually do not conform with the polluter-pays principle. Such measures include low-interest loans, accelerated write-off allowances, cash grants for investments in pollution abatement equipment, research and development. Those subsidies are granted to individuals or enterprises either indirectly (in the case of tax rebates, which result in a loss of tax revenue) or as disbursements from the budget of environmental departments, sometimes through special funds set up for the purpose. The reduction or removal of subsidies that induce polluting activities above the optimal level is also important in some countries.

Financial assistance may not be in violation of the polluter-pays principle if it is used to speed up a period of transition and is thus limited in time, or if it consists of payments for positive externalities. For instance, general energy-saving measures, which incidentally also lead to a decrease in the emissions of sulphur and nitrogen compounds, receive government support in a number of countries.

(a) *Bulgaria*: A National Fund and Regional Funds were set up in 1993 and an Ordinance on the Raising, Spending and Control of Environmental Protection Funds was adopted. Money is raised through fines, taxes, donations and other means. Projects of particular importance are financed from the national budget by decision of the Council of Ministers, acting on a proposal by the Ministry of the Environment. There is an acute shortage of investment on a national scale. Efforts are being made to attract donors willing to invest on a mutually beneficial basis. A Council of Ministers' Decree exempts waste treatment equipment and subsidiary parts, as well as air monitoring and control equipment and chemicals, from import taxes.

(b) *Canada*: The Income Tax Act allows accelerated write-off allowances to businesses investing in government-approved air pollution control devices.

(c) *Cyprus*: With the assistance of the World Bank, a special fund was created for the long-term financing of investments in industrial units including investments for pollution abatement equipment. The cost of the technical study for each investment is covered by the fund. In order to mitigate the impact of the recent legislation, cash grants are awarded to existing industries through government funds.

(d) *Czech Republic*: The State Environmental Fund has been set up to collect fees from individual polluters. These fees are then used for grants and loans (interest-free or with low interest rates) by the Ministry of the Environment to support measures leading to a decrease in emissions. The grants must not exceed 50% of the investment costs and are provided especially for non-profit organizations.

(e) *Denmark*: There are no low-interest loans or accelerated depreciation allowances, nor any general cash grants for environmental protection. About Dkr 500 million per year are given as subsidies to the development of bio-fuel technologies and investments in alternative energy production (wind, solar, power, biomass fuels, etc.).

(f) *Germany*: Commercial-scale demonstration projects in air quality control have been supported since 1979. In the first years support was granted in particular to projects concerned with upgrading existing plants to the state of the art. Later, the programme was extended to include new plants and broadened in scope to include waste management, water quality control, noise abatement, clean up of contaminated sites, and energy conservation. Funding amounts to up to 50% of the sum invested. Since 1991, interest subsidies have been the main form of support. The aim of this programme is to obtain knowledge of the measures' technical and economic feasibility to serve as a basis for the development of normative regulations. In addition, there are credit programmes subject to special terms to support environmental protection measures at, in particular, medium-sized companies. Measures in the fields of wind power, photovoltaics, co-generation of heat and power, energy analyses for buildings, efficient energy use, and renewable resources, are supported by direct subsidies, low-interest credits as well as special depreciation allowances.

(g) *Greece*: The installation of pollution control filters is subsidized by 40% through government funds.

(h) *Italy*: Incentives aimed at accelerating the renewal of the existing car fleet are presently under consideration. They should speed up the replacements of old vehicles with new ones complying with the European Community Directive that will enter into force as of January 1996 and the spreading of electric vehicles in specific sectors of urban transport.

(i) *Netherlands*: There are a limited number of financial incentives which promote certain kinds of environmentally friendly investments. These include subsidies for high efficiency, low-NO_x central heating boilers, and for wind power and cogeneration, which will, however, be largely cut or eliminated in 1995. Financial support is also granted to certain kinds of demonstration projects. In addition, there is an accelerated write-off allowance for investments in certain kinds of innovative environmental technologies. For the transport sector, financial incentives are provided for the rapid introduction of cleaner and less noisy trucks in anticipation of future stricter exhaust standards.

(j) *Norway*: Electric cars, in the country supplied through hydro-power, are exempt from the normal import duties for cars (approximately 100% of the price) in order to encourage their use. The first electric car was given type approval in 1992. Governmental funding of energy efficiency measures have decreased substantially over the last two years, due initially to the overall budgetary situation and a subsequent evaluation of the measures. The Government is now moving away from general grant schemes. In 1994, the work on energy efficiency will concentrate on information, education and grants to facilitate the introduction of energy efficient technology. At the local level the Government is encouraging the establishment of energy efficiency centres. During 1994 some five to seven centres will be established. For 1994 the Government has granted NKr 36 million for information and training connected to energy-saving measures. NKr 10 million are granted for the introduction of new energy technologies.

(k) *Poland*: The national Fund for Environmental Protection and Water Management and similar funds at the Voivodeship (provincial) and Gmina (community) level provide low-interest loans and subsidies for environmental projects that constitute a priority at the national or local level. The income of the funds includes the revenue from fees and fines, which is generally divided between the Gmina (10%), Voivodeship (54%) and national (36%) funds. In 1992 and 1993 the main air pollution related projects included the desulphurization and dedusting of waste gases, the production of cleaner fuels (biogas and wood briquettes), the development of alternative energy sources and fluidized bed combustion. Since 1991 the Environmental Protection Bank has been in operation. Its aim is to support the protection of the environment by providing credits, in particular for the installation of machinery, emission control equipment and emission measuring devises. Indirect subsidies are provided by granting rebates on income tax, turnover tax and an agricultural tax for environmental expenditure and investments.

(l) *Portugal*: Under the Government's Specific Programme for the Development of Portuguese Industry all industrial projects that contribute to the reduction of emissions to the environment are priority candidates for subsidies.

(m) *Russian Federation*: Investment loans from the federal Government are obtainable for measures designed to solve problems of environmental protection through the replacement of existing production lines by, or the conversion into, more efficient plants meeting ecological requirements. The chances of obtaining such loans, however, depend entirely on the initiative of the actual producers or organs of State authority of the region concerned. The assignment of centralized State capital investments to the execution of measures to protect the ambient air has been sharply reduced in recent years: whereas in 1990 such investments (at 1993 prices) amounted to R 285 billion, in 1992 they shrank to R 20 billion and in 1993 they totalled R 114 billion. Under the Act on the protection of the natural environment, a single system of extrabudgetary ecological funds, combining a federal ecological fund and republican, territorial, regional and local funds, has been established for the performance of urgent ecological tasks. The resources of the ecological funds are distributed as follows: 60% for the implementation of nature-protection measures of lo-

cal significance, 30% for measures to be implemented at the level of constituent tribunal territorial entities of the Federation, and 10% for the implementation of measures of federal significance.

(n) *Slovakia*: The revenue generated from pollution charges and fines is reserved for the fund for environmental investments. Subsidies from the State budget are also paid into this fund, there are no direct subsidies for environmentally sound technologies. Twice a year the Ministry of the Environment selects projects that correspond to environmental policy objectives.

(o) *Slovenia*: The Environmental Fund was set up in 1994 to support measures leading to a decrease in emissions. Money for the Fund is raised primarily from the national budget but the Fund also receives assistance from sources such as the World Bank. A large number of the projects are parallel to the Environmental Fund and subsidized directly through the national budget. These subsidies are provided especially for non-profit organizations in the public sector.

(p) *Sweden*: There are no low-interest loans or accelerated depreciation allowances, nor any general cash grants for environmental protection. About SKr 25 million per year are given as subsidies to the development of bio-fuel techniques and investments in alternative energy production (wind, solar power, biomass fuels, etc.). The liming of acidified lakes is mainly financed with the help of State grants (about SKr 150 million per year covering about 85% of the costs).

(q) *United Kingdom*: No direct subsidy is available to industry specifically for expenditure on investment in pollution control equipment or on research and development. When a local authority introduces a smoke control area it is required to pay private householders 70% of the costs of adapting their heating appliance to use smokeless fuel. The Government assists local authorities with 40% of those costs and also provides them with additional borrowing allocations to enable smoke control works to be brought forward. The area with the greatest scope for subsidies and financial assistance is energy efficiency. The Energy Efficiency Office's budget for 1994/95 increased to over £102 million. The budget of the Home Energy Efficiency Scheme, which provides grants to low-income households, the elderly and the disabled for the installation of basic energy efficiency measures, was almost doubled in April 1994. Provision for 1994 is now £75 million. The Energy Management Assistance Scheme provides help to smaller companies towards the cost of obtaining consultancy advice on energy efficiency. The Best Practice Programme provides authoritative and independent advice on energy efficiency in industrial processes, building design and management techniques. It also supports research and development. The Programme includes the promotion of combined heat and power (CHP); the target is to reach 5000 MW installed CHP capacity. A pilot programme aimed at stimulating investment in residential CHP by local authorities and housing associations has been run by the Energy Saving Trust. The Trust has been set up by the Department of the Environment, the Scottish Office, British Gas, the 12 regional electricity companies in England and Wales and Scottish Hydro-Electric to propose, develop and manage schemes financed by its members to promote the efficient use of energy.

C. MEASURES RELATED TO EMISSION CONTROL TECHNOLOGY

1. Technology requirements in legislation and regulations

A common approach for ensuring that appropriate control technology is applied to different polluting activities is to require the use of the so-called ''best available technology'' (BAT), ''state-of-the-art technology'' or ''best practicable means''. In some countries, the concept of best available or practicable technology is explicitly stated in environmental legislation, whereas others stipulate the use of best practicable technology in the permits and licences required in order to undertake potentially polluting activities. Several countries introduce best practicable technology into their air pollution policies by setting emission standards on the basis of the technical performance of those technologies.

(a) *Austria*: BAT requirements have been used since the first Clean Air Act of 1980. They now play a central role in major environmental laws such as the Industrial Code, which regulates the licensing of all operational plants. BAT reflects the level of development based on the knowledge about advanced technological processes, facilities and operational modes, whose proper function has been tested and proved. In the regulation especially comparable processes, facilities and operational modes have to be considered. The definition of BAT thus does not confine itself to nationally available technology but includes any international technology that is successfully used. BAT requirements in Austria are not mere guidelines but binding requirements. They are defined as emission limits for groups of sources. In cases where no BAT is defined by law, experts have to determine it in the course of the licensing process. The trend is to make BAT requirements explicit in the law.

(b) *Belgium*: In the early 1990s more stringent emission limit values were imposed on major industrial installations in the three regions. In Flanders, these are based on the draft EC directive on integrated pollution prevention, prescribing air quality objectives and emission standards for all industrial sectors, which reflect the most recent assessment of best available technology. In Wallonia a decree imposes best available technology not entailing excessive costs to all polluting industries; technical instructions on air quality, based on principles set out in German legislation, are under preparation.

(c) *Bulgaria*: The Clean Ambient Air Bill uses the concept of ''best practicable technology'' in formulating policies for emission standards.

(d) *Canada*: Federal environmental standards and guidelines are based on the use of state-of-the-art processes and control measures, although applications of specific technologies are not usually mandated.

(e) *Cyprus*: The concept of best practicable means is explicitly stated in the regulations for non-registrable processes. Within the framework of the licensing system provided by the environmental legislation, the competent authorities can impose limits as well as means based on the best practicable technology, which will be prescribed in the licence.

(f) *Czech Republic*: The concept of best available techniques not entailing excessive cost (BATNEEC) is laid down in the Clean Air Act and forms the basis for setting emission limits in the relevant regulations. It is also applied in the procedure for issuing construction and operation permits for potentially polluting emission sources.

(g) *Finland*: In practice, BAT is required through the licensing procedure. It is planned that the Air Pollution Control Act will be amended so that BAT always has to be taken into account.

(h) *Germany*: Emission limits are usually based on the state of the art. In general, industry is free to decide which technology to use to comply with the emission limits. The specification of emission limits follows the level of development of advanced processes, facilities or modes of operation. The experiences gained from pilot plants may also be utilized. Emission control provisions shall not result in problems being shifted to other areas; further ecological aspects such as the minimization and recycling of residuals, heat utilization, noise abatement and occupational safety must therefore be taken into account.

(i) *Netherlands*: The Environmental Protection Act states that a permit shall be subject to any regulations which are necessary to protect the environment. If there are adverse environmental effects which cannot be avoided by making the permit subject to such regulations, additional requirements are to be set in the permit to provide the greatest possible protection, unless this cannot be reasonably required. This principle also applies to the rules that can be laid down in general administrative orders. Furthermore, both the restrictions and regulations to which a permit is subject and the regulations laid down in general administrative orders have to be reconsidered regularly in the light of developments in the technological possibilities for protecting the environment and developments in environmental quality. If it is evident that it is possible to further restrict the adverse environmental effects, then this must be done.

(j) *Slovakia*: In accordance with the Clean Air Act emission standards must be set on the basis of best available technology not entailing excessive cost. These requirements are applied whether technology has to be imported or not.

(k) *Sweden*: In the licensing procedure of environmentally hazardous activities for stationary sources no technical requirements are given. However, the conditions for an installation should include reference to BAT as long as it is economically feasible.

(l) *Switzerland*: Emission standards are usually based on the state of the art. Emissions shall be limited as much as technology and operating conditions allow, provided this is economically feasible. A medium-sized and economically sound industrial plant is used as the criterion for assessing the economic feasibility of emission limitation. Emission limitation, therefore, is not governed by the weakest economic sector.

(m) *United Kingdom*: BATNEEC requirements are incorporated in emission limit values, but generally specific technology requirements are not prescribed. However, the guidance notes referred to in section A.5 above, will constitute the best practicable environmental option. Individual plant authorizations may require the fitting of specific abatement technology such as low-NO$_x$ burners.

(n) *United States*: There are multiple BAT requirements contained in the Clean Air Act. New major stationary sources of air pollution and major modifications to such sources are required by the CAA to obtain an air pollution permit before commencing construction. In addition, the CAA requires the Environmental Protection Agency (EPA) to develop new source performance standards (NSPS) for major industrial sources of the criteria pollutants. NSPS are technology-based emission standards for criteria pollutants based on best demonstrated technology for a particular source category or process that is economically feasible. NSPS have been established for over 60 categories of major sources. The 1990 CAA Amendments created two new types of technology-based standards: (i) maximum achievable control technology standards for hazardous air pollutants; and (ii) maximum control technology standards for solid waste combustion.

2.   Control technology requirements for stationary sources

Technological requirements form an integral part of the Sulphur, NO$_x$ and VOC Protocols. The following paragraphs summarize the requirements on emission control technologies for major stationary sources of air pollution. In most cases the timetable for the introduction differs between new and existing sources.

(a) *Bulgaria*: Legislation requires the introduction of more stringent standards for all existing sources by January 1996. Those sources that are retrofitted before that date should comply earlier with the stringent standards. This approach has led to an improvement in the non-ferrous metallurgy, chemical and petrochemical industries. The five-year interim period has proven to be unrealistic for large combustion plants (> 50 MW). The standards given by the Protocol on Further Reduction of Sulphur Emissions will be introduced into legislation in accordance with the required time-frames. Standards approved for 1995-2004 will reflect the state of the art and will be a step towards European Community standards. These will already be applied to new sources, licensed after December 1995.

(b) *Canada*: Emissions of acidifying compounds from provincial power companies have been greatly reduced using a variety of measures, such as flue gas scrubbers, wet limestone units, and sorbent injection, in some cases leading to a removal of 90% of the SO$_2$. For other sources such as smelters, provincial regulations on a plant-by-plant basis have resulted in the application of advanced process technology. By 1994, most smelters were using modern process technology for capturing

their SO$_2$ emissions. The NO$_x$ emission standard for thermal power plants has been tightened as part of the joint federal/provincial NO$_x$/VOC Management Plan, and a further review of those guidelines is scheduled for 1995. National NO$_x$ and SO$_2$ emission limits which incorporate overall plant thermal efficiency considerations have also been prepared for new stationary gas turbine engines. Standards for new NO$_x$ and VOC sources are being established in the light of the best available control technologies economically achievable. In addition, controls on evaporative losses from fuel handling and storage have been developed and changes to fuel properties are being investigated. Measures include lower volatility fuels in some jurisdictions, vapour balancing and recovery in bulk petrol distribution systems and development of additional petrol vapour recovery measures at the retail level.

(c) *Czech Republic*: Control technology requirements for stationary sources are based on the emission standards for new sources set by the Measure to the Clean Air Act. Emission limits are set especially for solid fuels for SO$_2$, NO$_x$, CO, hydrocarbons, and other substances. Emission limits for existing sources are set individually by the relevant air protection authority; however, by the end of 1998 all sources must conform to the emission limits for new sources.

(d) *Denmark*: For the reduction of emissions of SO$_2$, NO$_x$, VOC, heavy metals and persistent organic pollutants, requirements have been laid down in standards and licences. Many different measures have been taken at a large number of facilities: flue gas desulphurization is used in many power plants based on oil and coal. To remove SO$_2$ from the flue gas, both regenerative and non-regenerative processes are used. The non-regenerative processes utilize lime or limestone to convert SO$_2$ into gypsum or CaSO$_3$, while the regenerative processes produce sulphur acid. Low-NO$_x$ burners and staged combustions have been installed in many coal, oil and gas-fired plants. Almost independent of the feedstock properties, NO$_x$ emissions can be reduced by a factor of two. Further reduction of NO$_x$ emissions has been obtained by catalytic de-NO$_x$ units. Particulate emissions are reduced by using electrostatic precipitators and bag filters. For VOC control in refineries measures include: tightening of process equipment; floating roofs with secondary seals in tanks; and gas recovery in loading equipment. VOC control measures are also used in oil depots and harbours. For petrol distribution systems, stage 1 controls (terminals) are introduced in most installations. VOC emissions from the plastic and graphic industries are dealt with by using water-based prints and treating emissions.

(e) *Finland*: Sulphur emission standards for coal-fired power plants, which can be achieved with flue gas desulphurization units, were introduced in 1989. Technology-based emission limits have also been set for other fuels. The limit for NO$_x$ emissions for new coal-fired power plants with a capacity of more than 150 MW$_{th}$ requires selective catalytic reduction technology. The emission limits for smaller plants can be reached by modern power station and burner technologies. Technology-based emission limits have also been set for burning peat, wood, oil and gas.

(f) *Germany*: A comprehensive system of emission limits covers all relevant installations and pollutants. Existing plants must, in principle, meet the same requirements as new plants. Since 1985 legislation requires an effective and comprehensive retrofitting of existing plants. Operators of existing plants are granted transitional periods within which to bring their pollution control technology up to the level required for new plants. The criteria for the length of the transitional period are: type, quantity and hazardousness of the emissions, service life of the installation, and technical particularities. The period allowed as a general rule for retrofitting plants subject to licensing is five years.

(g) *Italy*: Guidelines, established in July 1990, set emission limits for existing plants and introduce deadlines for adaptation. They cover 289 pollutants (sulphur oxides, nitrogen oxides, suspended particles, carbon monoxide, carcinogenic substances, inorganic and organic substances) and indicate the abatement technologies available for a broad range of plant types, including combustion plants, driers, incinerators, cement factories, coke plants, foundries, and furnaces. For companies with several installations at least 35% of installed power has to be adapted by December 1997, at least 60% by December 1999 and retrofitting has to be completed by December 2002. Emission reductions can be obtained by modifying plant management practices, such as improving the quality of fuels, or by introducing combustion modifications and flue gas denitrification, desulphurization and deducting systems. In some cases, retrofitting projects may be accompanied by simultaneous repowering programmes with turbogas sets.

(h) *Netherlands*: Abatement technologies applied to meet standards or permit requirements include: flue gas desulphurization with 85% efficiency for large coal and oil-fired combustion installations ($\geq$ 300 MW_{th}); fluidized-bed combustion for new coal-fired installations ($\geq$ 300 MW_{th}); use of low-NO_x combustion technologies for new and existing installations; and selective catalytic reduction of NO_x at power plants.

(i) *Portugal*: A voluntary agreement between the Government and the industry association is in place to reduce the environmental impact of the pulp industry that includes the reduction of emissions of particulates and SO_2 to the air. This agreement has already led to process changes and the installation of electrostatic precipitators and wet scrubbers in four plants, out of a total of seven, with the consequent reduction in emissions of the target pollutants. The same type of measures is being introduced in the remaining plants.

(j) *Slovakia*: Under the Clean Air Act, emission standards for new sources apply immediately, whereas existing sources, i.e. those authorized before October 1991, have to meet the standards by January 1999.

(k) *Sweden*: For the reduction of emissions of SO_2, NO_x, VOC, heavy metals and persistent organic pollutants, requirements have been laid down in standards and licences. The guiding principle when considering applications for permits for industrial plants is that measures costing a maximum of SKr 30 per kg of sulphur and SKr 40 per kg of nitrous oxide are usually required. In pulp production, ways of reducing emissions of sulphur include: the installation of scrubbers; gas treatment including combustion of odorous gases; and increasing the dry content of black liquor. For VOC control in refineries measures include: tightening of process equipment; floating roofs with secondary seals in tanks; and gas recovery in loading equipment. VOC control measures are also used in oil depots and harbours. For petrol distribution systems, stage I controls (terminals) and stage II controls (petrol stations) are introduced in most installations. VOC emissions from plastic and graphic industries are dealt with by using water-based prints and treating the emissions.

(l) *Switzerland*: The emission standards apply not only to new plants, but also to existing plants. As a general rule, existing plants have to be retrofitted within a period of five years after the entry into force of emission limitations.

(m) *United States*: Final maximum achievable control technology (MACT) standards for hazardous air pollutant (HAP) emissions from chemical manufacturing, disposal of uranium mill tailings, coke ovens and dry-cleaning operations were issued in 1994. MACT standards for HAP emissions from aerospace manufacturing, magnetic tape manufacturing, petrol distribution, degreasing operations, industrial process cooling towers, paper and pulp manufacturing, chromium electroplating operations, and polymer and resins facilities were proposed in 1994.

3. Control technology requirements for mobile sources

As regards motor vehicles, most ECE countries use as a basis for national approval procedures the international regulations annexed to the 1958 Agreement concerning the adoption of uniform conditions of approval and reciprocal recognition of approval for motor vehicle equipment and parts (United Nations, ECE) currently applied by 25 ECE member States. The development of these regulations meets a continuing need to improve road safety and to reduce the damage to the environment at a time of continuing growth in motor vehicle traffic. Currently 94 regulations are in existence. They have been subsequently amended, or supplemented, in response to the concerns of society and to the changing technology. Under the uniform system so established, approval of vehicle types and components (including the conformity of production tests related to pollutant emissions for instance) is a prerequisite for marketing, including the import of vehicles or parts manufactured outside the ECE region, and in some countries it also suffices for the operation of imported vehicles. Some countries additionally require regular in-service controls and inspections as a prerequisite for continued operation of vehicles in road traffic. As of 20 February 1995, regulations concerning the emission of pollutants by motor vehicle engines were in force in the following countries:

(*a*) Regulation No. 15 (with four series of amendments and a supplement, gradually being replaced by Regulation No. 83) on gaseous pollutants from passenger cars and light-duty vehicles equipped with a positive-ignition engine using leaded petrol (or with a compression-ignition engine): Croatia; Romania; Russian Federation; and Yugoslavia;

(b) Regulation No. 24 (with three series of amendments) on visible pollutants from compression-ignition engines or from vehicles equipped with such engines: Belgium; Croatia; Czech Republic; Finland; France; Germany; Hungary; Italy; Luxembourg; Netherlands; Poland; Romania; Slovakia; Slovenia; Spain; Russian Federation; United Kingdom; and Yugoslavia;

(c) Regulation No. 40 (with one series of amendments) on gaseous pollutants from motor cycles equipped with a positive-ignition engine: Belgium; Croatia; Czech Republic; Finland; France; Germany; Hungary; Italy; Luxembourg; Netherlands; Norway; Poland; Romania; Russian Federation; Slovakia; Slovenia; United Kingdom; and Yugoslavia;

(d) Regulation No. 47 (in its original version) on gaseous pollutants from mopeds equipped with a positive-ignition engine: Belgium; Croatia; Czech Republic; Finland; France; Germany; Hungary; Italy; Luxembourg; Netherlands; Norway; Poland; Romania; Russian Federation; Slovakia; Slovenia; United Kingdom; and Yugoslavia;

(e) Regulation No. 49 (with two series of amendments) on emissions of pollutants (gaseous and particulate) by compression-ignition engines for heavy-duty vehicles: Belgium; Croatia; Czech Republic; Finland; France; Germany; Hungary; Italy; Luxembourg; Netherlands; Poland; Romania; Russian Federation; Slovakia; Slovenia; United Kingdom; and Yugoslavia;

(f) Regulation No. 67 (in its original version) on equipment for using liquefied petroleum gas in motor vehicle propulsion systems (safety requirements): Belgium; Czech Republic; Finland; Hungary; Italy; Netherlands; Norway; Poland; Romania; Slovakia; and United Kingdom;

(g) Regulation No. 83 (with one series of amendments; a second series of amendments was adopted in July 1994) on the approval of vehicles with regard to the emission of gaseous and particulate pollutants by the engine according to the engine fuel requirements: Belgium; Czech Republic; France; Germany; Hungary; Italy; Luxembourg; Netherlands; Poland; Romania; Slovakia; Slovenia; Spain; United Kingdom; and Yugoslavia;

(h) Regulation No. 84 (in its original version) on the approval of power-driven vehicles equipped with internal combustion engines with regard to the measurements of fuel consumption: Austria; Belgium; Czech Republic; Finland; France; Germany; Hungary; Italy; Luxembourg; Netherlands; Norway; Poland; Romania; Slovakia; Slovenia; Spain; United Kingdom and Yugoslavia;

(i) Regulation No. 85 (in its original version) on the approval of power-driven vehicles equipped with internal combustion engines with regard to the measurement of the net power: Belgium; Czech Republic; Finland; France; Germany; Hungary; Italy; Luxembourg; Netherlands; Norway; Poland; Romania; Slovakia; Slovenia; Spain; United Kingdom and Yugoslavia.

The following two draft regulations were adopted in 1994:

(a) Draft regulation on the emissions of pollutants (gaseous and particulate) by the compression-ignition engines to be installed in agricultural and forestry tractors will be enacted by the Governments of Italy and of the United Kingdom;

(b) Draft regulation on the emissions of carbon dioxide and the fuel consumption of passenger cars will be enacted by the Governments of France and Germany.

Requirements for mobile source emissions are also included in the Sulphur, NO_x and VOC Protocols. The following paragraphs summarize the requirements on emission control technologies for major categories of mobile emission sources.

(a) *Austria*: To meet the emission standards for vehicles it is necessary that petrol-fuelled passenger cars are equipped with a three-way catalytic converter; diesel-fuelled cars need an engine of the modern type.

(b) *Canada*: In 1988 vehicle emission standards were tightened and those for light-duty vehicles have been further tightened beginning with the 1994 model year. Measures required include improved three-way catalysts and advanced engine controls.

(c) *Denmark*: There are no requirements for technologies used for controlling emissions from mobile sources. However, new vehicles must meet the emission standards laid down in the relevant EC directives. In practice all new petrol-driven passenger cars have been equipped with closed-loop three-way catalysts and coal canisters since October 1990.

(d) *Germany*: Since January 1993, exhaust gas limits necessitating the use of three-way catalyst are applicable for all new otto-engine passenger cars. Also since January 1993 provisions concerning the evaporative losses of fuel have been in force. They can only be complied with through the use of a special device which captures the emissions and feeds them to the engine combustion process (on-board measures). In two further stages, 1996 and 1999, the 1993 limits for pollutant emissions from passenger cars are again to be reduced by 50% at each stage. The limit values to be complied with as from 1996 were agreed upon by the EC Environment Ministers in June 1993. A limit value for soot particles had been applicable since October 1990 for new diesel-engine passenger cars. As of January 1993 a more stringent limit has been in effect, which is due to be again tightened drastically in 1996. Particulate emissions of heavy-duty vehicles and buses are dealt with in an EC directive, to become effective in two stages, 1993 and 1996, which was adopted in March 1991. The standards are due to be tightened further in 1999.

(e) *Norway*: As of January 1989, the US-83 vehicle emission standard was made compulsory for petrol-fuelled passengers cars. As of October 1990 US-87 standards became compulsory for diesel passenger cars and all other light vehicles with a maximum payload of less than 750 kg. As of October 1992 the US-90 vehicle emission standard for light-duty trucks became compulsory for all those with a total weight of less than 3500 kg, and a maximum payload exceeding 760 kg. As of October 1993 the EC emission standard for heavy-duty vehicles became compulsory. As of January 1995 the EC directives on vehicle emission standards for petrol-fuelled and diesel-fuelled passenger cars and for light-duty trucks will come into force. Some of the standards are given in tables 13.1-3.

(f) *Poland*: A draft legal act has been prepared to set emission limits for vehicles so that they have to be fitted with catalytic converters. It applies to all vehicles with spark-ignition engines registered in Poland (i.e. also imported second-hand vehicles) after 1 July 1995 (excluding those with an engine capacity of less than 700 cm^3 registered before the end of 1996).

(g) *Slovenia*: To meet the emission standards for new vehicles petrol-fuelled passenger cars have to be equipped with a three-way catalytic converter.

(h) *Sweden*: There are no requirements for technologies used for controlling emissions from mobile sources. There are specific exhaust emission control regulations for passenger cars and new light and heavy commercial vehicles. To meet the exhaust emission control requirements for new vehicles different technical measures are used: three-way catalytic converter with closed loop and charcoal canister for passenger cars with spark-ignition engines; exhaust gas recirculation and oxidation catalytic converter for compression ignition engines; engine measures on heavy vehicles.

(i) *United States*: Standards reducing particulate emissions (soot) from old and new diesel-fuelled urban buses and refuelling emissions from light-duty trucks have been issued. New buses are required to reduce their emissions by 93% from uncontrolled levels starting with the 1994 model year. Old buses will have emission controls added whenever their engines are rebuilt or replaced. Standards were also proposed for smoke and nitrogen oxides from large diesel non-road vehicles such as farm and construction equipment.

4. The availability of unleaded fuel

All Parties that reported under this item noted that unleaded fuel was widely available. Most distribution facilities now offer unleaded fuel. Some Parties reported on the market share of unleaded fuel; this information has been included in table 12, in the last column that gives the fuel standard for unleaded petrol. In some countries leaded petrol or some type of petrol has been banned. In *Austria* only unleaded petrol has been available since November 1993; in *Canada* only unleaded petrol is available in nearly all stations since leaded petrol was phased out in the late 1980s; in *Germany* and *Switzerland* regular petrol is only available unleaded; in *Sweden* a complete ban of leaded petrol is expected before the end of 1994.

5. The role for technology-related research and development

Most Parties have special national programmes or projects to stimulate research and development of control technologies and so-called ''clean'' technologies that are expected to reduce air pollution.

(a) *Bulgaria*: There are two funds that promote research: the National Fund for Scientific Research and the Environmental Protection Fund. The latter is managed by a council headed by the Minister of the Environment. With a view to reducing emissions of sulphur and nitrogen oxides from combustion plants, the funds have financed the development of technologies for adding emulsifiers to liquid fuels, the use of ultrasound and fluidized-bed combustion technologies.

(b) *Canada*: The federal Government, in concert with the provinces and industry, has conducted many development and demonstration projects, and continues to undertake technology research. Recent examples include work on demonstrating advanced combustion systems to reduce NO$_x$ emissions, research into coal benefication and coal gasification, and support for fluidized-bed combustion demonstrations.

(c) *Germany*: During the period from 1987 to 1990 the federal Government supported 362 research and development projects with funds totalling about DM 450 million. The main focus of these projects was on improving emission control technologies and techniques designed to save energy. In addition to this, the federal Government has supported commercial-scale demonstration projects since 1979. The results from these projects form the basis for developing regulations.

(d) *Netherlands*: Research into control techniques, projects demonstrating low-emission technology and environmentally friendly energy production are being financed by Government. During the last three years the Government has financed major programmes for the demonstration of best available low-NO$_x$ technology for gas-powered engines, gas turbines, boilers and furnaces. Another programme is aimed at the demonstration of de-NO$_x$ techniques at four municipal waste incineration plants. The efficiency of inner floating roofs and double seals is being investigated. Other studies aim at demonstrating the applicability of vapour recovery techniques for petrol loading operations carried out by inland barges. Research financed by the Government also demonstrated the technical and economic feasibility of reducing fluoride emissions in the ceramic industry. Recent research has focused on private energy consumption. The energy intensity of a wide variety of activities has been investigated to determine the impact of a shift to low-energy consumption lifestyles.

(e) *Norway*: The State Pollution Control Authority gives financial support (up to 50%) to demonstration and development projects. The primary objective is to promote the development of technology and demonstration projects aimed at reducing pollution and waste. The total sum for the financial year of 1994 is NKr 47 million. In addition, the Research Council administers two research and development programmes for promoting solutions to environmental problems for process industries (e.g. metal smelters) and for promoting the export of environmental technology. The total financial contribution for these two programmes is NKr 20 million.

(f) *Russian Federation*: A section of the State scientific and technological programme is entitled ''The Ecological Security of Russia'' (1993-1995). In pursuit of the 23 targets of this programme, 27 research projects are in progress, the aggregate financing for which exceeds R 260 million. The projects cover a wide range of problems, including an analysis of the ecological, technical and economic characteristics of modern technologies in the main sectors of industry and gas-refining processes. In the course of these research efforts, a draft national programme for the application to industry of progressive nature-protection equipment and advanced technologies for the purpose of reducing transboundary air pollution will be prepared.

(g) *United Kingdom*: The Government has operated and continues to operate a number of schemes. Under the Environmental Technology Innovation Scheme, grants are made available to fund projects up to "proof of concept" stage. Ten projects have been completed and a further 19 projects are currently being supported. The Department of the Environment has offered a total of £5.35 million under the schemes. Most of these projects have focused on VOC emission abatement, but there are also projects on SO_2 abatement. In June 1994 the £16-million Environmental Technology Best Practice Programme, which will run over five years, was launched. This Programme will emphasize the provision and delivery of information rather than provide grant assistance to firms. It will aim to make the best environmental technology and techniques more widely known to potential users and suppliers. The emphasis will be on reduction of waste and pollution at source. As part of the Coal Research Programme, there are 17 projects on SO_2 emissions from coal combustion and on gasification technologies, 11 projects assessing formation mechanisms and control strategies for NO_x emissions, and a project on CO_2 emissions from coal-fired plants. The Air Pollution Abatement Review Group gives technological advice on stationary source abatement technology in support of policy. The Group comprises experts in abatement technologies from research institutes, industry, universities, government and professional bodies.

(h) *United States*: EPA has major research programmes to develop innovative, pollution prevention control techniques. There is also the Clean Coal Technology Program sponsored by the Department of Energy, a multi-million dollar public/private partnership designed to demonstrate technologies on a commercial scale that use coal with lower pollution (especially sulphur dioxide and nitrogen oxides) and sometimes energy conversion gains. Most of the projects under this programme are expected to be ready for commercial use by the year 2000.

D. MONITORING AND ASSESSMENT OF AIR POLLUTION EFFECTS

1. Monitoring of air quality and environmental effects

Air pollution monitoring systems may deal with emissions, deposition, air and precipitation quality and the environmental effects related to air pollution. They may be designed to provide information on local problems or those on a regional scale. The importance of automated monitoring is growing. Table 14.1 gives a description of national air quality monitoring activities and table 14.2 lists national monitoring stations for the major air pollut-

ants. The following paragraphs summarize national activities related to the systematic monitoring of effects of air pollutants:

(a) *Austria*: The "Bioindikator-Netz" is a needle and leaf sampling programme of the Federal Forest Research Institute on a 16 km x 16 km grid across all of the country. Its objective is to obtain information on the sulphur content and the main nutrients in foliage. The Forest Damage Monitoring System of the Federal Forest Research Institute is carried out on a 8.7 km x 8.7 km grid. It includes: periodic soil analysis, needle/leaf sampling and analysis, integrated air pollutant measurement, and crown condition assessment.

(b) *Canada*: Activities include monitoring of: concentrations and depositions of SO_2 and NO_x; changes in lake and stream chemistry; and forest health.

(c) *Netherlands*: In addition to the quantitative measurements of compounds, biological effects on plants and lichens are monitored. Integrated (multi-media) monitoring (air, groundwater, and soil) of forests is carried out within the framework of national acidification research in order to determine the relationship between air pollution, acid deposition and effects on trees. The air pollution monitoring network has been integrated with monitoring networks for rain water in 15 places.

(d) *Norway*: More than NKr 18 million is spent on monitoring the effects of air pollutants in 1994. The monitoring results give the basis for mapping critical loads and levels, and their exceedances.

Several Parties reported on the use of continuous emission monitoring (CEM) systems. In *Austria* these CEMs are installed at power plants and big industrial plants. In *Canada* they are applied to coal-fired power plants. As of January 1996 power plants, large heating facilities, cement plants, lime kilns, and waste combustion plants must have CEMs installed in the *Czech Republic*. In *Germany* for large combustion plants, CEMs are required in general. In *Poland* CEMs have to be applied at installations emitting more than 1200 kg of SO_2 or 800 kg of particulates per hour.

2. Research into air pollution effects and assessment of critical loads and levels

In addition to efforts within the framework of the Convention (see chap. IV, sect. A), there are numerous activities at the national level with respect to the assessment of effects of air pollutants, in particular where these provide a basis for determining critical loads and levels within their territories. On the basis of data collected by the Coordinating Center for Effects figures III.1 and III.2 present maps of critical loads for acidity and sulphur deposition.

(a) *Austria*: The research activities include studies concerning: the acidity control of remote alpine lakes; the atmospheric heavy metal depositions and the use of mosses as accumulation indicators; the concentrations of heavy metals and sulphur in bogs of the province of Salzburg; and the lindane concentrations in precipitation. The "Forschungsinitiative gegen das Waldsterben" is a programme of interdisciplinary forest decline research dealing mainly with the decline in forest ecosystems, especially Norway spruce and mixed oak.

(b) *Canada*: On the basis of monitoring and modelling, work has been initiated to investigate the impact of emissions on visibility. Research is undertaken on biological effects in lakes and rivers at five biomonitoring sites. The goal is to determine whether there are aquatic systems that will not be fully protected by current programmes. Other interdisciplinary research on ecological processes is also performed at the five calibrated watersheds, including research on wildlife. A priority is to produce an assessment of fresh water acidification caused by atmospheric deposition of nitrogen pollutants. Research activities on the threat of acid rain and airborne pollutants to forests focus on investigating the link between air pollution and direct effects on forest vegetation, and estimating critical loads for forests. Also, research is under way on the direct effects of acidic pollutants in gaseous and aerosol form on human health and the risk to human health posed by exposure to acidic pollutants. Population and field studies, inhalation toxicology studies and clinical human studies are being carried out. Current plans include a comprehensive scientific assessment, to be prepared by 1997, to provide the basis for the next steps aimed at meeting new target loads. In addition, research is being conducted into the effects of ground-level ozone on vegetation and human health.

(c) *Czech Republic*: Critical load mapping is concentrated on forest ecosystems and the effects of atmospheric deposition of sulphur and nitrogen compounds. The assessment is carried out for the EMEP grid cells. The critical loads have been assessed for over two thirds of the national territory.

(d) *Denmark*: Action to determine critical loads include the mapping and integrated monitoring of terrestrial ecosystems, monitoring of air pollutants, deposition calculations and analyses of the consequences of reduction scenario, covering the effects in fresh water. Mapping includes both acidification aspects and the potential damage of excess nutrient loads resulting from high nitrogen deposition levels. Work is planned on heavy metals and xenobiotic substances.

(e) *Finland*: The development of calculation methods for depicting critical loads of aquatic and terrestrial ecosystems as a function of sulphur and nitrogen deposition has been given the highest priority. Existing data for lakes and forests have been used to test calculation methods. The dynamic Simulation Model for Acidification's Regional Trends (SMART) has been applied to those seven catchments for which relevant soil and catchment data are available. The use of dynamic models makes it possible to analyse the time scale within which the critical loads have to be achieved in order to protect ecosystems from damage.

(f) *Italy*: The Agency for New Technology, Energy and Environment (ENEA) has commenced critical load mapping activities. First results are expected in early 1995.

(g) *Netherlands*: The Priority Programme on Acidification was started in 1985. The third and final phase of this programme started in 1992 and will end in 1994. The topics that have been or are being researched in this programme include: exposure-effect relationships; effectiveness of abatement techniques by an integrated acidification model; chemical mechanisms by which the damage occurs; quantification of effects; combination stress; nitrogen cycle and forest soils; and critical loads.

(h) *Norway*: In 1994 approximately NKr 3 million will be spent on activities directly related to the assessment of critical loads and levels. Around 60 projects have been carried out. These projects comprise mapping of critical loads and levels, reports on the proposed critical loads and levels criteria related to effects on biota, tests of critical loads and levels on specific Norwegian ecosystems, indicator species or societies. The projects and scientific work have been carried out by the five largest research institutes on air, aquatic and terrestrial environment and by four Norwegian universities. The research activities into air pollutants and their effects comprise a wide range of topics from transport and deposition of air pollutants to effect-oriented studies.

(i) *Poland*: In areas where the concentrations of pollutants have been considerably in excess of the norms, notably the highly industrialized area of Upper Silesia, epidemiological research on the local population has been conducted for years. Also, studies of other environmental impacts and estimates of the associated losses have been undertaken.

(j) *Russian Federation*: The research in progress has made it possible to determine critical load values for a number of areas in the European part of the Russian Federation. Maps were prepared on the EMEP grid system on a scale of 150 x 150 km^2.

(k) *Spain*: A research group has been established under the Ministry of Industry and Energy to update critical load and level values. Since 1993 several surveys have been carried out to evaluate damage to crops and forest induced by ozone on the coast of the Mediterranean.

(l) *Sweden*: The Environmental Protection Agency has conducted research into the effects of air pollution since the 1970s. A four-year integrated research programme ''Acidifying Substances and Groundlevel Ozone—Effects and Critical Loads'' was started in 1993. For 1993/94 a budget of SKr 9.25 million has been allocated to such programmes, mainly focusing on: the role of organic acids in the acidification of soils and waters; effects of ground-level ozone on forest trees; recovery and future development of soil and water acidification; methods for determining critical loads for nitrogen and sulphur compounds; and the practical use of the critical load and level concept on a regional/local scale. During 1993/94 a new research programme on metals in urban and rural environments has been formulated. One major part of the programme concerns the effects and critical loads of metals in soils and waters, and projects within this field were to be initiated during 1994. Furthermore, the Agency runs a programme to determine critical loads of nitrogen and to study the acidification of the very sensitive surface waters of northern Scandinavia.

(m) *Switzerland*: High priority was given from 1991 to 1993 to mapping critical loads of acidity for forest soils and alpine lakes at a high spatial resolution of 1 x 1 km^2. The critical loads of acidity have been calculated with the steady state mass balance approach adapted to alpine areas with high precipitation amounts. In 1992 work was started to apply more complex steady state multi-layer soil models for assessing critical loads of acidity for forest soils. This work is not yet completed. First applications of dynamic models are currently explored at the Swiss Federal Institute for Forest, Snow and Landscape and at the Institute for Applied Plant Biology. Critical loads for nitrogen have been calculated and mapped by applying the mass balance and the empirical approach. Work has been started to map the critical levels for ozone and their exceedances for agricultural crops and for forests.

(n) *United Kingdom*: National networks have been established to monitor both wet and dry deposition of NO_x and SO_2 so as to allow production of national critical load exceedance maps. Substantial effort and financial resources (ca. £1.6 million for 1993/94) have underpinned the critical load mapping process. Since 1990 around 1,600 water samples from freshwater sites have been analysed to produce critical load maps for acidity. Researchers have developed the "Diatom" method of pH reconstruction of freshwater lakes and efforts are now focusing on this method to obtain critical loads for nutrient nitrogen. A state-of-the-art report reviewing the impacts of nitrogen deposition on the terrestrial environment has recently been published. Research is currently under way to underpin the mass-balance approach to critical load evaluation for both acidification and eutrophication. Longer-term field experiments looking at the effects of ozone on crops, semi-natural vegetation and forests are ongoing, as are manipulative experiments looking at the impact of enhanced nitrogen deposition on moorlands and forests. There is evidence of an increase in the incidence of respiratory complaints, including that of asthma. The role of ambient levels of air pollution in this increase is not clear. As a result a £5 million research programme has been commissioned to investigate the possible links between both indoor and outdoor air quality and respiratory disorders.

(o) *United States*: The majority of research has been focused historically on the health effects associated with air pollution. However, in recent years extensive research has been initiated on environmental effects associated with the deposition of acidic compounds and hazardous air pollutants. A study is under way to determine the feasibility and effectiveness of acid deposition standards or standards to protect sensitive and critically sensitive aquatic and terrestrial resources.

Chapter IV

INTERNATIONAL ACTIVITIES

A. ACTIVITIES WITHIN THE FRAMEWORK OF THE CONVENTION

Table 15 summarizes the status of the Convention on Long-range Transboundary Air Pollution and its related protocols:

(a) The Convention on Long-range Transboundary Air Pollution, adopted in Geneva on 13 November 1979 (E/ECE/1010), entered into force on 16 March 1983. As of 28 February 1995, with the accession to the Convention by Latvia and Lithuania in 1994, 38 States and the European Community were Parties to the Convention.

(b) The Protocol on Long-term Financing of the Cooperative Programme for Monitoring and Evaluation of the Long-range Transmission of Air Pollutants in Europe (EMEP), adopted in Geneva on 28 September 1984 (ECE/EB.AIR/11) and in force from 28 January 1988, has been ratified by 35 Parties.

(c) The Protocol on the Reduction of Sulphur Emissions or their Transboundary Fluxes by at least 30%, adopted in Helsinki on 8 July 1985 (ECE/EB.AIR/12) and in force from 2 September 1987, has been ratified by 21 Parties.

(d) The Protocol concerning the Control of Emissions of Nitrogen Oxides or their Transboundary Fluxes, adopted in Sofia on 31 October 1988 (ECE/EB.AIR/21) and in force since 14 February 1991, has been ratified by 25 Parties.

(e) The Protocol concerning the Control of Emissions of Volatile Organic Compounds or their Transboundary Fluxes was adopted in Geneva on 18 November 1991 (ECE/EB.AIR/30) and has been signed by 23 Parties and ratified by 11 Parties.

(f) The Protocol on Further Reduction of Sulphur Emissions was adopted in Oslo on 14 June 1994 (ECE/EB.AIR/40) and has been signed by 28 Parties to the Convention.

Activities carried out under the auspices of the Executive Body for the Convention have been programmed in the annual work-plans as approved by the Executive Body from 1983. The fifth phase of the Cooperative Programme for Monitoring and Evaluation of the Long-range Transmission of Air Pollutants in Europe (EMEP) covered the years 1990-1994. EMEP was established in 1977 with the cooperation of the World Meteorological Organization (WMO) and the United Nations Environment Programme (UNEP). It is now financed by mandatory contributions through a United Nations Trust Fund and coordinated on behalf of the Executive Body by the EMEP Steering Body. At the end of 1993, 32 countries reported air and precipitation monitoring data to the Chemical Coordinating Centre of EMEP (see table 16). However, the current monitoring network does not cover satisfactorily all parts of the EMEP area and the full basic monitoring programme (compounds linked to acidification and ozone) is carried out at less than one quarter of all EMEP stations.

The Working Group on Effects coordinates research and monitoring activities aimed at obtaining a better understanding of the environmental effects of sulphur and nitrogen compounds and other major air pollutants. These activities are carried out by five International Cooperative Programmes which study the effects of air pollution on forests, agricultural crops, surface waters, on selected ecosystems and materials. Table 16 gives an overview of the participation in the International Cooperative Programmes under the Convention. Their main objective is to assess the present status of the environment, evaluate occurring changes and their trends and to establish relevant dose/effect relationships, thus substantiating and providing for an effect-based approach to controlling emissions of air pollutants. In recent years, in particular in connection with the preparation of the Protocol on Further Reduction of Sulphur Emissions, the determination of critical loads and levels of air pollutants has been of special importance. Mapping of critical levels and loads and their exceedances is coordinated by the Task Force on Mapping; the Coordination Center for Effects provides scientific and technical support and produces relevant maps in cooperation with Programme Centres and National Focal Points.

The Working Group on Technology (established in 1991) prepared the annex on control technologies for sulphur emissions from stationary sources to the Protocol on Further Reduction of Sulphur Emissions and updated the technical annex to the 1988 Sofia Protocol related to control technologies for emissions of nitrogen oxides from stationary and mobile sources. When performing these activities the Working Group took into account the output of the Fifth Seminar on Control Technology for Emissions from Stationary Sources, held in Nuremberg (Germany), the objectives of the ECE Project "Energy Efficiency 2000", and the results of regular expert assessments of performance of relevant technologies for air pollution abatement. The Working Group also prepared scientific and technical inputs for the development of possible future protocols on persistent organic pollutants and heavy metals.

B. ACTIVITIES AIMED AT ENHANCING THE EXCHANGE OF CONTROL TECHNOLOGY

Within the framework of the Convention, the Working Group on Technology organized a series of target-oriented workshops to facilitate the exchange of technology addressing the need and potential for information exchange, relevant basic engineering services and training for plant operators from selected industrial branches. With a view to facilitating the trade in technology, the Working Group has also initiated activities aimed at strengthening and harmonizing legal frameworks for air pollution abatement technology in countries in transition. On the global level numerous activities in this field are under way. For instance, the multilateral fund of the Montreal Protocol on Substances that Deplete the Ozone Layer supports training and demonstration programmes in the use of alternate chemicals and technologies that do not deplete stratospheric ozone.

Many Parties have taken measures related to air pollution control technology cooperation. They include the organization of training programmes, financial cooperation and trade measures aimed at enhancing the exchange of technology:

(a) *Austria* has been, since 1991, granting financial support to projects in the eastern neighbouring countries by means of the "East-Ecofund". Over the past three years, more than US$ 50 million were provided for over 70 projects to carry out feasibility studies and planning activities for in-plant improvements in the recipient countries. Financial support covers air and water cleaning as well as energy saving projects. The two most recent examples are the planning of desulphurization facilities in the power plants of Novaky (*Slovakia*) and Sostanj (*Slovenia*).

(b) *Canada* has held targeted workshops with international participation in pulp mill sludge combustion and ozone depleting substance destruction technologies. Future workshops are planned in biological gas cleaning, advanced removal of particulates, and expert systems in environmental protection. The National Environmental Technology Advancement Program is a technology inflow program which seeks to examine, import, adapt and further develop foreign-based technologies for Canadian conditions and applications. The Technologies for Environmental Solutions Program promotes the demonstration of developed pollution control technologies. While the venue of a demonstration is usually within Canada, foreign locations are also promoted in the interest of enhancing technology export opportunities. Foreign Affairs and International Trade Canada has instituted several databases devoted to aiding Canadian companies access export markets for pollution control technologies.

(c) The First North American Conference and Exhibition on Emerging Clean Air Technologies and Business Opportunities was held in cooperation with the *United States* and *Mexico* Government Departments, in September 1994, in Toronto (Canada). Environment Canada and the United States EPA meet annually to review research and development programmes in air pollution control.

(d) *Cyprus*: Air pollution control information from international data banks can easily be accessed from this country. Entrepreneurs and technical consultants in *Cyprus* cooperate with industrialized countries on the basis of the free market principles. The Government as well as the private sector regularly organize programmes and seminars on air pollution control.

(e) In the *Czech Republic*, a number of technological facilities, developed in advanced economies, are under construction. This work is being financed through domestic and foreign loans.

(f) *Germany* provides permanent technical assistance to the *Czech Republic* for the introduction of new technologies, especially fluidized-bed combustion, sulphur-removal from combustion products and monitoring of air pollution. This cooperation is centred primarily on concrete projects in border areas.

(g) *Denmark*, between 1991 and mid-1994, spent about DKr 550 million on bilateral environmental projects in central and eastern Europe, about Dkr 290 million on the reduction of emissions of sulphur, nitrogen oxides and VOCs. About 220 projects have been put into operation. In the area of direct investments in control technology about Dkr 50 million were spent on VOC-recycling equipment, precipitators, low-NO_x burners, and control systems for SO_2 and NO_x, etc. Another 240 million were invested in alternative energy production and energy efficiency. The recipient countries were primarily the *Czech Republic, Estonia, Latvia, Lithuania, Poland* and *the Russian Federation*, while a few projects were started in *Hungary, Slovakia* and *Ukraine*. The work is carried out in close collaboration with the responsible authorities in the recipient countries.

(h) The Ministry of Environment of *Finland* has granted Fmk 185 million for investment in environmental protection and energy efficiency in *Estonia, Latvia, Lithuania, Poland* and the *Russian Federation*. Support has covered about 190 technical assistance projects, a large share of which dealt with air pollution control.

(i) In the context of cooperation between *Germany* and the *Russian Federation*, a comprehensive plan for the reduction of carbon dioxide emissions is being prepared. It includes the selection of technologies and know-how, the evaluation of their use in the Russian Federation, and the establishment of contacts between Russian and German firms.

(j) In the context of the *Netherlands* bilateral Programme for Cooperation with Central and Eastern Europe, technical assistance related to energy and environmental protection has been provided. Initiatives to be highlighted are a number of cooperation programmes and projects in *Bulgaria, Hungary* and *Poland*: application of low-NO$_x$ burners for renovating a power plant; master plan for emission reduction in the steel industry; installation of desulphurization equipment in a power plant with financial aid from the Netherlands Electricity Board; and training programmes and on-site energy auditing.

(k) Within the framework of cooperation between *Norway* and the *Russian Federation*, a project has been prepared to train operators of polluting enterprises. As a result, output will increase while environmental pollution will be reduced, without special expenditure, through a more effective use of raw materials and equipment.

(l) *Poland*: A large number of multilateral and bilateral programmes involving the transfer of know-how are under way in Poland and only some examples are cited below. In cooperation with the World Bank and the Global Environment Facility a plan is being implemented to manage and monitor atmospheric pollution in the Krakow/Katowice region. It includes the training of personnel and pilot projects to switch from coal to gas in the heating of public buildings. Among the projects supported by the *European Community* PHARE programme have been: the start-up of production of fluidized-bed combustion boilers in a Polish firm; the purchase of the licence for the construction of German desulphurization equipment; and the provision of nine mobile laboratories for the monitoring of air pollution. In the framework of the programme for the promotion of clean production, sponsored by *Norway* and implemented by non-governmental organizations, a series of training courses involving specialists from industry were organized and projects introducing clean technologies into industrial enterprises were set up. In 1992 this resulted in the signing of the ''Declaration on clean production'' by industry representatives in the presence of the Environment Minister. The cooperation with the *United States* led to the installation of desulphurization equipment in two boilers, using United States technology of wet desulphurization.

(m) *Sweden* has been active in assisting the introduction of fuel conversions from fossil to biomass fuels, and in conjunction therewith feasible boiler technology, in the Baltic region. In the joint projects both technology improvements and training programmes are included. A joint programme with *Estonia* was agreed upon. The financing of the reconstruction of boilers used in district heating comes from the World Bank and different countries with Sweden contributing US$ 10 million.

(n) The *United Kingdom* operates a small programme known as the Environmental Know How Fund providing £5 million over three years from 1992. The Fund's main objective is to support the transfer of skills and expertise to the countries of central and eastern Europe including, as resources permit, the Commonwealth of Independent States (CIS). The aim is to contribute to improved environmental management, to institution building and to long-term environmental improvement. Projects supported or under consideration in the field of air pollution and energy efficiency cover *inter alia*: clean coal technologies in *Ukraine* and *Roma-

nia; economic instruments in *Poland*; traffic planning in Budapest (*Hungary*); and energy efficiency in *Hungary*.

(o) In the *United States,* a major effort is under way under the auspices of the Clean Coal Technology Program to transfer emission control technologies to appropriate Parties in central and eastern Europe and the CIS. The United States has held conferences to inform these countries. The latest information on new emission reduction technologies and emission limits in the United States continues to be available on the Technology Transfer Network that is accessible through the Internet electronic mail system.

C. OTHER BILATERAL ACTIVITIES IN THE ECE REGION

Besides a number of multilateral initiatives listed in section D, several Parties are engaged in bilateral programmes within the ECE region for air pollution abatement:

(a) *Austria* has concluded a series of bilateral treaties on cooperation in environmental matters with its neighbouring countries in the eastern part of Europe. They include programmes to: provide technical and organizational assistance; enhance energy efficiency and encourage the use of renewable energy sources; collect and exchange environmental data and information; and develop indigenous environmental counselling as well as educational capacities and structures. Treaties are in force with the *Czech Republic, Hungary* and *Poland*. A memorandum of understanding on bilateral cooperation has been concluded with *Slovakia* and *India*.

(b) *Bulgaria* and *Romania* signed, in 1992, an agreement for cooperation in environmental protection. In December 1993 the two countries signed a memorandum about the technical reconstruction of major stationary sources along the lower Danube. It is expected that this will be supported by financial assistance from the *European Community*.

(c) The Canada/United States Air Quality Agreement covers, *inter alia*, the reduction of sulphur dioxide emissions. In addition, joint efforts continue in both countries to address the problem of the deposition of hazardous air pollutants into the Great Lakes.

(d) A joint course of action between the *Czech Republic, Germany* and *Poland* to reduce the emissions of air pollutants in the ''black triangle'', a region comprising the industrial regions Saxony, Bohemia and Upper Silesia, was agreed upon. In this framework joint measurements of sulphur dioxide, nitrogen oxides and ozone have been carried out along the borders. Automatic data transfer from the individual monitoring stations is under preparation.

(e) Cooperation between the *Czech Republic* and *Slovakia* focuses on the exchange of information on the effectiveness of individual legislative regulations and measures for amending this legislation, especially as the two countries still have the same air protection legislation.

(f) *Finland* has concluded bilateral agreements with *Estonia* and the *Russian Federation* on a 50% reduction in sulphur emissions by 1997 and 1995 respectively, based on 1980 levels. Further reductions are considered on the basis of the critical load concept.

(g) *Germany* has concluded a number of environmental agreements with: the *Czech Republic, Estonia, Hungary, Latvia, Lithuania, Poland, Romania, the Russian Federation, Slovakia* and *Ukraine*. The contractual cooperation initiated with the Soviet Union is being continued with the various CIS republics. The aim is to improve environmental conditions, in particular air quality, and to provide a framework of investigations into harmful environmental impacts. For instance, one of the tasks of the Polish-German Environmental Council is to identify measures to reduce pollution in the border region. For this purpose, a government commission will prepare proposals for environmentally sound development in the border region, draw up a transboundary action plan and develop proposals for specific measures to be taken. Funds totalling DM 2.5 million have been provided by the German Government for the establishment of air pollution measurement networks in Budapest and Sofia.

(h) The *Netherlands* has signed memoranda of understanding which provide a basis for cooperation in the field of air pollution with *Hungary, Poland*, the *Russian Federation, Ukraine* and the *United States*. Under these memoranda, information regarding acidification and its abatement is exchanged.

(i) *Norway* has bilateral agreements on environmental cooperation with the *Czech Republic, Hungary, Poland*, the *Russian Federation*, and *Slovakia*. Projects include monitoring, assessment of critical loads, assessment of health effects, development of abatement programmes and education in approaches to cleaner production. In all cooperating countries an educational school project on acid rain has been initiated to increase young people's knowledge and awareness.

(j) *Poland*: Bilateral agreements in the field of environment are in force with all the seven neighbouring States. In 1992 an agreement was signed with *Belarus*, article two of which details cooperation in protecting the atmosphere from pollution. A 1974 agreement concerning air pollution, signed with the former Czechoslovakia, provides the basis for cooperation with the *Czech Republic*. In 1992 an agreement was signed with *Lithuania* establishing cooperation, *inter alia*, on environmental monitoring and transboundary pollution. An agreement on cooperation in the field of environment with *Germany* was signed in 1994 covering: the exchange of legal expertise, the collection, analysis and exchange of data, education, technology cooperation, and strategy development. The agreement with the *Russian Federation*, signed in 1993, aims at enhancing cooperation on atmospheric protection and environmental monitoring. With *Slovakia* an agreement on cooperation on air pollution matters and integrated monitoring, especially in border areas, was signed in 1994; and a similar agreement with the *Ukraine* was also signed in 1994.

(k) The *United States* has also initiated a multi-million dollar effort with the *Russian Federation* to as-sist it in reviewing and updating its air quality management system.

D. OTHER MULTILATERAL ACTIVITIES AT THE REGIONAL AND GLOBAL LEVEL

Besides ongoing cooperation under the Convention, there are many other multilateral initiatives in the ECE region of importance for air pollution abatement. This includes, in particular, the other ECE conventions: the Convention on Environmental Impact Assessment in a Transboundary Context adopted in Espoo (Finland) in February 1991 and signed by 29 countries and the European Community; the Convention on the Transboundary Effects of Industrial Accidents, adopted in Helsinki in March 1992 and signed by 27 countries and the European Community; and the Convention on the Protection and Use of Transboundary Watercourses and International Lakes, adopted in Helsinki in March 1992 and signed by 26 countries and the European Community. In addition, air pollution problems are dealt with in the framework of: the Convention on the Alps adopted in November 1991 in Salzburg (Austria) and now signed by nine countries; the Convention on the Protection of the Marine Environment in the Baltic Sea Area (Helsinki, 1974); the 1992 Convention for the Protection of the Marine Environment of the North-East Atlantic; the International Convention for the Prevention of Pollution from Ships (MARPOL, London, 1973); and the Nordic Convention on the Protection of the Environment, (Stockholm, 1974).

Other multilateral initiatives include: the Arctic Monitoring and Assessment Programme (AMAP); the Air Pollution Group under the European Free Trade Association (EFTA); the Central European Initiative (CEI), which provides a framework for six countries and, in 1993, completed a detailed inventory of air pollution emission sources; the cooperation of Nordic countries, which for air pollution, is carried out by the Nordic Committee of Senior Officials for Environmental Affairs under the Nordic Council of Ministers; and the regular meetings of Environment Ministers of the four German-speaking countries (Austria, Germany, Liechtenstein, Switzerland), which called for a 70-80% reduction in ozone precursors based on 1980 levels.

Besides the efforts to reduce air pollution at the regional levels, international cooperation at the global level has progressed considerably. Measures taken under global programmes will often also produce beneficial results for concerns dealt with under the Convention. This applies for instance to the linkages between abating carbon dioxide emissions and decreasing sulphur emissions. The main event at the global level over the last years has been the United Nations Conference on Environment and Development (UNCED) held in Rio de Janeiro (Brazil), June 1992. The most important output of that Conference was the Rio Declaration on Environment and Development and Agenda 21. In chapter 9, the latter makes an explicit reference to the Convention and its protocols, stressing that "these programmes need to be continued and enhanced, and their experience needs to be shared with other regions of the world".

Negotiated in the preparatory phase of UNCED, the United Nations Framework Convention on Climate Change (UNFCCC) was adopted at United Nations Headquarters, New York, in May 1992 and entered into force in March 1994. All Parties to the Convention on Long-range Transboundary Air Pollution except two (Bosnia and Herzegovina, and Turkey) have also signed the UNFCCC; as of 2 February 1995, 27 Parties to the Convention on Long-range Transboundary Air Pollution (Austria, Canada, Czech Republic, Denmark, Finland, France, Germany, Greece, Hungary, Iceland, Ireland, Italy, Liechtenstein, Luxembourg, Netherlands, Norway, Poland, Portugal, Romania, Russian Federation, Slovakia, Spain, Sweden, Switzerland, United Kingdom, United States, and the European Community) had ratified UNFCCC (A/AC.237/INF.15/Rev.2).

Also of relevance is the cooperation under the Vienna Convention for the Protection of the Ozone Layer (adopted in 1985) and its Montreal Protocol on Substances that Deplete the Ozone Layer (adopted in 1987) and the Rio Convention on Biological Diversity (adopted in 1992). Most Parties have joined these agreements as well.

Chapter V

CONCLUSIONS

A. STATUS OF IMPLEMENTATION OF THE 1985 HELSINKI PROTOCOL ON THE REDUCTION OF SULPHUR EMISSIONS OR THEIR TRANSBOUNDARY FLUXES BY AT LEAST 30%

Table 17 is based on the emission data in table 1 that had been submitted by Parties to the Convention by 16 January 1995. Parties to the 1985 Helsinki Protocol are shown shaded in table 17. Figure V shows sulphur emissions in 1993, or a previous year if no data were available for 1993, as a percentage of 1980 levels separately for Parties and non-Parties to the Protocol. In some cases even data for emissions dating from before 1992 had to be used. Among the Parties to the Protocol, Italy, Liechtenstein, and Luxembourg have not reported sulphur emission levels for years after 1991; Luxembourg has not reported data on its sulphur emissions after 1985. This limits the possibility of evaluating the status of implementation.

Taken as a whole, the 21 Parties to the 1985 Helsinki Protocol reduced 1980 sulphur emissions by 48% by 1993 (using the latest available figure, where no data were available for 1993). In the whole of Europe, including non-Parties to the Protocol, that sum of emissions is below 30,000 kt which corresponds to a reduction of 45% compared to 1980. Also individually, based on the latest available data, all Parties to the Sulphur Protocol have reached the reduction target. Also four non-Parties to the Protocol have achieved sulphur emission reductions of 30% or more. Twelve Parties have achieved reductions of at least 50%; two of these have actually reduced their sulphur emissions by 80% or more.

Given that the target year for the Helsinki Protocol is 1993, it can be concluded that all Parties to that Protocol have reached the target of reducing emissions by at least 30%.

B. STATUS OF IMPLEMENTATION OF THE 1988 SOFIA PROTOCOL CONCERNING THE CONTROL OF EMISSIONS OF NITROGEN OXIDES OR THEIR TRANSBOUNDARY FLUXES

Table 18 is based on the emission data in table 2 that had been submitted by Parties to the Convention by 16 January 1995. Parties to the 1988 Sofia Protocol are shown shaded in table 18. Figure VI shows nitrogen oxide emissions in 1993, or a previous year if no data were available for 1993, as a percentage of 1987 levels, or 1978 for the United States, separately for Parties and non-Parties to the Protocol. In some cases even data for emissions dating from before 1992 had to be used. Among the Parties to the Protocol, Italy, Liechtenstein, Luxembourg, Spain, and the European Community have not reported NO_x emission levels for years after 1991; Luxembourg and the European Community have not reported data for 1990 or 1991 either. In addition, Liechtenstein, Luxembourg, and the European Community have not reported emission data for 1987, their base year for the reduction target under the Sofia Protocol. The lack of data severely limits the possibility of evaluating the status of implementation.

Concerning the emissions of nitrogen oxides the general reference year is 1987 with the exception of the United States that chose to relate its emission target to 1978. For all Parties to the Convention overall emissions of NO_x had been stabilized by 1990 at the 1987 level and by 1993 (or an earlier year, where no figures are available for 1993) they had been reduced by 4%. Taking the sum of emissions of Parties to the NO_x Protocol in 1993, or a previous year, where no recent data are available, also a slight reduction of 4% compared to 1987 can be noted. Eighteen of the 25 Parties to the 1988 Sofia Protocol have reached the target and stabilized emissions at 1987, or in the case of the United States 1978, levels or reduced emissions below that level according to the latest emission data reported. Among the other cases three cannot be evaluated because of a lack of data for the base year and the three remaining Parties to the Protocol have increased emissions by 4 to 41% above 1987 levels. Six Parties to the Convention (including one non-Party to the Sofia Protocol) have reduced NO_x emissions by more than 25%. All but one of these are countries with economies in transition. It can also be noted that, in general, in southern Europe NO_x emissions have increased, in some cases significantly, above 1987 levels.

Concerning obligations under article 2, paragraph 2, of the Sofia Protocol, nine Parties (Belarus, France, Hungary, Liechtenstein, Luxembourg, Russian Federation, Ukraine, United States and the European Community) to the Protocol have not submitted any information on emission standards for NO_x in the context of this major review. For other Parties the responses to the questionnaire under this item was incomplete. For those Parties that did submit data it can be concluded that emission standards have been set in most cases for new sources in the power generation sector (see table 13.2). Fewer Parties have reported on emission standards for mobile sources. Concerning the availability of unleaded fuel, based on the responses received, it can be concluded that the requirement of article 4 has been largely fulfilled and unleaded fuel is available throughout the ECE region (see chap. III, sect. C.4).

Emission projections

TABLE 8.1

Emission projections of sulphur

(Thousands of tonnes of SO$_2$)

	1995	2000	2005	2010
Bulgaria				
1- baseline lower limit	1220	1320	1034	861
2- baseline scenario				
3- baseline upper limit	1380	1374	1230	1127
Croatia				
1- baseline lower limit	150	130	120	100
2- baseline scenario				
3- baseline upper limit	170	150	140	120
Cyprus				
1- baseline lower limit	49	60	58	60
2- baseline scenario	50	62	62	62
3- baseline upper limit	52	65	65	65
Denmark				
1- baseline lower limit	169	90	90	
2- baseline scenario				
3- baseline upper limit		111		
Finland				
1- baseline lower limit				
2- baseline scenario				
3- baseline upper limit		116	116	116
Germany				
1- baseline lower limit				
2- baseline scenario				
3- baseline upper limit		990		
Italy				
1- baseline lower limit				
2- baseline scenario	1535	1209	1142	
3- baseline upper limit				
Netherlands				
1- baseline lower limit		86		76
2- baseline scenario				
3- baseline upper limit		92		85

	1995	2000	2005	2010
Norway				
1- baseline lower limit				
2- baseline scenario	44	42		48
3- baseline upper limit				
Poland				
1- baseline lower limit	2459	2163	2013	1801
2- baseline scenario				
3- baseline upper limit	2640	2344	2344	2135
Slovakia				
1- baseline lower limit		217	175	170
2- baseline scenario		270	250	220
3- baseline upper limit		337	295	240
Slovenia				
1- baseline lower limit	180	92	45	37
2- baseline scenario	180	92	45	37
3- baseline upper limit				
Spain				
1- baseline lower limit				
2- baseline scenario				
3- baseline upper limit		2143		
Sweden				
1- baseline lower limit				
2- baseline scenario	100	107	103	113
3- baseline upper limit				
United Kingdom				
1- baseline lower limit	2853	2050	1890	1889
2- baseline scenario	2951	2320	2100	2115
3- baseline upper limit	3049	2596	2300	2332

Sweden : rough estimate for 2010.

TABLE 8.2

Emission projections of nitrogen oxides

(Thousands of tonnes of NO$_2$)

	1995	2000	2005	2010		1995	2000	2005	2010
Bulgaria					**Spain**				
1- baseline lower limit	270	300	280	200	1- baseline lower limit				
2- baseline scenario					2- baseline scenario				
3- baseline upper limit	300	380	350	290	3- baseline upper limit	892	892		
Cyprus					**Sweden**				
1- baseline lower limit	14	17	19	19	1- baseline lower limit				
2- baseline scenario	15	18	20	20	2- baseline scenario	376	312	303	311
3- baseline upper limit	16	19	21	21	3- baseline upper limit				
Denmark					**United Kingdom**				
1- baseline lower limit	254	203	192		1- baseline lower limit	2336	1790	1639	1659
2- baseline scenario					2- baseline scenario	2460	2000	1842	1860
3- baseline upper limit					3- baseline upper limit	2585	2204	2046	2061
Finland									
1- baseline lower limit									
2- baseline scenario									
3- baseline upper limit		224	224	224					

Sweden : rough estimate for 2010.

	1995	2000	2005	2010
Germany				
1- baseline lower limit			1850	
2- baseline scenario				
3- baseline upper limit		2200	2150	
Italy				
1- baseline lower limit				
2- baseline scenario	2128	2098	2060	
3- baseline upper limit				
Netherlands				
1- baseline lower limit		346		227
2- baseline scenario				
3- baseline upper limit		366		288
Norway				
1- baseline lower limit				
2- baseline scenario	213	206		208
3- baseline upper limit				
Slovakia				
1- baseline lower limit		156		
2- baseline scenario		175		
3- baseline upper limit		190		
Slovenia				
1- baseline lower limit				
2- baseline scenario	53	45	38	31
3- baseline upper limit				

TABLE 8.3

Emission projections of ammonia

(Thousands of tonnes of NH₃)

	1995	2000	2005	2010
Bulgaria				
1- baseline lower limit	125	130	130	130
2- baseline scenario				
3- baseline upper limit	140	143	140	140
Denmark				
1- baseline lower limit	121	103		
2- baseline scenario				
3- baseline upper limit				
Finland				
1- baseline lower limit				
2- baseline scenario				
3- baseline upper limit		32	23	23
Germany				
1- baseline lower limit		620	600	
2- baseline scenario				
3- baseline upper limit		680	650	
Netherlands				
1- baseline lower limit		86		70
2- baseline scenario				
3- baseline upper limit		94		75
Norway				
1- baseline lower limit				
2- baseline scenario	40	41		
3- baseline upper limit				
Sweden				
1- baseline lower limit				
2- baseline scenario	69	68	67	66
3- baseline upper limit				
United Kingdom				
1- baseline lower limit		340		
2- baseline scenario		382		
3- baseline upper limit		423		

TABLE 8.4

Emission projections of non-methane volatile organic compounds

(Thousands of tonnes)

	1995	2000	2005	2010		1995	2000	2005	2010
Bulgaria					**United Kingdom**				
1- baseline lower limit	342	337	256	245	1- baseline lower limit	2081	1496	1315	1247
2- baseline scenario					2- baseline scenario	2100	1519	1340	1276
3- baseline upper limit	357	357	276	265	3- baseline upper limit	2119	1543	1365	1306

Netherlands : excluding nature.

United Kingdom : emissions from road transport only.

	1995	2000	2005	2010
Denmark				
1- baseline lower limit		112		
2- baseline scenario				
3- baseline upper limit				
Finland				
1- baseline lower limit		151	108	108
2- baseline scenario				
3- baseline upper limit		151	151	151
Germany				
1- baseline lower limit			930	
2- baseline scenario				
3- baseline upper limit		1900	1750	
Netherlands				
1- baseline lower limit		245		230
2- baseline scenario		248		233
3- baseline upper limit		253		245
Norway				
1- baseline lower limit				
2- baseline scenario	281	241		167
3- baseline upper limit				
Slovakia				
1- baseline lower limit				
2- baseline scenario		95		
3- baseline upper limit				
Slovenia				
1- baseline lower limit				
2- baseline scenario	36	33	30	25
3- baseline upper limit				
Spain				
1- baseline lower limit				
2- baseline scenario				
3- baseline upper limit		668		
Sweden				
1- baseline lower limit				
2- baseline scenario	445	342	287	
3- baseline upper limit				

TABLE 8.5

Emission projections of methane

(Thousands of tonnes of CH$_4$)

	1995	2000	2005	2010
Bulgaria				
1- baseline lower limit	440	440	400	390
2- baseline scenario				
3- baseline upper limit	450	450	420	420
Denmark				
1- baseline lower limit	382	355	354	
2- baseline scenario				
3- baseline upper limit				
Germany				
1- baseline lower limit			2650	
2- baseline scenario				
3- baseline upper limit		4700	3200	
Netherlands				
1- baseline lower limit		750		580
2- baseline scenario				701
3- baseline upper limit		870		725
Norway				
1- baseline lower limit				
2- baseline scenario	289	291		273
3- baseline upper limit				
Sweden				
1- baseline lower limit				
2- baseline scenario	335	300	296	
3- baseline upper limit				
United Kingdom				
1- baseline lower limit				
2- baseline scenario	4811	4257	3993	3730
3- baseline upper limit				

Netherlands : excluding nature.

TABLE 8.6

Emission projections of carbon monoxide

(Thousands of tonnes of CO)

	1995	2000	2005	2010
Bulgaria				
1- baseline lower limit	810	830	760	600
2- baseline scenario				
3- baseline upper limit	820	850	800	750
Denmark				
1- baseline lower limit	727	647	562	
2- baseline scenario				
3- baseline upper limit				
Germany				
1- baseline lower limit			3750	
2- baseline scenario				
3- baseline upper limit		6050	5350	
Netherlands				
1- baseline lower limit		570		570
2- baseline scenario				
3- baseline upper limit		630		670
Norway				
1- baseline lower limit				
2- baseline scenario	773	602		576
3- baseline upper limit				
Sweden				
1- baseline lower limit				
2- baseline scenario	1164	760	631	
3- baseline upper limit				
United Kingdom				
1- baseline lower limit	5456	3248	1839	1342
2- baseline scenario	5513	3324	1884	1379
3- baseline upper limit	5570	3400	1928	1417

United Kingdom : emissions from road transport only.

EMISSIONS OF MAJOR AIR POLLUTANTS
BY MAJOR SOURCE CATEGORY

SOURCE CATEGORY DESCRIPTION

Definition of the EMEP/CORINAIR source category split used:

Source category 1:   Public power, cogeneration and district heating plants.
Source category 2:   Commercial, institutional and residential combustion plants.
Source category 3:   Industrial combustion plants and processes with combustion.
Source category 4:   Non-combustion processes.
Source category 5:   Extraction and distribution of fossil fuels.
Source category 6:   Solvent use.
Source category 7:   Road transport.
Source category 8:   Other transport.
Source category 9:   Waste treatment and disposal.
Source category 10:   Agriculture.
Source category* 11:   Nature.

---

* From now on, and for statistical purposes, Sc. or sc. = source category.

TABLE 9.1

National annual emissions of sulphur by source category

(Thousands of tonnes of SO$_2$)

Austria	1985	1990	1991	1992	1993	2000
1 - Public power, cogeneration, district heating	50.0	15.5	15.8	16.4	17.7	
2 - Commercial, institutional, residential combustion	39.0	19.9	19.9	16.3	16.1	
3 - Industrial combustion and processes	92.9	47.7	40.7	35.2	28.7	
4 - Non combustion processes	0.2	0.2	0.2	0.2		
5 - Extraction and distribution of fossil fuels						
6 - Solvent use						
7 - Road transport	11.6	6.3	6.9	7.3	7.7	
8 - Other transport	0.8	0.3	0.3	0.3	0.3	
9 - Waste treatment and disposal	0.2	0.1	0.1	0.1	0.1	
10 - Agriculture						
11 - Nature						
TOTAL	194.7	90.0	83.9	75.8	70.6	

Belgium	1985	1990	1991	1992	1993	2000
1 - Public power, cogeneration, district heating	124.8	94.7	89.7	83.1		
2 - Commercial, institutional, residential combustion	64.0	36.6	38.9	36.6		
3 - Industrial combustion and processes	121.6	122.7	120.3	115.1		
4 - Non combustion processes	72.8	44.4	56.2	50.6		
5 - Extraction and distribution of fossil fuels	0.0	0.0	0.0	0.0		
6 - Solvent use	0.0	0.0	0.0	0.0		
7 - Road transport	15.3	14.2	14.5	14.9		
8 - Other transport		0.3	0.3	0.4		
9 - Waste treatment and disposal	1.1	3.6	3.5	3.3		
10 - Agriculture	0.0	0.0	0.0	0.0		
11 - Nature	0.0	0.0	0.0	0.0		
TOTAL	399.5	316.6	323.5	303.9		

Bulgaria	1985	1990	1991	1992	1993	2000
1 - Public power, cogeneration, district heating	1010.0	1452.5	1182.0	667.4	1119.3	909.0
2 - Commercial, institutional, residential combustion	142.0	120.6	110.0	109.5	148.6	100.0
3 - Industrial combustion and processes	759.0	326.4	300.0	285.6	102.0	300.0
4 - Non combustion processes	112.0	80.7	42.0	26.7	30.3	35.0
5 - Extraction and distribution of fossil fuels	14.0	13.2	13.0	13.0		13.0
6 - Solvent use						
7 - Road transport	5.0	10.3	8.0	7.2	5.6	7.0
8 - Other transport	8.0	16.3	12.0	10.5	16.3	10.0
9 - Waste treatment and disposal						
10 - Agriculture						
11 - Nature						
TOTAL	2050.0	2020.0	1667.0	1120.0	1422.1	1374.0

Croatia	1985	1990	1991	1992	1993	2000
1 - Public power, cogeneration, district heating		69.4				
2 - Commercial, institutional, residential combustion		19.6				
3 - Industrial combustion and processes		75.2				
4 - Non combustion processes		0.9				
5 - Extraction and distribution of fossil fuels		0.0				
6 - Solvent use		0.0				
7 - Road transport		6.6				
8 - Other transport		6.3				
9 - Waste treatment and disposal		2.0				
10 - Agriculture		0.0				
11 - Nature		0.0				
TOTAL		180.0				

TABLE 9.1 (*continued*)

Cyprus	1985	1990	1991	1992	1993	2000
1 - Public power, cogeneration, district heating	28.7	44.0	28.3	30.3	30.5	47.0
2 - Commercial, institutional, residential combustion	0.3	0.4	0.4	0.4	0.5	0.5
3 - Industrial combustion and processes	3.4	4.2	7.0	6.7	4.9	6.0
4 - Non combustion processes						
5 - Extraction and distribution of fossil fuels						
6 - Solvent use						
7 - Road transport	1.7	1.4	2.9	5.1	3.6	4.4
8 - Other transport	2.0	1.2	2.5	2.9	3.1	4.1
9 - Waste treatment and disposal						
10 - Agriculture						
11 - Nature						
TOTAL	36.2	51.2	41.1	45.5	42.5	62.0

Czech Republic	1985	1990	1991	1992	1993	2000
1 - Public power, cogeneration, district heating		955.8				
2 - Commercial, institutional, residential combustion		427.6				
3 - Industrial combustion and processes		425.9				
4 - Non combustion processes		60.0				
5 - Extraction and distribution of fossil fuels						
6 - Solvent use						
7 - Road transport						
8 - Other transport		5.9				
9 - Waste treatment and disposal		0.9				
10 - Agriculture						
11 - Nature						
TOTAL		1876.0				

Denmark	1985	1990	1991	1992	1993	2000
1 - Public power, cogeneration, district heating	204.9	125.0	181.4	135.0	104.4	56.3
2 - Commercial, institutional, residential combustion	39.2	7.5	8.2	7.0	7.2	2.8
3 - Industrial combustion and processes	67.3	26.2	29.8	28.1	31.6	24.3
4 - Non combustion processes	0.3	0.3	0.1	0.0	0.1	
5 - Extraction and distribution of fossil fuels						
6 - Solvent use						
7 - Road transport	11.7	6.4	6.6	6.6	1.6	3.0
8 - Other transport	16.1	14.5	15.8	12.1	12.1	3.8
9 - Waste treatment and disposal						
10 - Agriculture						
11 - Nature						
TOTAL	339.0	180.0	242.0	189.0	157.0	90.0

European Community	1985	1990	1991	1992	1993	2000
1 - Public power, cogeneration, district heating		6436.0				
2 - Commercial, institutional, residential combustion		759.5				
3 - Industrial combustion and processes		2965.2				
4 - Non combustion processes		525.1				
5 - Extraction and distribution of fossil fuels		43.9				
6 - Solvent use		0.3				
7 - Road transport		497.1				
8 - Other transport		385.8				
9 - Waste treatment and disposal		72.3				
10 - Agriculture		1.4				
11 - Nature		573.0				
TOTAL		12259.5				

TABLE 9.1 (*continued*)

Finland	1985	1990	1991	1992	1993	2000
1 - Public power, cogeneration, district heating		73.4				
2 - Commercial, institutional, residential combustion		20.2				
3 - Industrial combustion and processes		95.5				
4 - Non combustion processes		59.9				
5 - Extraction and distribution of fossil fuels		0.0				
6 - Solvent use						
7 - Road transport		3.9				
8 - Other transport		7.1				
9 - Waste treatment and disposal						
10 - Agriculture						
11 - Nature						
TOTAL		260.0				

France	1985	1990	1991	1992	1993	2000
1 - Public power, cogeneration, district heating		343.7	446.7	332.1		
2 - Commercial, institutional, residential combustion		116.2	131.3	119.4		
3 - Industrial combustion and processes		514.1	467.4	446.9		
4 - Non combustion processes		110.9	113.6	113.3		
5 - Extraction and distribution of fossil fuels		23.8	23.8	21.9		
6 - Solvent use		0.0	0.0	0.0		
7 - Road transport		145.3	151.8	157.9		
8 - Other transport		24.6	24.3	24.2		
9 - Waste treatment and disposal		19.2	19.1	22.6		
10 - Agriculture		0.0	0.0	0.0		
11 - Nature		2.5	0.3	0.6		
TOTAL		1300.4	1378.5	1239.0		

Germany	1985	1990	1991	1992	1993	2000
1 - Public power, cogeneration, district heating		4060.0	3316.0	2913.0		
2 - Commercial, institutional, residential combustion		593.0	400.0	346.0		
3 - Industrial combustion and processes		881.0	616.0	541.0		
4 - Non combustion processes						
5 - Extraction and distribution of fossil fuels		0.0	0.0			
6 - Solvent use						
7 - Road transport		66.0	73.0	75.0		
8 - Other transport		33.0	25.0	21.0		
9 - Waste treatment and disposal						
10 - Agriculture						
11 - Nature						
TOTAL		5633.0	4430.0	3896.0		

Greece	1985	1990	1991	1992	1993	2000
1 - Public power, cogeneration, district heating	359.0					
2 - Commercial, institutional, residential combustion	14.0					
3 - Industrial combustion and processes	109.0					
4 - Non combustion processes	18.0					
5 - Extraction and distribution of fossil fuels	0.0					
6 - Solvent use						
7 - Road transport	0.0					
8 - Other transport						
9 - Waste treatment and disposal	0.0					
10 - Agriculture						
11 - Nature	0.0					
TOTAL	500.0					

Table 9.1 (*continued*)

Hungary	1985	1990	1991	1992	1993	2000
1 - Public power, cogeneration, district heating	504.0	423.0	243.4	168.3		
2 - Commercial, institutional, residential combustion	362.1	263.0	407.5	442.7		
3 - Industrial combustion and processes	487.3	268.0	217.1	182.4		
4 - Non combustion processes		18.0	15.5	10.0		
5 - Extraction and distribution of fossil fuels						
6 - Solvent use						
7 - Road transport	21.1	16.0	13.4	12.9		
8 - Other transport						
9 - Waste treatment and disposal						
10 - Agriculture	29.1	22.0	16.0	11.0		
11 - Nature						
TOTAL	1403.6	1010.0	912.9	827.3		

Ireland	1985	1990	1991	1992	1993	2000
1 - Public power, cogeneration, district heating		103.0	104.9	96.6		
2 - Commercial, institutional, residential combustion		30.4	31.5	25.4		
3 - Industrial combustion and processes		38.7	35.0	30.7		
4 - Non combustion processes		0.0	1.1	0.7		
5 - Extraction and distribution of fossil fuels		0.0	0.0	0.0		
6 - Solvent use		0.0	0.0	0.0		
7 - Road transport		5.2	5.7	5.8		
8 - Other transport		0.6	0.9	0.9		
9 - Waste treatment and disposal		0.0	0.0	0.0		
10 - Agriculture		0.0				
11 - Nature		0.0				
TOTAL		177.9	179.1	160.1		

Italy	1985	1990	1991	1992	1993	2000
1 - Public power, cogeneration, district heating	1005.5	765.5				
2 - Commercial, institutional, residential combustion	213.5	82.0				
3 - Industrial combustion and processes	721.0	573.8				
4 - Non combustion processes	176.8	104.9				
5 - Extraction and distribution of fossil fuels	0.0	0.0				
6 - Solvent use						
7 - Road transport	74.9	103.0				
8 - Other transport	48.9	48.2				
9 - Waste treatment and disposal	3.8	4.3				
10 - Agriculture						
11 - Nature	0.0	569.6				
TOTAL	2244.4	2251.3				

Netherlands	1985	1990	1991	1992	1993	2000
1 - Public power, cogeneration, district heating	63.0	43.7	35.0	29.0		16.0
2 - Commercial, institutional, residential combustion	9.0	4.1	5.0	6.0		2.0
3 - Industrial combustion and processes	98.0	43.3	76.0	72.0		59.0
4 - Non combustion processes	59.0	73.6	32.0	29.0		
5 - Extraction and distribution of fossil fuels		0.1				
6 - Solvent use		0.3				
7 - Road transport	11.0	13.0	13.0	14.0		15.0
8 - Other transport	18.0	16.9	14.0	14.0		
9 - Waste treatment and disposal	3.0	4.8	3.0	4.0		
10 - Agriculture		1.4				
11 - Nature						
TOTAL	261.0	201.2	177.0	167.0		92.0

TABLE 9.1 (*continued*)

Norway	1985	1990	1991	1992	1993	2000
1 - Public power, cogeneration, district heating	0.3	0.4	0.3	0.3	0.2	0.0
2 - Commercial, institutional, residential combustion	7.2	3.4	2.3	2.0	1.8	2.0
3 - Industrial combustion and processes	24.0	7.7	7.2	6.5	6.0	4.0
4 - Non combustion processes	47.1	30.6	25.5	20.1	21.2	26.0
5 - Extraction and distribution of fossil fuels					0.0	1.0
6 - Solvent use						
7 - Road transport	4.3	3.6	3.3	3.4	3.0	2.0
8 - Other transport	14.8	7.8	6.7	5.2	4.6	7.0
9 - Waste treatment and disposal						
10 - Agriculture						
11 - Nature						
TOTAL	98.0	53.5	45.4	37.0	36.7	42.0

Poland	1985	1990	1991	1992	1993	2000
1 - Public power, cogeneration, district heating	1935.0	1589.0	1480.0	1320.0	1290.0	
2 - Commercial, institutional, residential combustion	860.0	444.0	455.0	456.0	750.0	
3 - Industrial combustion and processes	1290.0	1006.0	899.0	877.0	535.0	
4 - Non combustion processes	129.0	94.0	90.0	86.0	100.0	
5 - Extraction and distribution of fossil fuels	0.0	0.0			0.0	
6 - Solvent use	0.0	0.0			0.0	
7 - Road transport	86.0	140.0	90.0	91.0	50.0	
8 - Other transport						
9 - Waste treatment and disposal						
10 - Agriculture					0.0	
11 - Nature						
TOTAL	4300.0	3273.0	2996.0	2996.0	2725.0	

Portugal	1985	1990	1991	1992	1993	2000
1 - Public power, cogeneration, district heating		174.6	184.8	234.3	177.1	
2 - Commercial, institutional, residential combustion		4.3	4.5	4.9	4.9	
3 - Industrial combustion and processes		75.9	71.9	76.0	76.7	
4 - Non combustion processes		10.9	11.0	11.1	11.1	
5 - Extraction and distribution of fossil fuels		0.0	0.0	0.0	0.0	
6 - Solvent use		0.0	0.0	0.0	0.0	
7 - Road transport		13.8	15.0	16.6	17.5	
8 - Other transport		3.0	3.0	3.0	3.1	
9 - Waste treatment and disposal		0.0	0.0	0.0	0.0	
10 - Agriculture		0.0	0.0	0.0	0.0	
11 - Nature		0.0	0.0	0.0	0.0	
TOTAL		282.4	290.1	345.8	290.3	

Romania	1985	1990	1991	1992	1993	2000
1 - Public power, cogeneration, district heating				210.3		
2 - Commercial, institutional, residential combustion				20.1		
3 - Industrial combustion and processes				304.6		
4 - Non combustion processes				5.8		
5 - Extraction and distribution of fossil fuels						
6 - Solvent use						
7 - Road transport				12.2		
8 - Other transport				5.9		
9 - Waste treatment and disposal						
10 - Agriculture						
11 - Nature						
TOTAL				558.9		

TABLE 9.1 (*continued*)

Russian Federation	1985	1990	1991	1992	1993	2000
1 - Public power, cogeneration, district heating	2671.0			1470.0		
2 - Commercial, institutional, residential combustion						
3 - Industrial combustion and processes	1610.0					
4 - Non combustion processes	680.0					
5 - Extraction and distribution of fossil fuels				227.8		
6 - Solvent use						
7 - Road transport						
8 - Other transport						
9 - Waste treatment and disposal						
10 - Agriculture						
11 - Nature						
TOTAL	6191.0	4460.0		3839.0		

Slovakia	1985	1990	1991	1992	1993	2000
1 - Public power, cogeneration, district heating				261.0		
2 - Commercial, institutional, residential combustion				81.0		
3 - Industrial combustion and processes						
4 - Non combustion processes				34.0		
5 - Extraction and distribution of fossil fuels						
6 - Solvent use						
7 - Road transport				2.0		
8 - Other transport				1.0		
9 - Waste treatment and disposal				1.0		
10 - Agriculture						
11 - Nature						
TOTAL				380.0		

Slovenia	1985	1990	1991	1992	1993	2000
1 - Public power, cogeneration, district heating	171.2	153.5	136.9	151.3	147.8	
2 - Commercial, institutional, residential combustion	26.3	17.2	21.7	19.6	18.1	
3 - Industrial combustion and processes	40.2	21.5	19.0	15.1	13.4	
4 - Non combustion processes						
5 - Extraction and distribution of fossil fuels						
6 - Solvent use						
7 - Road transport	2.5	2.7	2.4	2.3	2.8	
8 - Other transport						
9 - Waste treatment and disposal						
10 - Agriculture						
11 - Nature						
TOTAL	240.2	194.9	180.0	188.3	182.1	

Spain	1985	1990	1991	1992	1993	2000
1 - Public power, cogeneration, district heating	1642.0	1461.4				1339.0
2 - Commercial, institutional, residential combustion	57.0	98.0				45.0
3 - Industrial combustion and processes	360.0	476.4				599.0
4 - Non combustion processes	63.0	38.0				
5 - Extraction and distribution of fossil fuels						
6 - Solvent use						
7 - Road transport	67.3	69.3				160.0
8 - Other transport		17.0				
9 - Waste treatment and disposal		41.8				
10 - Agriculture						
11 - Nature						
TOTAL	2189.3	2202.0				2143.0

TABLE 9.1 (*continued*)

Sweden	1985	1990	1991	1992	1993	2000
1 - Public power, cogeneration, district heating		16.0	15.0	14.0	13.0	20.0
2 - Commercial, institutional, residential combustion		16.0	9.0	8.0	8.0	8.0
3 - Industrial combustion and processes		22.0	18.0	13.0	15.0	10.0
4 - Non combustion processes		39.0	42.0	40.0	40.0	38.0
5 - Extraction and distribution of fossil fuels		0.0	0.0	0.0	0.0	0.0
6 - Solvent use						
7 - Road transport		8.0	4.0	3.0	3.0	2.0
8 - Other transport		29.0	23.0	22.0	22.0	27.0
9 - Waste treatment and disposal		2.0	2.0	2.0	2.0	2.0
10 - Agriculture						
11 - Nature		0.0	0.0	0.0	0.0	0.0
TOTAL		132.0	113.0	102.0	103.0	107.0

Switzerland	1985	1990	1991	1992	1993	2000
1 - Public power, cogeneration, district heating		1.2	1.0	1.0	1.0	
2 - Commercial, institutional, residential combustion		14.8	14.6	14.6	14.6	
3 - Industrial combustion and processes		34.3	33.4	31.9	30.8	
4 - Non combustion processes		4.0	4.0	4.0	4.0	
5 - Extraction and distribution of fossil fuels						
6 - Solvent use						
7 - Road transport		4.0	4.6	3.5	3.0	
8 - Other transport		0.6	0.6	0.6	0.6	
9 - Waste treatment and disposal		3.4	3.4	3.4	3.4	
10 - Agriculture		0.3	0.3	0.3	0.3	
11 - Nature						
TOTAL		62.6	61.9	59.3	57.7	

United Kingdom	1985	1990	1991	1992	1993	2000
1 - Public power, cogeneration, district heating	2627.0	2722.0	2534.0	2427.0	2104.0	1379.0
2 - Commercial, institutional, residential combustion	330.0	208.0	198.0	187.0	188.0	118.0
3 - Industrial combustion and processes	632.0	694.0	698.0	741.0	633.0	594.0
4 - Non combustion processes	26.0	19.0	18.0	14.0	14.0	
5 - Extraction and distribution of fossil fuels	2.0	2.0	3.0	3.0	3.0	
6 - Solvent use						
7 - Road transport	45.0	63.0	58.0	62.0	64.0	40.0
8 - Other transport	57.0	65.0	65.0	65.0	63.0	
9 - Waste treatment and disposal					0.0	
10 - Agriculture						
11 - Nature						
TOTAL	3726.0	3782.0	3574.0	3500.0	3069.0	2320.0

United States	1985	1990	1991	1992	1993	2000
1 - Public power, cogeneration, district heating	14736.0	14398.0	14319.0	14371.0		
2 - Commercial, institutional, residential combustion	524.0	542.0	552.0	534.0		
3 - Industrial combustion and processes	2875.0	2818.0	2848.0	2803.0		
4 - Non combustion processes	2207.0	1991.0	1957.0	1919.0		
5 - Extraction and distribution of fossil fuels						
6 - Solvent use						
7 - Road transport	521.0	674.0	698.0	712.0		
8 - Other transport	320.0	241.0	248.0	245.0		
9 - Waste treatment and disposal	35.0	37.0	37.0	37.0		
10 - Agriculture						
11 - Nature						
TOTAL	21218.0	20701.0	20659.0	20621.0		

TABLE 9.1 (*concluded*)

Yugoslavia	1985	1990	1991	1992	1993	2000
1 - Public power, cogeneration, district heating	404.0	446.6	391.2	335.0	358.0	556.6
2 - Commercial, institutional, residential combustion						
3 - Industrial combustion and processes	21.0	19.8	13.0	10.4	14.0	47.6
4 - Non combustion processes						
5 - Extraction and distribution of fossil fuels						
6 - Solvent use						
7 - Road transport						
8 - Other transport						
9 - Waste treatment and disposal						
10 - Agriculture						
11 - Nature						
TOTAL	478.0	508.0	223.0	396.0	401.0	680.0

Comments :

Bulgaria. Data for 1980.

Denmark. 1985 : source category 7 based on sales.

European Community : not including emissions from the former GDR.

Finland. 1990 : preliminary data.

Germany. 1990, 1991, 1992 : source category 3 includes source category 4.
    1992 : preliminary data .

Hungary. Source category 7 includes source category 8.
    1985 : source category 3 includes source category 4.

Ireland. 1991, 1992 : estimate.

Netherlands. 1992 : provisional data.
        2000 : source category 3 includes source category 4 ;
            source category 7 includes source category 8.

Norway. Source category 1 includes waste combustion with energy generation.
        Source category 3 includes gas turbines in the North Sea.
        Source category 5 includes gas flaring and VOC from leakage from petrol handling.
        Source category 7 includes cars and motor cycles.
        Source category 8 includes mobile oil platforms.

Poland. 1985, 1991, 1992, 1993 : source category 7 includes source category 8.
    1990 : according to the EMEP/CORINAIR methodology.

Slovakia. 1992 : source category 1 includes source category 3.

Spain. 2000 : source category 7 includes source category 8.

Sweden. 1991, 1992, 1993 : estimate for source category 9.
    1993 : estimate for source category 3.

Yugoslavia. Source category 1 includes source category 2.
        Source category 3 includes source category 4.

TABLE 9.2

National annual emissions of nitrogen oxides by source category

(Thousands of tonnes of NO$_2$)

Austria	1985	1990	1991	1992	1993	2000
1 - Public power, cogeneration, district heating	22.0	11.1	11.4	11.8	9.4	
2 - Commercial, institutional, residential combustion	9.6	11.7	12.5	11.7	11.9	
3 - Industrial combustion and processes	47.6	44.2	40.7	38.4	33.7	
4 - Non combustion processes	9.3	2.5	2.6	2.0	1.2	
5 - Extraction and distribution of fossil fuels						
6 - Solvent use						
7 - Road transport	149.0	145.3	142.0	130.0	119.0	
8 - Other transport	6.4	6.4	6.4	6.3	6.3	
9 - Waste treatment and disposal	1.4	0.7	0.6	0.6	0.6	
10 - Agriculture						
11 - Nature						
TOTAL	245.3	221.9	216.2	200.8	182.1	

Belgium	1985	1990	1991	1992	1993	2000
1 - Public power, cogeneration, district heating	45.1	58.9	58.9	57.0		
2 - Commercial, institutional, residential combustion	19.4	15.3	16.2	15.8		
3 - Industrial combustion and processes	39.1	66.2	62.6	63.4		
4 - Non combustion processes	28.0	4.9	8.3	7.1		
5 - Extraction and distribution of fossil fuels	0.0	0.0	0.0	0.0		
6 - Solvent use	0.0	0.0	0.0	0.0		
7 - Road transport	182.3	190.4	192.8	199.2		
8 - Other transport		4.0	4.0	4.1		
9 - Waste treatment and disposal	1.1	3.3	3.4	3.2		
10 - Agriculture	0.0	0.0	0.0	0.0		
11 - Nature	0.0	0.0	0.0	0.0		
TOTAL	315.1	343.0	346.1	349.9		

Bulgaria	1985	1990	1991	1992	1993	2000
1 - Public power, cogeneration, district heating		86.3	71.5	70.2	66.4	70.0
2 - Commercial, institutional, residential combustion		5.6	4.9	4.8	8.0	5.0
3 - Industrial combustion and processes		71.5	54.9	41.2	29.3	42.0
4 - Non combustion processes		29.2	22.8	19.2	27.1	18.0
5 - Extraction and distribution of fossil fuels		17.5	10.5	8.6		9.0
6 - Solvent use						
7 - Road transport		136.6	87.2	94.0	77.9	196.0
8 - Other transport		29.3	21.2	22.0	29.3	40.0
9 - Waste treatment and disposal						
10 - Agriculture						
11 - Nature						
TOTAL		376.0	273.0	260.0	238.0	380.0

Croatia	1985	1990	1991	1992	1993	2000
1 - Public power, cogeneration, district heating		9.3				
2 - Commercial, institutional, residential combustion		4.8				
3 - Industrial combustion and processes		18.3				
4 - Non combustion processes		1.3				
5 - Extraction and distribution of fossil fuels		0.0				
6 - Solvent use		0.0				
7 - Road transport		27.8				
8 - Other transport		21.5				
9 - Waste treatment and disposal		0.1				
10 - Agriculture		0.0				
11 - Nature		0.3				
TOTAL		83.4				

TABLE 9.2 (*continued*)

Cyprus	1985	1990	1991	1992	1993	2000
1 - Public power, cogeneration, district heating	2.5	3.4	3.6	4.0	4.2	6.3
2 - Commercial, institutional, residential combustion	0.0	0.0	0.0	0.0	0.0	0.0
3 - Industrial combustion and processes	1.9	1.9	1.9	1.9	1.9	1.9
4 - Non combustion processes						
5 - Extraction and distribution of fossil fuels						
6 - Solvent use						
7 - Road transport	3.8	5.4	6.5	6.3	6.6	8.7
8 - Other transport	0.5	0.7	0.7	0.8	0.8	1.1
9 - Waste treatment and disposal						
10 - Agriculture						
11 - Nature						
TOTAL	8.6	11.4	12.6	13.0	13.5	18.0

Czech Republic	1985	1990	1991	1992	1993	2000
1 - Public power, cogeneration, district heating		217.2				
2 - Commercial, institutional, residential combustion		97.6				
3 - Industrial combustion and processes		215.0				
4 - Non combustion processes		8.0				
5 - Extraction and distribution of fossil fuels						
6 - Solvent use						
7 - Road transport		151.6				
8 - Other transport		51.4				
9 - Waste treatment and disposal		1.1				
10 - Agriculture						
11 - Nature		0.1				
TOTAL		742.0				

Denmark	1985	1990	1991	1992	1993	2000
1 - Public power, cogeneration, district heating	119.4	89.6	131.2	89.0	92.5	59.7
2 - Commercial, institutional, residential combustion	9.1	5.8	6.2	5.8	6.1	4.9
3 - Industrial combustion and processes	15.4	13.6	14.5	14.1	14.6	16.7
4 - Non combustion processes	0.8	0.8	0.8	0.6	0.6	0.6
5 - Extraction and distribution of fossil fuels	2.9	3.8	5.2	5.7	5.4	10.4
6 - Solvent use						
7 - Road transport	91.4	98.8	101.5	100.3	88.4	61.5
8 - Other transport	54.5	57.0	59.1	58.6	56.7	49.0
9 - Waste treatment and disposal						
10 - Agriculture						
11 - Nature						
TOTAL	294.0	269.0	319.0	274.0	264.0	203.0

European Community	1985	1990	1991	1992	1993	2000
1 - Public power, cogeneration, district heating		2246.2				
2 - Commercial, institutional, residential combustion		457.9				
3 - Industrial combustion and processes		1328.1				
4 - Non combustion processes		192.7				
5 - Extraction and distribution of fossil fuels		75.8				
6 - Solvent use		0.9				
7 - Road transport		6235.5				
8 - Other transport		1461.9				
9 - Waste treatment and disposal		112.9				
10 - Agriculture		32.5				
11 - Nature		48.8				
TOTAL		12193.2				

TABLE 9.2 (*continued*)

Finland	1985	1990	1991	1992	1993	2000
1 - Public power, cogeneration, district heating		60.6				
2 - Commercial, institutional, residential combustion		13.4				
3 - Industrial combustion and processes		31.1				
4 - Non combustion processes		4.0				
5 - Extraction and distribution of fossil fuels						
6 - Solvent use						
7 - Road transport		119.0				
8 - Other transport		55.7				
9 - Waste treatment and disposal						
10 - Agriculture						
11 - Nature						
TOTAL		284.0				

France	1985	1990	1991	1992	1993	2000
1 - Public power, cogeneration, district heating		105.9	148.4	121.7		
2 - Commercial, institutional, residential combustion		88.6	93.0	96.7		
3 - Industrial combustion and processes		164.3	146.5	142.6		
4 - Non combustion processes		30.8	29.5	29.0		
5 - Extraction and distribution of fossil fuels		3.5	4.5	3.8		
6 - Solvent use		0.0	0.0	0.0		
7 - Road transport		1037.8	1044.6	1051.6		
8 - Other transport		129.1	128.2	127.8		
9 - Waste treatment and disposal		23.9	24.6	25.2		
10 - Agriculture		0.0	0.0	0.0		
11 - Nature		5.5	0.8	1.4		
TOTAL		1589.4	1620.1	1599.9		

Germany	1985	1990	1991	1992	1993	2000
1 - Public power, cogeneration, district heating		609.0	572.0	526.0		
2 - Commercial, institutional, residential combustion		119.0	133.0	148.0		
3 - Industrial combustion and processes		317.0	278.0	275.0		
4 - Non combustion processes						
5 - Extraction and distribution of fossil fuels		2.0	2.0	2.0		
6 - Solvent use						
7 - Road transport		1656.0	1638.0	1641.0		
8 - Other transport		330.0	311.0	312.0		
9 - Waste treatment and disposal						
10 - Agriculture						
11 - Nature						
TOTAL		3033.0	2934.0	2904.0		

Greece	1985	1990	1991	1992	1993	2000
1 - Public power, cogeneration, district heating	146.0					
2 - Commercial, institutional, residential combustion	2.0					
3 - Industrial combustion and processes	12.0					
4 - Non combustion processes	28.0					
5 - Extraction and distribution of fossil fuels	0.0					
6 - Solvent use						
7 - Road transport	120.0					
8 - Other transport						
9 - Waste treatment and disposal	0.0					
10 - Agriculture						
11 - Nature	0.0					
TOTAL	308.0					

TABLE 9.2 *(continued)*

Hungary	1985	1990	1991	1992	1993	2000
1 - Public power, cogeneration, district heating	61.6	45.0	25.3	23.4		
2 - Commercial, institutional, residential combustion	33.0	29.0	35.3	37.3		
3 - Industrial combustion and processes	48.8	20.0	20.1	15.0		
4 - Non combustion processes		21.0	19.0	10.0		
5 - Extraction and distribution of fossil fuels						
6 - Solvent use						
7 - Road transport	110.5	116.0	98.4	94.3		
8 - Other transport						
9 - Waste treatment and disposal						
10 - Agriculture	8.6	7.0	5.0	3.2		
11 - Nature						
TOTAL	262.5	238.0	203.1	183.2		

Ireland	1985	1990	1991	1992	1993	2000
1 - Public power, cogeneration, district heating		46.4	45.0	51.5		
2 - Commercial, institutional, residential combustion		6.7	6.7	6.4		
3 - Industrial combustion and processes		11.3	10.9	10.0		
4 - Non combustion processes		1.7	2.1	2.1		
5 - Extraction and distribution of fossil fuels		0.0	0.0	0.0		
6 - Solvent use		0.0	0.0	0.0		
7 - Road transport		44.0	46.2	46.7		
8 - Other transport		5.0	7.7	7.4		
9 - Waste treatment and disposal		0.7	0.6	0.6		
10 - Agriculture		0.0				
11 - Nature		0.0				
TOTAL		115.7	119.2	124.6		

Italy	1985	1990	1991	1992	1993	2000
1 - Public power, cogeneration, district heating	379.1	407.3				
2 - Commercial, institutional, residential combustion	150.1	58.9				
3 - Industrial combustion and processes	143.0	303.3				
4 - Non combustion processes	153.5	12.3				
5 - Extraction and distribution of fossil fuels	0.0	0.2				
6 - Solvent use						
7 - Road transport	858.2	946.0				
8 - Other transport	48.4	278.3				
9 - Waste treatment and disposal	4.1	34.2				
10 - Agriculture	0.0	0.5				
11 - Nature	4.6	12.0				
TOTAL	1741.0	2053.0				

Netherlands	1985	1990	1991	1992	1993	2000
1 - Public power, cogeneration, district heating	80.0	76.3	68.0	69.0		31.0
2 - Commercial, institutional, residential combustion	44.0	31.3	41.0	43.0		56.0
3 - Industrial combustion and processes	82.0	39.7	92.0	86.0		55.0
4 - Non combustion processes	25.0	61.1	16.0	11.0		
5 - Extraction and distribution of fossil fuels		1.6				
6 - Solvent use		0.9				
7 - Road transport	262.0	272.0	266.0	262.0		145.0
8 - Other transport	75.0	49.1	74.0	74.0		79.0
9 - Waste treatment and disposal	5.0	5.3	5.0	5.0		
10 - Agriculture		23.7				
11 - Nature		15.0				
TOTAL	573.0	576.0	561.0	550.0		366.0

TABLE 9.2 (*continued*)

Norway	1985	1990	1991	1992	1993	2000
1 - Public power, cogeneration, district heating	0.4	1.0	1.0	1.2	1.2	1.0
2 - Commercial, institutional, residential combustion	3.4	3.0	2.5	2.3	2.3	2.0
3 - Industrial combustion and processes	26.0	27.7	30.2	33.0	29.1	36.0
4 - Non combustion processes	11.6	9.3	7.9	6.6	7.1	8.0
5 - Extraction and distribution of fossil fuels		9.0	5.8	5.0	5.4	15.0
6 - Solvent use						
7 - Road transport	99.3	83.9	80.5	79.8	81.4	55.0
8 - Other transport	75.7	96.7	92.6	91.6	98.5	94.0
9 - Waste treatment and disposal						
10 - Agriculture						
11 - Nature						
TOTAL	216.0	230.6	220.4	220.0	225.0	210.0

Poland	1985	1990	1991	1992	1993	2000
1 - Public power, cogeneration, district heating		493.0	398.0	376.0	380.0	
2 - Commercial, institutional, residential combustion		43.0	39.0	44.0	130.0	
3 - Industrial combustion and processes		348.0	321.0	271.0	160.0	
4 - Non combustion processes		75.0	54.0	43.0	30.0	
5 - Extraction and distribution of fossil fuels		0.0			0.0	
6 - Solvent use		0.0			0.0	
7 - Road transport	385.0	402.0	393.0	396.0	420.0	
8 - Other transport						
9 - Waste treatment and disposal		84.0			20.0	
10 - Agriculture		0.0			0.0	
11 - Nature		1.0				
TOTAL	1500.0	1446.0	1205.0	1205.0	1330.0	

Portugal	1985	1990	1991	1992	1993	2000
1 - Public power, cogeneration, district heating		50.2	53.0	62.0	51.8	
2 - Commercial, institutional, residential combustion		3.0	3.2	3.3	3.3	
3 - Industrial combustion and processes		27.0	25.6	26.1	26.1	
4 - Non combustion processes		4.4	4.9	4.5	4.7	
5 - Extraction and distribution of fossil fuels		0.0	0.0	0.0	0.0	
6 - Solvent use		0.0	0.0	0.0	0.0	
7 - Road transport		106.7	115.1	125.9	132.2	
8 - Other transport		24.0	23.9	24.2	24.8	
9 - Waste treatment and disposal		0.0	0.0	0.0	0.0	
10 - Agriculture		0.0	0.0	0.0	0.0	
11 - Nature		5.5	6.9	1.8	1.8	
TOTAL		220.8	232.5	247.9	244.8	

Romania	1985	1990	1991	1992	1993	2000
1 - Public power, cogeneration, district heating				194.1		
2 - Commercial, institutional, residential combustion				8.7		
3 - Industrial combustion and processes				82.2		
4 - Non combustion processes				2.4		
5 - Extraction and distribution of fossil fuels						
6 - Solvent use						
7 - Road transport				153.2		
8 - Other transport						
9 - Waste treatment and disposal						
10 - Agriculture				2.8		
11 - Nature						
TOTAL				443.4		

TABLE 9.2 (*continued*)

Russian Federation	1985	1990	1991	1992	1993	2000
1 - Public power, cogeneration, district heating				649.2		
2 - Commercial, institutional, residential combustion						
3 - Industrial combustion and processes						
4 - Non combustion processes						
5 - Extraction and distribution of fossil fuels				75.0		
6 - Solvent use						
7 - Road transport		973.8	844.3	785.7		
8 - Other transport						
9 - Waste treatment and disposal						
10 - Agriculture						
11 - Nature						
TOTAL		2675.0	2570.8	2298.0		

Slovakia	1985	1990	1991	1992	1993	2000
1 - Public power, cogeneration, district heating				103.0		
2 - Commercial, institutional, residential combustion				10.0		
3 - Industrial combustion and processes						
4 - Non combustion processes				23.0		
5 - Extraction and distribution of fossil fuels						
6 - Solvent use						
7 - Road transport				46.0		
8 - Other transport				9.0		
9 - Waste treatment and disposal				1.0		
10 - Agriculture						
11 - Nature						
TOTAL				192.0		

Slovenia	1985	1990	1991	1992	1993	2000
1 - Public power, cogeneration, district heating	17.8	15.4	14.0	14.7	15.1	
2 - Commercial, institutional, residential combustion	0.9	1.1	1.2	1.4	1.4	
3 - Industrial combustion and processes	5.0	4.0	3.4	3.1	2.6	
4 - Non combustion processes						
5 - Extraction and distribution of fossil fuels						
6 - Solvent use						
7 - Road transport	26.3	32.7	31.1	31.4	37.4	
8 - Other transport						
9 - Waste treatment and disposal						
10 - Agriculture						
11 - Nature						
TOTAL	50.0	53.2	49.7	50.6	56.5	

Spain	1985	1990	1991	1992	1993	2000
1 - Public power, cogeneration, district heating	265.5	249.0				246.0
2 - Commercial, institutional, residential combustion	13.0	21.3				20.0
3 - Industrial combustion and processes	39.5	169.2				200.0
4 - Non combustion processes	67.5	14.6				
5 - Extraction and distribution of fossil fuels						
6 - Solvent use						
7 - Road transport	453.5	511.9				426.0
8 - Other transport		246.0				
9 - Waste treatment and disposal		34.2				
10 - Agriculture		1.0				
11 - Nature		9.7				
TOTAL	839.0	1256.9				892.0

TABLE 9.2 (*continued*)

Sweden	1985	1990	1991	1992	1993	2000
1 - Public power, cogeneration, district heating		16.0	16.0	14.0	19.0	16.0
2 - Commercial, institutional, residential combustion		13.0	13.0	12.0	13.0	9.0
3 - Industrial combustion and processes		23.0	23.0	18.0	19.0	15.0
4 - Non combustion processes		23.0	24.0	28.0	28.0	22.0
5 - Extraction and distribution of fossil fuels		0.0	0.0	0.0	0.0	0.0
6 - Solvent use						
7 - Road transport		172.0	165.0	159.0	150.0	95.0
8 - Other transport		149.0	154.0	157.0	160.0	153.0
9 - Waste treatment and disposal		2.0	2.0	2.0	2.0	2.0
10 - Agriculture		0.0	0.0	0.0	0.0	0.0
11 - Nature		0.2	0.0	1.0	0.0	0.0
TOTAL		398.0	397.0	391.0	391.0	312.0

Switzerland	1985	1990	1991	1992	1993	2000
1 - Public power, cogeneration, district heating		0.3	0.3	0.3	0.3	
2 - Commercial, institutional, residential combustion		9.3	9.2	7.4	8.6	
3 - Industrial combustion and processes		31.8	30.9	25.0	26.3	
4 - Non combustion processes		2.3	2.2	2.2	2.2	
5 - Extraction and distribution of fossil fuels						
6 - Solvent use						
7 - Road transport		119.2	111.7	105.6	96.0	
8 - Other transport		17.2	17.0	17.0	12.7	
9 - Waste treatment and disposal		3.7	3.7	3.7	3.7	
10 - Agriculture						
11 - Nature						
TOTAL		183.8	175.0	161.2	149.8	

United Kingdom	1985	1990	1991	1992	1993	2000
1 - Public power, cogeneration, district heating	775.0	777.0	718.0	694.0	671.0	569.0
2 - Commercial, institutional, residential combustion	136.0	124.0	135.0	132.0	133.0	73.0
3 - Industrial combustion and processes	253.0	242.0	244.0	236.0	229.0	250.0
4 - Non combustion processes	13.0	9.0	9.0	9.0	9.0	
5 - Extraction and distribution of fossil fuels	66.0	82.0	85.0	88.0	88.0	
6 - Solvent use						
7 - Road transport	1015.0	1434.0	1450.0	1398.0	1432.0	946.0
8 - Other transport	164.0	175.0	178.0	177.0	174.0	
9 - Waste treatment and disposal	12.0	12.0	12.0	12.0	12.0	
10 - Agriculture	5.0	4.0	4.0	4.0	4.0	
11 - Nature						
TOTAL	2438.0	2860.0	2835.0	2750.0	2752.0	2000.0

United States	1985	1990	1991	1992	1993	2000
1 - Public power, cogeneration, district heating	6057.0	6828.0	6787.0	6775.0		
2 - Commercial, institutional, residential combustion	639.0	664.0	676.0	665.0		
3 - Industrial combustion and processes	3107.0	3207.0	3269.0	3196.0		
4 - Non combustion processes	622.0	809.0	804.0	798.0		
5 - Extraction and distribution of fossil fuels						
6 - Solvent use						
7 - Road transport	7360.0	7091.0	6999.0	6783.0		
8 - Other transport	2358.0	2579.0	2512.0	2587.0		
9 - Waste treatment and disposal	196.0	195.0	193.0	195.0		
10 - Agriculture						
11 - Nature						
TOTAL	20339.0	21373.0	21240.0	20999.0		

TABLE 9.2 (*concluded*)

Yugoslavia	1985	1990	1991	1992	1993	2000
1 - Public power, cogeneration, district heating	50.5	59.2	50.9	44.1	47.6	76.8
2 - Commercial, institutional, residential combustion						
3 - Industrial combustion and processes	4.9	4.6	8.0	2.4	10.0	8.4
4 - Non combustion processes						
5 - Extraction and distribution of fossil fuels						
6 - Solvent use						
7 - Road transport						
8 - Other transport						
9 - Waste treatment and disposal						
10 - Agriculture						
11 - Nature						
TOTAL	58.0	66.0	57.0	49.0	54.0	88.3

Comments :

Denmark. 1985 : source category 7 based on sales.

European Community : not including emissions from the former GDR.

Finland. 1990 : preliminary data.

Germany. 1990, 1991, 1992 : source category 3 includes source category 4.
          1992 : preliminary data.

Hungary. 1985, 1991, 1992 : source category 7 includes source category 8.
          1985 : source category 3 includes source category 4.

Ireland. 1991, 1992 : estimate.

Netherlands. 1992 : provisional data.
          2000 : source category 3 includes source category 4.
               Based on the baseline scenario.

Norway. Source category 1 includes waste combustion with energy generation.
          Source category 3 includes gas turbines in the North Sea.
          Source category 5 includes gas flaring and VOC from leakage from petrol handling.
          Source category 7 includes cars and motor cycles.
          Source category 8 includes mobile oil platforms.

Poland. 1985, 1991, 1992, 1993 : source category 7 includes source category 8.
          1990 : according to the EMEP/CORINAIR methodology.

Slovakia. 1992 : source category 1 includes source category 3.
          1992 : source category 7 and source category 8 according to the COPERT method.

Spain. 2000 : source category 7 includes source category 8.

Sweden. 1991, 1992 : estimate for source category 9.
          1993 : estimate for source category 3, 7, 8 and 9.

Yugoslavia. Source category 1 includes source category 2.
          Source category 3 includes source category 4.

TABLE 9.3

National annual emissions of ammonia by source category

(Thousands of tonnes of NH$_3$)

Austria	1985	1990	1991	1992	1993	2000
1 - Public power, cogeneration, district heating		0.1	0.1	0.1	0.1	
2 - Commercial, institutional, residential combustion		0.1	0.1	0.1	0.1	
3 - Industrial combustion and processes		0.1	0.1	0.1	0.1	
4 - Non combustion processes		5.0	5.0	5.0	5.0	
5 - Extraction and distribution of fossil fuels						
6 - Solvent use						
7 - Road transport		1.0	1.0	2.0	3.0	
8 - Other transport						
9 - Waste treatment and disposal		7.0	7.0	7.0	7.0	
10 - Agriculture		78.0	78.0	78.0	78.0	
11 - Nature		7.6	7.6	7.6	7.6	
TOTAL		98.9	98.9	99.9	100.9	

Belgium	1985	1990	1991	1992	1993	2000
1 - Public power, cogeneration, district heating	0.0	0.0	0.0	0.0		
2 - Commercial, institutional, residential combustion	0.0	0.0	0.0	0.0		
3 - Industrial combustion and processes	0.0	0.0	0.0	0.0		
4 - Non combustion processes	2.6	2.7	2.1	1.1		
5 - Extraction and distribution of fossil fuels	0.0	0.0	0.0	0.0		
6 - Solvent use	0.0	0.0	0.0	0.0		
7 - Road transport	0.1	0.1	0.2	0.2		
8 - Other transport		0.0	0.0	0.0		
9 - Waste treatment and disposal	0.0	0.0	0.0	0.0		
10 - Agriculture	71.1	75.8	75.8	75.6		
11 - Nature	0.0	0.0	0.0	0.0		
TOTAL	73.8	78.6	78.0	76.9		

Bulgaria	1985	1990	1991	1992	1993	2000
1 - Public power, cogeneration, district heating						
2 - Commercial, institutional, residential combustion						
3 - Industrial combustion and processes						
4 - Non combustion processes		9.6			13.2	
5 - Extraction and distribution of fossil fuels						
6 - Solvent use						
7 - Road transport		0.5			0.0	
8 - Other transport		0.0				
9 - Waste treatment and disposal		25.7			25.6	
10 - Agriculture		288.4			181.0	
11 - Nature						
TOTAL		323.7			219.8	

Czech Republic	1985	1990	1991	1992	1993	2000
1 - Public power, cogeneration, district heating		0.1				
2 - Commercial, institutional, residential combustion		0.9				
3 - Industrial combustion and processes		0.0				
4 - Non combustion processes		2.5				
5 - Extraction and distribution of fossil fuels						
6 - Solvent use						
7 - Road transport		0.8				
8 - Other transport						
9 - Waste treatment and disposal						
10 - Agriculture		100.8				
11 - Nature						
TOTAL		105.1				

TABLE 9.3 (*continued*)

Denmark	1985	1990	1991	1992	1993	2000
1 - Public power, cogeneration, district heating						
2 - Commercial, institutional, residential combustion						
3 - Industrial combustion and processes						
4 - Non combustion processes						
5 - Extraction and distribution of fossil fuels						
6 - Solvent use						
7 - Road transport	0.1	0.1	0.1		0.1	0.1
8 - Other transport	0.0	0.0	0.0			0.0
9 - Waste treatment and disposal						
10 - Agriculture	152.0	140.0	134.0		126.0	103.0
11 - Nature						
TOTAL	152.0	140.0	134.0		126.1	103.0

European Community	1985	1990	1991	1992	1993	2000
1 - Public power, cogeneration, district heating		0.1				
2 - Commercial, institutional, residential combustion		1.0				
3 - Industrial combustion and processes		0.1				
4 - Non combustion processes		97.0				
5 - Extraction and distribution of fossil fuels		0.0				
6 - Solvent use		0.0				
7 - Road transport		9.6				
8 - Other transport		0.1				
9 - Waste treatment and disposal		23.1				
10 - Agriculture		3338.5				
11 - Nature		57.0				
TOTAL		3526.6				

Finland	1985	1990	1991	1992	1993	2000
1 - Public power, cogeneration, district heating						
2 - Commercial, institutional, residential combustion						
3 - Industrial combustion and processes						
4 - Non combustion processes		1.3				
5 - Extraction and distribution of fossil fuels						
6 - Solvent use						
7 - Road transport		0.2				
8 - Other transport						
9 - Waste treatment and disposal		0.3				
10 - Agriculture		39.2				
11 - Nature						
TOTAL		41.0				

France	1985	1990	1991	1992	1993	2000
1 - Public power, cogeneration, district heating						
2 - Commercial, institutional, residential combustion						
3 - Industrial combustion and processes						
4 - Non combustion processes		16.6	14.9	13.7		
5 - Extraction and distribution of fossil fuels						
6 - Solvent use		0.0	0.0	0.0		
7 - Road transport		0.8	0.9	1.0		
8 - Other transport						
9 - Waste treatment and disposal		1.8	1.8	1.8		
10 - Agriculture		625.9	617.5	606.4		
11 - Nature						
TOTAL		645.1	635.0	622.8		

TABLE 9.3 (*continued*)

Germany	1985	1990	1991	1992	1993	2000
1 - Public power, cogeneration, district heating		3.0	3.0	3.0		
2 - Commercial, institutional, residential combustion		3.0	1.0	1.0		
3 - Industrial combustion and processes		1.0	1.0	11.0		
4 - Non combustion processes		16.0	9.0			
5 - Extraction and distribution of fossil fuels						
6 - Solvent use						
7 - Road transport		7.0	12.0	17.0		
8 - Other transport		0.0	0.0	0.0		
9 - Waste treatment and disposal						
10 - Agriculture		729.0	640.0	616.0		
11 - Nature						
TOTAL		759.0	666.0	648.0		

Ireland	1985	1990	1991	1992	1993	2000
1 - Public power, cogeneration, district heating		0.0				
2 - Commercial, institutional, residential combustion		0.0				
3 - Industrial combustion and processes		0.0				
4 - Non combustion processes		0.0				
5 - Extraction and distribution of fossil fuels		0.0				
6 - Solvent use		0.0				
7 - Road transport		0.0				
8 - Other transport		0.0				
9 - Waste treatment and disposal		6.2				
10 - Agriculture		120.0				
11 - Nature		0.0				
TOTAL		126.2				

Italy	1985	1990	1991	1992	1993	2000
1 - Public power, cogeneration, district heating	0.1	0.1				
2 - Commercial, institutional, residential combustion	0.0	0.0				
3 - Industrial combustion and processes	0.0	0.1				
4 - Non combustion processes	9.5	23.0				
5 - Extraction and distribution of fossil fuels						
6 - Solvent use						
7 - Road transport	0.3	0.6				
8 - Other transport	0.0	0.0				
9 - Waste treatment and disposal	8.9	11.0				
10 - Agriculture	404.1	348.9				
11 - Nature	85.5	0.0				
TOTAL	508.4	383.7				

Netherlands	1985	1990	1991	1992	1993	2000
1 - Public power, cogeneration, district heating						
2 - Commercial, institutional, residential combustion		1.0				
3 - Industrial combustion and processes		0.0				
4 - Non combustion processes	7.0	3.9	4.5	5.0		3.0
5 - Extraction and distribution of fossil fuels						
6 - Solvent use		0.0				
7 - Road transport		0.4				
8 - Other transport		0.1				
9 - Waste treatment and disposal	9.0	0.0	10.5	11.0		11.0
10 - Agriculture	242.0	190.0	205.6	155.0		72.0
11 - Nature		9.0				
TOTAL	258.0	204.5	221.0	170.0		86.0

TABLE 9.3 (*continued*)

Norway	1985	1990	1991	1992	1993	2000
1 - Public power, cogeneration, district heating						
2 - Commercial, institutional, residential combustion						
3 - Industrial combustion and processes						
4 - Non combustion processes		0.5	0.3	0.4	0.4	0.0
5 - Extraction and distribution of fossil fuels						
6 - Solvent use						
7 - Road transport		0.2	0.4	0.4	0.5	2.0
8 - Other transport		0.0			0.0	
9 - Waste treatment and disposal						
10 - Agriculture		37.8	38.4	39.0	39.0	38.0
11 - Nature						
TOTAL		38.5	39.1	39.0	39.9	41.0

Poland	1985	1990	1991	1992	1993	2000
1 - Public power, cogeneration, district heating		1.0	1.0		1.0	
2 - Commercial, institutional, residential combustion		0.2			1.0	
3 - Industrial combustion and processes		0.3			1.0	
4 - Non combustion processes		35.4	20.0		20.0	
5 - Extraction and distribution of fossil fuels			0.0		0.0	
6 - Solvent use			0.0		0.0	
7 - Road transport		0.1	0.0		1.0	
8 - Other transport		0.0				
9 - Waste treatment and disposal		43.0	25.0		25.0	
10 - Agriculture		459.0	397.0		336.0	
11 - Nature		42.0	27.0			
TOTAL		581.0	470.0		382.0	

Portugal	1985	1990	1991	1992	1993	2000
1 - Public power, cogeneration, district heating		0.0	0.0	0.0	0.0	
2 - Commercial, institutional, residential combustion		0.0	0.0	0.0	0.0	
3 - Industrial combustion and processes		0.0	0.0	0.0	0.0	
4 - Non combustion processes		6.0	5.9	5.9	5.9	
5 - Extraction and distribution of fossil fuels		0.0	0.0	0.0	0.0	
6 - Solvent use		0.0	0.0	0.0	0.0	
7 - Road transport		0.0	0.1	0.1	0.1	
8 - Other transport		0.0	0.0	0.0	0.0	
9 - Waste treatment and disposal		0.0	0.0	0.0	0.0	
10 - Agriculture		86.9	86.9	86.9	86.9	
11 - Nature		0.0	0.0	0.0	0.0	
TOTAL		92.9	92.9	92.8	92.8	

Russian Federation	1985	1990	1991	1992	1993	2000
1 - Public power, cogeneration, district heating						
2 - Commercial, institutional, residential combustion						
3 - Industrial combustion and processes						
4 - Non combustion processes	37.6	45.5	63.5	53.3		
5 - Extraction and distribution of fossil fuels						
6 - Solvent use						
7 - Road transport						
8 - Other transport						
9 - Waste treatment and disposal						
10 - Agriculture	1239.0	1146.0	1097.0	1031.0		
11 - Nature						
TOTAL				1084.3		

TABLE 9.3 (*continued*)

Slovakia	1985	1990	1991	1992	1993	2000
1 - Public power, cogeneration, district heating						
2 - Commercial, institutional, residential combustion						
3 - Industrial combustion and processes						
4 - Non combustion processes				2.0		
5 - Extraction and distribution of fossil fuels						
6 - Solvent use						
7 - Road transport				0.1		
8 - Other transport						
9 - Waste treatment and disposal						
10 - Agriculture				59.0		
11 - Nature						
TOTAL				61.0		

Spain	1985	1990	1991	1992	1993	2000
1 - Public power, cogeneration, district heating						
2 - Commercial, institutional, residential combustion						
3 - Industrial combustion and processes		0.0				
4 - Non combustion processes		15.6				
5 - Extraction and distribution of fossil fuels						
6 - Solvent use						
7 - Road transport		0.4				
8 - Other transport		0.0				
9 - Waste treatment and disposal						
10 - Agriculture		308.3				
11 - Nature						
TOTAL		324.3				

Sweden	1985	1990	1991	1992	1993	2000
1 - Public power, cogeneration, district heating						
2 - Commercial, institutional, residential combustion						
3 - Industrial combustion and processes		1.0	1.0	1.0	1.0	1.0
4 - Non combustion processes						
5 - Extraction and distribution of fossil fuels						
6 - Solvent use						
7 - Road transport		0.0	0.0	0.0	0.0	0.0
8 - Other transport		0.0	0.0	0.0	0.0	0.0
9 - Waste treatment and disposal		28.0	28.0	28.0	28.0	28.0
10 - Agriculture		45.0	44.0	43.0	42.0	39.0
11 - Nature		0.0	0.0	0.0	0.0	0.0
TOTAL		74.0	73.0	72.0	71.0	68.0

Switzerland	1985	1990	1991	1992	1993	2000
1 - Public power, cogeneration, district heating						
2 - Commercial, institutional, residential combustion						
3 - Industrial combustion and processes						
4 - Non combustion processes		1.1	1.0	1.8	1.8	
5 - Extraction and distribution of fossil fuels						
6 - Solvent use		0.1	0.1	0.1	0.1	
7 - Road transport						
8 - Other transport						
9 - Waste treatment and disposal		4.9	4.9	4.9	4.9	
10 - Agriculture		55.4	55.0	55.0	55.8	
11 - Nature						
TOTAL		61.5	61.0	61.8	62.6	

TABLE 9.3 (*concluded*)

United Kingdom	1985	1990	1991	1992	1993	2000
1 - Public power, cogeneration, district heating					0.0	
2 - Commercial, institutional, residential combustion					4.2	
3 - Industrial combustion and processes					0.0	
4 - Non combustion processes					7.3	
5 - Extraction and distribution of fossil fuels						
6 - Solvent use						
7 - Road transport					1.7	
8 - Other transport					0.0	
9 - Waste treatment and disposal					71.5	
10 - Agriculture					297.0	
11 - Nature						
TOTAL					381.7	

Comments :

Denmark. 1985 : source category 7 based on sales.

European Community : not including emissions from the former GDR.

Finland. 1990 : preliminary data.

Germany. 1992 : source category 3 includes source category 4 ; preliminary data.

Netherlands. 1985 : data for 1986.
          1985, 1990, 1991, 1992, 2000 : including emissions from human beings, pet animals
                                        and the use of cleaning products.
          1992 : provisional data.
          2000 : based on the baseline scenario.

Norway. Source category 7 includes cars and motor cycles.
          Source category 8 includes mobile oil platforms.

Poland. 1991, 1993 : source category 7 includes source category 8.
          1990 : according to the EMEP/CORINAIR methodology.

Russian Federation. 1985 : source category 4 data for 1986.

Sweden. 1991, 1992, 1993 : estimate for source category 9.
          1990, 1991, 1992, 1993, 2000 : source category 3 includes source category 4.

United Kingdom. 1993 : source category 9 = 33-110 kt ;
                  Source category 10 = 294-300 kt ;
                  Total = 340-423 kt.

TABLE 9.4

National annual emissions of non-methane volatile organic compounds by source category

(Thousands of tonnes)

Austria	1985	1990	1991	1992	1993	2000
1 - Public power, cogeneration, district heating	0.5	0.5	0.6	0.6	0.8	
2 - Commercial, institutional, residential combustion	75.4	98.9	101.4	100.8	98.2	
3 - Industrial combustion and processes	3.5	3.6	3.6	3.2	3.2	
4 - Non combustion processes	12.8	12.5	12.2	12.1	11.9	
5 - Extraction and distribution of fossil fuels	14.5	15.8	16.7	16.4	15.8	
6 - Solvent use	118.0	130.0	124.0	122.0	120.0	
7 - Road transport	147.0	129.5	126.9	114.0	105.0	
8 - Other transport	2.1	1.7	1.7	1.7	1.7	
9 - Waste treatment and disposal	25.8	25.8	25.8	25.8	25.8	
10 - Agriculture	12.0	12.0	6.0	6.0	6.0	
11 - Nature						
TOTAL	411.6	430.3	418.9	402.6	388.4	

Belgium	1985	1990	1991	1992	1993	2000
1 - Public power, cogeneration, district heating	3.0	0.4	0.4	0.4		
2 - Commercial, institutional, residential combustion	16.9	7.3	7.8	7.9		
3 - Industrial combustion and processes	13.3	6.2	5.9	6.2		
4 - Non combustion processes	28.6	54.3	43.8	41.3		
5 - Extraction and distribution of fossil fuels	60.0	13.6	17.7	17.8		
6 - Solvent use	82.4	89.9	85.6	86.5		
7 - Road transport	185.4	188.7	197.2	204.0		
8 - Other transport	0.0	3.5	3.3	4.0		
9 - Waste treatment and disposal	17.0	0.2	0.0	0.2		
10 - Agriculture	253.3	0.8	0.8	0.8		
11 - Nature	28.1	29.5	29.5	29.3		
TOTAL	688.1	394.4	392.2	398.5		

Bulgaria	1985	1990	1991	1992	1993	2000
1 - Public power, cogeneration, district heating		0.5	0.5	0.4	0.5	0.4
2 - Commercial, institutional, residential combustion		17.0	17.0	12.7	20.5	10.0
3 - Industrial combustion and processes		9.0	8.0	8.5	1.5	8.0
4 - Non combustion processes		29.8	29.5	25.0	15.7	20.0
5 - Extraction and distribution of fossil fuels		4.4	4.0	3.0	1.7	3.0
6 - Solvent use		40.8	38.0	42.0	72.7	32.0
7 - Road transport		73.6	70.0	73.4	52.6	74.0
8 - Other transport		5.6	5.0	4.9	5.6	5.6
9 - Waste treatment and disposal		6.5			6.5	
10 - Agriculture		30.2	33.0	28.7	21.9	45.0
11 - Nature		176.0			176.0	
TOTAL		392.0	205.0	199.0	375.2	180.0

Czech Republic	1985	1990	1991	1992	1993	2000
1 - Public power, cogeneration, district heating		5.1				
2 - Commercial, institutional, residential combustion		57.2				
3 - Industrial combustion and processes		2.3				
4 - Non combustion processes		115.4				
5 - Extraction and distribution of fossil fuels		5.3				
6 - Solvent use		185.0				
7 - Road transport		56.2				
8 - Other transport		7.2				
9 - Waste treatment and disposal		0.3				
10 - Agriculture		100.0				
11 - Nature		40.2				
TOTAL		574.3				

TABLE 9.4 (*continued*)

Denmark	1985	1990	1991	1992	1993	2000
1 - Public power, cogeneration, district heating	0.9	1.0	1.2	1.2	1.2	
2 - Commercial, institutional, residential combustion	8.9	8.6	9.3	9.3	9.5	
3 - Industrial combustion and processes	0.8	0.9	0.9	0.9	0.9	
4 - Non combustion processes	3.7	3.7	3.9	4.2	4.4	
5 - Extraction and distribution of fossil fuels	6.6	6.6	6.2	5.3	5.0	
6 - Solvent use	33.8	33.8	33.8	33.8	33.9	
7 - Road transport	89.6	95.0	97.1	95.9	78.3	
8 - Other transport	12.8	13.4	13.2	13.1	13.2	
9 - Waste treatment and disposal						
10 - Agriculture	2.0	2.0	2.0	2.0	2.0	
11 - Nature	9.3	9.3	9.3	9.3	9.3	
TOTAL	169.0	174.3	177.0	175.0	158.0	

European Community	1985	1990	1991	1992	1993	2000
1 - Public power, cogeneration, district heating		37.3				
2 - Commercial, institutional, residential combustion		420.7				
3 - Industrial combustion and processes		51.6				
4 - Non combustion processes		880.6				
5 - Extraction and distribution of fossil fuels		960.9				
6 - Solvent use		3700.7				
7 - Road transport		5135.7				
8 - Other transport		460.5				
9 - Waste treatment and disposal		211.0				
10 - Agriculture		611.5				
11 - Nature		2631.4				
TOTAL		15101.7				

Finland	1985	1990	1991	1992	1993	2000
1 - Public power, cogeneration, district heating		1.0				
2 - Commercial, institutional, residential combustion		33.0				
3 - Industrial combustion and processes		1.0				
4 - Non combustion processes		19.5				
5 - Extraction and distribution of fossil fuels		18.0				
6 - Solvent use		47.5				
7 - Road transport		73.1				
8 - Other transport		13.0				
9 - Waste treatment and disposal		3.0				
10 - Agriculture						
11 - Nature						
TOTAL		209.1				

France	1985	1990	1991	1992	1993	2000
1 - Public power, cogeneration, district heating		1.3	2.0	1.7		
2 - Commercial, institutional, residential combustion		214.2	214.5	214.8		
3 - Industrial combustion and processes		7.3	6.6	6.4		
4 - Non combustion processes		100.1	98.9	100.5		
5 - Extraction and distribution of fossil fuels		122.5	127.0	125.3		
6 - Solvent use		635.6	608.9	601.8		
7 - Road transport		1169.8	1150.1	1129.1		
8 - Other transport		121.8	121.7	121.6		
9 - Waste treatment and disposal		19.0	20.5	20.4		
10 - Agriculture		10.5	10.5	10.4		
11 - Nature		461.8	431.9	439.3		
TOTAL		2864.0	2792.6	2771.3		

TABLE 9.4 (*continued*)

Germany	1985	1990	1991	1992	1993	2000
1 - Public power, cogeneration, district heating		9.0	9.0	9.0		
2 - Commercial, institutional, residential combustion		113.0	101.0	95.0		
3 - Industrial combustion and processes		145.0	133.0	131.0		
4 - Non combustion processes						
5 - Extraction and distribution of fossil fuels		205.0	191.0	185.0		
6 - Solvent use		1170.0	1163.0	1141.0		
7 - Road transport		1236.0	1173.0	1125.0		
8 - Other transport		88.0	78.0	79.0		
9 - Waste treatment and disposal						
10 - Agriculture						
11 - Nature						
TOTAL		2966.0	2848.0	2765.0		

Greece	1985	1990	1991	1992	1993	2000
1 - Public power, cogeneration, district heating	1.0					
2 - Commercial, institutional, residential combustion	0.0					
3 - Industrial combustion and processes	6.0					
4 - Non combustion processes	4.0					
5 - Extraction and distribution of fossil fuels	245.0					
6 - Solvent use	30.0					
7 - Road transport	115.0					
8 - Other transport						
9 - Waste treatment and disposal	18.0					
10 - Agriculture						
11 - Nature	196.0					
TOTAL	614.0					

Hungary	1985	1990	1991	1992	1993	2000
1 - Public power, cogeneration, district heating			1.0			
2 - Commercial, institutional, residential combustion						
3 - Industrial combustion and processes						
4 - Non combustion processes						
5 - Extraction and distribution of fossil fuels			25.0			
6 - Solvent use			45.0			
7 - Road transport			72.5			
8 - Other transport						
9 - Waste treatment and disposal						
10 - Agriculture						
11 - Nature						
TOTAL			143.5			

Ireland	1985	1990	1991	1992	1993	2000
1 - Public power, cogeneration, district heating		0.2	0.2	0.3		
2 - Commercial, institutional, residential combustion		8.0	8.4	5.8		
3 - Industrial combustion and processes		0.3	0.3	0.2		
4 - Non combustion processes		0.7	0.7	0.8		
5 - Extraction and distribution of fossil fuels		3.1	2.5	2.6		
6 - Solvent use		21.4	24.0	24.0		
7 - Road transport		62.3	63.8	65.0		
8 - Other transport		1.2	1.4	1.3		
9 - Waste treatment and disposal		4.7	3.6	3.6		
10 - Agriculture		78.5				
11 - Nature		16.6				
TOTAL		197.0	105.0	103.6		

TABLE 9.4 (*continued*)

Italy

	1985	1990	1991	1992	1993	2000
1 - Public power, cogeneration, district heating	7.0	4.0				
2 - Commercial, institutional, residential combustion	36.8	20.9				
3 - Industrial combustion and processes	3.3	11.0				
4 - Non combustion processes	87.7	101.6				
5 - Extraction and distribution of fossil fuels	72.9	133.1				
6 - Solvent use	479.1	537.6				
7 - Road transport	806.4	953.7				
8 - Other transport	20.7	130.9				
9 - Waste treatment and disposal	12.2	112.6				
10 - Agriculture	3.3	396.2				
11 - Nature	241.7	152.2				
TOTAL	1771.1	2553.8				

Netherlands

	1985	1990	1991	1992	1993	2000
1 - Public power, cogeneration, district heating	0.0	0.7	0.0	1.0		145.0
2 - Commercial, institutional, residential combustion	15.0	16.6	13.0	8.0		
3 - Industrial combustion and processes	5.0	1.2	5.0	10.0		
4 - Non combustion processes	227.0	77.1	209.0	224.0		
5 - Extraction and distribution of fossil fuels		1.3				
6 - Solvent use		145.3				
7 - Road transport	217.0	183.6	165.0	159.0		77.0
8 - Other transport	9.0	22.8	10.0	10.0		23.0
9 - Waste treatment and disposal		3.1				
10 - Agriculture	24.0	5.1	24.0	24.0		
11 - Nature	3.0	3.4	3.0	3.0		3.0
TOTAL	500.0	460.2	429.0	439.0		248.0

Norway

	1985	1990	1991	1992	1993	2000
1 - Public power, cogeneration, district heating	0.1	0.3	0.3	0.3	0.3	0.0
2 - Commercial, institutional, residential combustion	8.0	8.9	7.9	7.8	7.8	8.0
3 - Industrial combustion and processes	1.1	2.3	2.4	2.7	2.7	2.0
4 - Non combustion processes	7.0	11.0	10.1	12.0	11.0	14.0
5 - Extraction and distribution of fossil fuels	66.2	95.0	103.9	114.8	123.6	121.0
6 - Solvent use	40.1	31.6	31.6	31.6	31.6	30.0
7 - Road transport	81.6	88.1	84.5	81.9	78.7	47.0
8 - Other transport	16.5	14.3	14.1	14.0	14.2	20.0
9 - Waste treatment and disposal						
10 - Agriculture						
11 - Nature						
TOTAL	221.0	251.5	254.8	265.0	270.0	242.0

Poland

	1985	1990	1991	1992	1993	2000
1 - Public power, cogeneration, district heating		2.0	9.0	3.0	3.0	
2 - Commercial, institutional, residential combustion		99.0	99.0	62.0	124.0	
3 - Industrial combustion and processes		11.0	157.0	27.0	27.0	
4 - Non combustion processes		88.0	66.0	56.0	53.0	
5 - Extraction and distribution of fossil fuels		51.0	26.0	22.0	37.0	
6 - Solvent use		230.0	205.0	192.0	179.0	
7 - Road transport	330.0	248.0	272.0	307.0		
8 - Other transport		73.0	73.0	62.0		
9 - Waste treatment and disposal						
10 - Agriculture		34.0	34.0	34.0	34.0	
11 - Nature	289.0	270.0	290.0	279.0	281.0	
TOTAL	1439.0	1295.0	1231.0	1058.0	1058.0	

TABLE 9.4 (*continued*)

Portugal	1985	1990	1991	1992	1993	2000
1 - Public power, cogeneration, district heating		0.4	0.4	0.5	0.4	
2 - Commercial, institutional, residential combustion		10.4	10.6	10.6	10.6	
3 - Industrial combustion and processes		4.0	3.8	3.8	3.8	
4 - Non combustion processes		25.2	24.4	25.2	25.3	
5 - Extraction and distribution of fossil fuels		7.6	7.6	8.5	8.7	
6 - Solvent use		67.1	67.1	67.1	67.1	
7 - Road transport		81.1	86.8	93.9	97.9	
8 - Other transport		5.9	5.9	5.9	6.0	
9 - Waste treatment and disposal		0.0	0.0	0.0	0.0	
10 - Agriculture		4.0	4.0	4.0	4.0	
11 - Nature		438.1	452.5	400.2	400.2	
TOTAL		643.9	663.1	619.7	624.0	

Romania	1985	1990	1991	1992	1993	2000
1 - Public power, cogeneration, district heating				21.1		
2 - Commercial, institutional, residential combustion				3.2		
3 - Industrial combustion and processes				24.3		
4 - Non combustion processes				0.8		
5 - Extraction and distribution of fossil fuels						
6 - Solvent use						
7 - Road transport				59.3		
8 - Other transport						
9 - Waste treatment and disposal						
10 - Agriculture				0.8		
11 - Nature						
TOTAL				109.5		

Russian Federation	1985	1990	1991	1992	1993	2000
1 - Public power, cogeneration, district heating						
2 - Commercial, institutional, residential combustion						
3 - Industrial combustion and processes						
4 - Non combustion processes				191.2		
5 - Extraction and distribution of fossil fuels	895.0			665.0		
6 - Solvent use				110.0		
7 - Road transport		1978.2	1796.8	1595.2		
8 - Other transport						
9 - Waste treatment and disposal						
10 - Agriculture						
11 - Nature	5500.0	5500.0	5500.0	5500.0	5500.0	
TOTAL						

Slovakia	1985	1990	1991	1992	1993	2000
1 - Public power, cogeneration, district heating				1.0		
2 - Commercial, institutional, residential combustion				10.0		
3 - Industrial combustion and processes						
4 - Non combustion processes				31.0		
5 - Extraction and distribution of fossil fuels						
6 - Solvent use				39.0		
7 - Road transport				35.0		
8 - Other transport				1.0		
9 - Waste treatment and disposal				8.0		
10 - Agriculture						
11 - Nature						
TOTAL				125.0		

TABLE 9.4 (*continued*)

Slovenia	1985	1990	1991	1992	1993	2000
1 - Public power, cogeneration, district heating		0.8				
2 - Commercial, institutional, residential combustion		1.1				
3 - Industrial combustion and processes		0.1				
4 - Non combustion processes		4.3				
5 - Extraction and distribution of fossil fuels		2.6				
6 - Solvent use		7.6				
7 - Road transport		18.7				
8 - Other transport						
9 - Waste treatment and disposal						
10 - Agriculture						
11 - Nature						
TOTAL		35.2				

Spain	1985	1990	1991	1992	1993	2000
1 - Public power, cogeneration, district heating	35.8	9.4				
2 - Commercial, institutional, residential combustion	18.7	59.2				
3 - Industrial combustion and processes	24.4	10.8				
4 - Non combustion processes	21.0	78.6				
5 - Extraction and distribution of fossil fuels		57.8				
6 - Solvent use	327.0	302.2				
7 - Road transport	489.0	449.1				
8 - Other transport		39.4				
9 - Waste treatment and disposal	368.0	22.9				
10 - Agriculture		82.1				
11 - Nature	876.0	775.5				
TOTAL	2141.0	1887.0				

Sweden	1985	1990	1991	1992	1993	2000
1 - Public power, cogeneration, district heating		3.0	4.0	4.0	5.0	5.0
2 - Commercial, institutional, residential combustion		141.0	140.0	136.0	149.0	113.0
3 - Industrial combustion and processes		6.0	6.0	6.0	11.0	13.0
4 - Non combustion processes		67.0	66.0	65.0	65.0	60.0
5 - Extraction and distribution of fossil fuels		18.0	16.0	13.0	11.0	10.0
6 - Solvent use		98.0	95.0	91.0	83.0	50.0
7 - Road transport		163.0	189.0	149.0	128.0	49.0
8 - Other transport		37.0		37.0	37.0	42.0
9 - Waste treatment and disposal						
10 - Agriculture						
11 - Nature		377.0	377.0	377.0	377.0	377.0
TOTAL		910.0	893.0	878.0	866.0	719.0

Switzerland	1985	1990	1991	1992	1993	2000
1 - Public power, cogeneration, district heating		0.0	0.0	0.0	0.0	
2 - Commercial, institutional, residential combustion		10.2	10.2	10.2	10.2	
3 - Industrial combustion and processes		3.1	3.1	3.1	3.1	
4 - Non combustion processes		17.8	17.8	16.4	16.4	
5 - Extraction and distribution of fossil fuels		17.8	17.7	17.2	14.0	
6 - Solvent use		180.1	179.3	165.2	162.4	
7 - Road transport		59.2	52.8	53.0	47.5	
8 - Other transport		8.0	8.0	8.0	8.0	
9 - Waste treatment and disposal		0.9	0.9	0.9	0.9	
10 - Agriculture						
11 - Nature						
TOTAL		297.0	289.7	274.0	262.5	

TABLE 9.4 (*concluded*)

United Kingdom	1985	1990	1991	1992	1993	2000
1 - Public power, cogeneration, district heating	12.0	13.0	13.0	12.0	0.0	
2 - Commercial, institutional, residential combustion	74.0	41.0	40.0	37.0	33.0	
3 - Industrial combustion and processes	3.0	3.0	3.0	3.0	3.0	
4 - Non combustion processes	291.0	295.0	295.0	295.0	295.0	
5 - Extraction and distribution of fossil fuels	285.0	337.0	342.0	345.0	351.0	
6 - Solvent use	752.0	752.0	752.0	752.0	752.0	
7 - Road transport	855.0	1007.0	1001.0	949.0	957.0	398.0
8 - Other transport	25.0	26.0	26.0	26.0	26.0	
9 - Waste treatment and disposal	57.0	57.0	57.0	57.0	57.0	
10 - Agriculture	80.0	80.0	80.0	80.0	80.0	
11 - Nature						
TOTAL	2435.0	2612.0	2609.0	2556.0	2565.0	1519.0

United States	1985	1990	1991	1992	1993	2000
1 - Public power, cogeneration, district heating	37.0	32.0	30.0	29.0		
2 - Commercial, institutional, residential combustion	1352.0	396.0	386.0	357.0		
3 - Industrial combustion and processes	104.0	258.0	262.0	254.0		
4 - Non combustion processes						
5 - Extraction and distribution of fossil fuels	4095.0	5050.0	5054.0	4981.0		
6 - Solvent use	5058.0	5454.0	5454.0	5454.0		
7 - Road transport	8612.0	6330.0	6179.0	5533.0		
8 - Other transport	2038.0	1923.0	1869.0	1930.0		
9 - Waste treatment and disposal	1395.0	2034.0	1998.0	2079.0		
10 - Agriculture						
11 - Nature						
TOTAL	22691.0	21477.0	21232.0	20617.0		

Comments :

Belgium. 1985 : NMVOCs emissions include CH4.

Czech Republic. 1990 : preliminary data for source category 6 and 10.

Denmark. 1985 : source category 7 based on sales.

European Community : not including emissions from the former GDR.

Finland. 1990 : preliminary data.

Germany. 1990, 1991, 1992 : source category 3 includes source category 4.
        1992 : preliminary data.

Greece. 1985 : NMVOCs emissions include CH4. Source category 11 includes agriculture.

Hungary. 1991 : source category 7 includes source category 8. Source category 1 includes sc. 2.

Netherlands. NMVOCs emissions exclude CH4 and CFC.
        Source category 4 includes source category 5 and 6.
        1992 : provisional data.
        2000 : based on the baseline scenario.

Norway. Source category 1 includes waste combustion with energy generation.
        Source category 3 includes gas turbines in the North Sea.
        Source category 5 includes gas flaring and VOCs from leakage from petrol handling.
        Source category 7 includes cars and motor cycles.
        Source category 8 includes mobile oil platforms.

Poland. 1985 : source category 7 includes source category 8.
        1990 : according to the EMEP/CORINAIR methodology.

Slovakia. 1992 : source category 1 includes source category 3.

Sweden. 1991 : source category 7 includes source category 8. Estimate.
        1993 : estimate for source category 6, 7 and 8.

Switzerland : source category 7 includes CH4 emissions.

TABLE 9.5

National annual emissions of methane by source category

(Thousands of tonnes of CH$_4$)

Austria	1985	1990	1991	1992	1993	2000
1 - Public power, cogeneration, district heating		0.1	0.1	0.1	0.1	
2 - Commercial, institutional, residential combustion		7.8	9.5	10.3	10.1	
3 - Industrial combustion and processes		1.0	1.0	1.0	1.0	
4 - Non combustion processes						
5 - Extraction and distribution of fossil fuels		91.8	92.0	92.6	92.6	
6 - Solvent use						
7 - Road transport		14.8	16.2	16.2	16.6	
8 - Other transport		0.5	0.5	0.5	0.5	
9 - Waste treatment and disposal		228.2	228.2	228.2	228.2	
10 - Agriculture		258.6	258.6	258.6	258.6	
11 - Nature		207.6	207.6	207.6	207.6	
TOTAL		810.4	813.7	815.1	815.3	

Belgium	1985	1990	1991	1992	1993	2000
1 - Public power, cogeneration, district heating		0.1	0.2	0.1		
2 - Commercial, institutional, residential combustion		4.4	4.7	4.8		
3 - Industrial combustion and processes		5.1	3.9	3.9		
4 - Non combustion processes		14.1	13.9	11.7		
5 - Extraction and distribution of fossil fuels		46.7	48.9	50.0		
6 - Solvent use		0.0	0.0	0.0		
7 - Road transport		9.4	9.4	9.9		
8 - Other transport		0.0	0.0	0.0		
9 - Waste treatment and disposal		4.9	4.9	5.8		
10 - Agriculture		270.0	284.2	320.9		
11 - Nature		15.4	16.5	12.3		
TOTAL		370.0	386.6	419.5		

Bulgaria	1985	1990	1991	1992	1993	2000
1 - Public power, cogeneration, district heating		0.5	17.7	17.9	0.5	19.0
2 - Commercial, institutional, residential combustion		18.4			22.5	
3 - Industrial combustion and processes		4.3			1.4	
4 - Non combustion processes		2.7	2.0	2.0	1.2	2.0
5 - Extraction and distribution of fossil fuels		261.4	196.0	193.4	420.0	200.0
6 - Solvent use						
7 - Road transport		1.7	3.4	4.2	1.2	5.0
8 - Other transport		0.3				
9 - Waste treatment and disposal		61.9	46.5	46.1	61.9	50.0
10 - Agriculture		236.0	176.9	175.8	155.5	174.0
11 - Nature		2.2				
TOTAL		589.3	442.0	439.0	664.2	450.0

Czech Republic	1985	1990	1991	1992	1993	2000
1 - Public power, cogeneration, district heating		5.1				
2 - Commercial, institutional, residential combustion		57.1				
3 - Industrial combustion and processes		0.7				
4 - Non combustion processes		1.4				
5 - Extraction and distribution of fossil fuels		844.8				
6 - Solvent use						
7 - Road transport		2.6				
8 - Other transport		0.3				
9 - Waste treatment and disposal		34.3				
10 - Agriculture		507.5				
11 - Nature		94.7				
TOTAL		1548.6				

TABLE 9.5 (*continued*)

Denmark	1985	1990	1991	1992	1993	2000
1 - Public power, cogeneration, district heating	0.9	0.9	1.1	1.0	1.0	2.2
2 - Commercial, institutional, residential combustion	6.5	6.1	6.6	6.6	6.7	7.1
3 - Industrial combustion and processes	0.7	0.7	0.8	0.7	0.8	0.9
4 - Non combustion processes	0.0	0.0	0.0	0.0	0.0	0.0
5 - Extraction and distribution of fossil fuels	12.1	12.0	13.4	13.4	12.7	14.1
6 - Solvent use						
7 - Road transport	1.7	1.8	1.8	1.8	1.6	1.2
8 - Other transport	1.0	1.1	1.0	1.0	1.0	1.2
9 - Waste treatment and disposal	121.6	121.6	121.6	121.6	121.6	66.2
10 - Agriculture	262.0	262.0	262.0	262.0	262.0	262.0
11 - Nature	354.0	354.0	354.0	354.0	354.0	354.0
TOTAL	760.0	760.0	762.0	762.0	761.0	709.0

European Community	1985	1990	1991	1992	1993	2000
1 - Public power, cogeneration, district heating		22.9				
2 - Commercial, institutional, residential combustion		266.2				
3 - Industrial combustion and processes		38.5				
4 - Non combustion processes		50.6				
5 - Extraction and distribution of fossil fuels		4503.7				
6 - Solvent use		0.0				
7 - Road transport		142.3				
8 - Other transport		14.0				
9 - Waste treatment and disposal		6306.9				
10 - Agriculture		9834.2				
11 - Nature		6594.5				
TOTAL		27773.9				

Finland	1985	1990	1991	1992	1993	2000
1 - Public power, cogeneration, district heating		1.0				
2 - Commercial, institutional, residential combustion		6.5				
3 - Industrial combustion and processes		2.1				
4 - Non combustion processes						
5 - Extraction and distribution of fossil fuels		0.1				
6 - Solvent use						
7 - Road transport		1.9				
8 - Other transport		7.6				
9 - Waste treatment and disposal		67.1				
10 - Agriculture		163.0				
11 - Nature						
TOTAL		249.2				

France	1985	1990	1991	1992	1993	2000
1 - Public power, cogeneration, district heating		1.1	1.7	1.3		
2 - Commercial, institutional, residential combustion		149.9	150.7	149.7		
3 - Industrial combustion and processes		6.6	6.6	6.5		
4 - Non combustion processes		5.9	5.1	5.1		
5 - Extraction and distribution of fossil fuels		352.2	345.8	333.4		
6 - Solvent use		0.0	0.0	0.0		
7 - Road transport		22.3	21.9	21.9		
8 - Other transport		0.6	0.6	0.6		
9 - Waste treatment and disposal		729.0	1041.8	1022.7		
10 - Agriculture		2410.2	2370.2	2319.5		
11 - Nature		191.1	186.9	187.5		
TOTAL		3868.8	4131.2	4048.3		

TABLE 9.5 (*continued*)

Germany	1985	1990	1991	1992	1993	2000
1 - Public power, cogeneration, district heating		9.0	9.0	9.0		
2 - Commercial, institutional, residential combustion		110.0	110.0	112.0		
3 - Industrial combustion and processes		32.0	27.0	29.0		
4 - Non combustion processes						
5 - Extraction and distribution of fossil fuels		1539.0	1515.0	1530.0		
6 - Solvent use						
7 - Road transport		70.0	75.0	83.0		
8 - Other transport		4.0	4.0	3.0		
9 - Waste treatment and disposal		2398.0	2565.0	2677.0		
10 - Agriculture		2053.0	1809.0	1721.0		
11 - Nature						
TOTAL		6215.0	6114.0	6164.0		

Ireland	1985	1990	1991	1992	1993	2000
1 - Public power, cogeneration, district heating		0.0				
2 - Commercial, institutional, residential combustion		3.6				
3 - Industrial combustion and processes		0.2				
4 - Non combustion processes		0.0				
5 - Extraction and distribution of fossil fuels		10.2				
6 - Solvent use		0.0				
7 - Road transport		1.2				
8 - Other transport		0.0				
9 - Waste treatment and disposal		138.3				
10 - Agriculture		642.6				
11 - Nature		53.9				
TOTAL		850.0				

Italy	1985	1990	1991	1992	1993	2000
1 - Public power, cogeneration, district heating	7.4	3.8				
2 - Commercial, institutional, residential combustion	13.0	16.7				
3 - Industrial combustion and processes	2.0	9.5				
4 - Non combustion processes	9.9	7.6				
5 - Extraction and distribution of fossil fuels	459.1	347.5				
6 - Solvent use						
7 - Road transport	47.2	25.2				
8 - Other transport	1.7	8.2				
9 - Waste treatment and disposal	862.9	1302.8				
10 - Agriculture	448.3	1765.5				
11 - Nature	412.0	291.4				
TOTAL	2263.5	3778.2				

Netherlands	1985	1990	1991	1992	1993	2000
1 - Public power, cogeneration, district heating	0.0	0.5	0.0	1.0		132.0
2 - Commercial, institutional, residential combustion	8.0	1.9	8.0	10.0		
3 - Industrial combustion and processes	2.0	1.6	3.0	5.0		
4 - Non combustion processes		8.1				
5 - Extraction and distribution of fossil fuels	166.0	0.9	169.0	166.0		
6 - Solvent use		0.0				
7 - Road transport	9.0	6.4	7.0	6.0		
8 - Other transport	0.0	0.2	0.0	0.0		
9 - Waste treatment and disposal	328.0	378.0	380.0	378.0		223.0
10 - Agriculture	512.0	520.0	512.0	498.0		400.0
11 - Nature	121.0	122.7	121.0	121.0		121.0
TOTAL	1146.0	1040.4	1200.0	1185.0		876.0

TABLE 9.5 (*continued*)

Norway	1985	1990	1991	1992	1993	2000
1 - Public power, cogeneration, district heating		0.1	0.1	0.1	0.1	0.0
2 - Commercial, institutional, residential combustion		11.0	9.8	9.8	9.7	10.0
3 - Industrial combustion and processes		2.6	2.8	3.0	3.1	3.0
4 - Non combustion processes		7.0	1.1	8.4	5.6	7.0
5 - Extraction and distribution of fossil fuels		7.8	14.5	8.9	9.7	12.0
6 - Solvent use						
7 - Road transport		1.9	1.8	1.7	1.7	1.0
8 - Other transport		1.2	1.1	1.2	1.2	2.0
9 - Waste treatment and disposal		166.7	165.1	165.5	168.0	163.0
10 - Agriculture		91.1	92.5	94.4	94.4	93.0
11 - Nature						
TOTAL		289.4	288.8	293.0	293.6	291.0

Poland	1985	1990	1991	1992	1993	2000
1 - Public power, cogeneration, district heating		2.0		1.0	1.0	
2 - Commercial, institutional, residential combustion		94.0		19.0	19.0	
3 - Industrial combustion and processes		16.0		3.0	3.0	
4 - Non combustion processes		9.0		14.0	14.0	
5 - Extraction and distribution of fossil fuels		2914.0		2333.0	1705.0	
6 - Solvent use					0.0	
7 - Road transport		4.0			9.0	
8 - Other transport		1.0				
9 - Waste treatment and disposal		814.0		510.0	540.0	
10 - Agriculture		1861.0		767.0	699.0	
11 - Nature		392.0				
TOTAL		6107.0		3647.0	2990.0	

Portugal	1985	1990	1991	1992	1993	2000
1 - Public power, cogeneration, district heating		0.4	0.4	0.5	0.4	
2 - Commercial, institutional, residential combustion		6.9	7.1	7.1	7.1	
3 - Industrial combustion and processes		2.9	2.8	2.8	2.8	
4 - Non combustion processes		1.5	1.4	1.6	1.6	
5 - Extraction and distribution of fossil fuels		2.0	1.9	1.6	1.6	
6 - Solvent use		0.0	0.0	0.0	0.0	
7 - Road transport		1.4	1.5	1.6	1.6	
8 - Other transport		0.2	0.2	0.2	0.2	
9 - Waste treatment and disposal		35.2	35.2	35.2	35.2	
10 - Agriculture		191.0	191.0	191.0	191.0	
11 - Nature		137.3	139.8	130.6	130.6	
TOTAL		378.7	381.2	372.0	371.9	

Romania	1985	1990	1991	1992	1993	2000
1 - Public power, cogeneration, district heating						
2 - Commercial, institutional, residential combustion						
3 - Industrial combustion and processes						
4 - Non combustion processes				750.0		
5 - Extraction and distribution of fossil fuels				674.0		
6 - Solvent use						
7 - Road transport						
8 - Other transport						
9 - Waste treatment and disposal						
10 - Agriculture						
11 - Nature						
TOTAL				1424.0		

TABLE 9.5 (*continued*)

Russian Federation	1985	1990	1991	1992	1993	2000
1 - Public power, cogeneration, district heating						
2 - Commercial, institutional, residential combustion						
3 - Industrial combustion and processes						
4 - Non combustion processes						
5 - Extraction and distribution of fossil fuels	627.0	622.0	618.0	524.0		
6 - Solvent use						
7 - Road transport						
8 - Other transport						
9 - Waste treatment and disposal						
10 - Agriculture	4190.0					
11 - Nature	8100.0					
TOTAL	12900.0					

Slovakia	1985	1990	1991	1992	1993	2000
1 - Public power, cogeneration, district heating				1.0		
2 - Commercial, institutional, residential combustion				9.0		
3 - Industrial combustion and processes						
4 - Non combustion processes						
5 - Extraction and distribution of fossil fuels				124.0		
6 - Solvent use						
7 - Road transport				1.0		
8 - Other transport				0.2		
9 - Waste treatment and disposal				96.0		
10 - Agriculture				106.0		
11 - Nature						
TOTAL				337.0		

Slovenia	1985	1990	1991	1992	1993	2000
1 - Public power, cogeneration, district heating		0.8				
2 - Commercial, institutional, residential combustion		1.1				
3 - Industrial combustion and processes		0.2				
4 - Non combustion processes						
5 - Extraction and distribution of fossil fuels		47.3				
6 - Solvent use						
7 - Road transport						
8 - Other transport						
9 - Waste treatment and disposal		32.4				
10 - Agriculture						
11 - Nature						
TOTAL		81.8				

Spain	1985	1990	1991	1992	1993	2000
1 - Public power, cogeneration, district heating		8.9				
2 - Commercial, institutional, residential combustion		44.2				
3 - Industrial combustion and processes		7.1				
4 - Non combustion processes		3.9				
5 - Extraction and distribution of fossil fuels		683.7				
6 - Solvent use						
7 - Road transport		11.4				
8 - Other transport		1.5				
9 - Waste treatment and disposal		506.7				
10 - Agriculture		861.4				
11 - Nature		856.2				
TOTAL		2985.0				

TABLE 9.5 (*concluded*)

Sweden	1985	1990	1991	1992	1993	2000
1 - Public power, cogeneration, district heating		1.0	1.0	1.0	2.0	2.0
2 - Commercial, institutional, residential combustion		10.0	10.0	10.0	10.0	10.0
3 - Industrial combustion and processes		4.0	4.0	4.0	4.0	5.0
4 - Non combustion processes		0.0	0.0	0.0	0.0	0.0
5 - Extraction and distribution of fossil fuels		0.0	0.0	0.0	0.0	0.0
6 - Solvent use						
7 - Road transport		19.0	18.0	16.0	14.0	7.0
8 - Other transport		4.0	4.0	4.0	4.0	4.0
9 - Waste treatment and disposal		97.0	97.0	97.0	97.0	67.0
10 - Agriculture		205.0	205.0	205.0	205.0	205.0
11 - Nature		1691.0	1691.0	1691.0	1691.0	1691.0
TOTAL		2031.0	2030.0	2028.0	2027.0	1991.0

Switzerland	1985	1990	1991	1992	1993	2000
1 - Public power, cogeneration, district heating						
2 - Commercial, institutional, residential combustion						
3 - Industrial combustion and processes						
4 - Non combustion processes						
5 - Extraction and distribution of fossil fuels		27.4	26.8	24.6	25.5	
6 - Solvent use						
7 - Road transport						
8 - Other transport						
9 - Waste treatment and disposal		48.1	48.0	48.0	45.6	
10 - Agriculture		158.0	158.0	158.0	158.0	
11 - Nature						
TOTAL		233.5	232.8	230.6	229.1	

United Kingdom	1985	1990	1991	1992	1993	2000
1 - Public power, cogeneration, district heating	3.0	3.0	3.0	3.0	3.0	
2 - Commercial, institutional, residential combustion	84.0	50.0	52.0	46.0	50.0	
3 - Industrial combustion and processes	9.0	9.0	9.0	9.0	8.0	
4 - Non combustion processes					0.0	
5 - Extraction and distribution of fossil fuels	1243.0	1238.0	1241.0	1158.0	1067.0	
6 - Solvent use						
7 - Road transport	9.0	10.0	10.0	10.0	11.0	
8 - Other transport					0.0	
9 - Waste treatment and disposal	1944.0	1971.0	1984.0	1991.0	1997.0	
10 - Agriculture	1560.0	1545.0	1525.0	1517.0	1516.0	
11 - Nature						
TOTAL	4854.0	4828.0	4825.0	4736.0	4652.0	

Comments:

Denmark. 1995: source category 7 based on sales.

European Community: not including emissions from the former GDR.

Finland. 1990: preliminary data.

Germany. 1990, 1991, 1992: source category 3 includes source category 4.
1992: preliminary data.

Netherlands. 1992: provisional data.
2000: source category 1 includes source category 2, 3, 4, 5, 6, 7 and 8; based on the baseline scenario.

Norway. Source category 1 includes waste combustion with energy generation.
Source category 3 includes gas turbines in the North Sea.
Source category 5 includes gas flaring and VOC from leakage from petrol handling.
Source category 7 includes cars and motor cycles.
Source category 8 includes mobiles oil platforms.

Poland. 1993: source category 7 includes source category 8.
1990: according to the EMEP/CORINAIR methodology.

Slovakia. 1992: source category 1 includes source category 3.

Sweden. 1991, 1992, 1993: estimate for source category 3, 9 and 10.

Switzerland. 1990, 1991, 1992, 1993: CH4 emissions from source category 7 included in NMVOCs
emissions from source category 7.

TABLE 9.6

National annual emissions of carbon monoxide by source category

(Thousands of tonnes of CO)

Austria	1985	1990	1991	1992	1993	2000
1 - Public power, cogeneration, district heating	5.0	8.9	9.6	8.3	8.8	
2 - Commercial, institutional, residential combustion	646.4	805.2	829.8	805.0	772.0	
3 - Industrial combustion and processes	274.1	230.7	205.2	204.0	220.6	
4 - Non combustion processes	24.1	24.0	16.2	16.0	0.4	
5 - Extraction and distribution of fossil fuels						
6 - Solvent use						
7 - Road transport	635.0	442.0	410.0	348.0	292.0	
8 - Other transport	3.0	2.1	2.1	2.1	2.1	
9 - Waste treatment and disposal	0.2	0.2	0.2	0.2	0.2	
10 - Agriculture	60.0	60.0	30.0	30.0	30.0	
11 - Nature						
TOTAL	1647.8	1573.1	1503.1	1413.6	1326.1	

Belgium	1985	1990	1991	1992	1993	2000
1 - Public power, cogeneration, district heating		2.3	2.5	10.2		
2 - Commercial, institutional, residential combustion		92.9	98.5	101.4		
3 - Industrial combustion and processes		23.8	38.2	38.3		
4 - Non combustion processes		10.3	0.0	0.0		
5 - Extraction and distribution of fossil fuels		0.0	0.0	0.0		
6 - Solvent use		0.0	0.0	0.0		
7 - Road transport		976.3	973.2	1008.3		
8 - Other transport		2.0	1.9	2.3		
9 - Waste treatment and disposal		16.1	16.1	16.2		
10 - Agriculture		0.0	0.0	0.0		
11 - Nature		0.0	0.0	0.0		
TOTAL		1123.7	1130.4	1176.7		

Bulgaria	1985	1990	1991	1992	1993	2000
1 - Public power, cogeneration, district heating		13.2	9.6	9.1	4.0	15.0
2 - Commercial, institutional, residential combustion		272.6	200.9	189.3	332.6	210.0
3 - Industrial combustion and processes		105.0	76.1	72.5	5.0	90.0
4 - Non combustion processes		48.0	35.2	33.2	91.4	40.0
5 - Extraction and distribution of fossil fuels		0.2				
6 - Solvent use						
7 - Road transport		371.9	268.2	263.0	263.7	360.0
8 - Other transport		14.6	11.2	10.0	14.6	20.0
9 - Waste treatment and disposal		64.3			64.3	
10 - Agriculture		0.5	52.8	45.9	0.3	85.0
11 - Nature		10.7			10.2	
TOTAL		901.0	654.0	623.0	786.1	820.0

Czech Republic	1985	1990	1991	1992	1993	2000
1 - Public power, cogeneration, district heating		25.2				
2 - Commercial, institutional, residential combustion		333.8				
3 - Industrial combustion and processes		278.3				
4 - Non combustion processes		82.5				
5 - Extraction and distribution of fossil fuels						
6 - Solvent use						
7 - Road transport		154.2				
8 - Other transport		9.1				
9 - Waste treatment and disposal		5.1				
10 - Agriculture		0.1				
11 - Nature		0.0				
TOTAL		888.0				

TABLE 9.6 (*continued*)

Denmark	1985	1990	1991	1992	1993	2000
1 - Public power, cogeneration, district heating	35.0	37.3	39.5	43.1	46.7	22.3
2 - Commercial, institutional, residential combustion	143.0	139.9	151.5	151.4	154.1	168.2
3 - Industrial combustion and processes	4.6	4.2	4.4	4.2	4.3	4.8
4 - Non combustion processes						
5 - Extraction and distribution of fossil fuels	34.5	34.4	44.5	43.2	37.4	44.1
6 - Solvent use						
7 - Road transport	496.1	526.2	556.1	542.6	444.1	378.2
8 - Other transport	27.4	28.3	28.0	27.8	27.9	29.1
9 - Waste treatment and disposal						
10 - Agriculture						
11 - Nature						
TOTAL	741.0	770.0	824.0	812.0	715.0	647.0

European Community	1985	1990	1991	1992	1993	2000
1 - Public power, cogeneration, district heating		224.7				
2 - Commercial, institutional, residential combustion		4535.1				
3 - Industrial combustion and processes		2964.0				
4 - Non combustion processes		2359.4				
5 - Extraction and distribution of fossil fuels		37.4				
6 - Solvent use		1.0				
7 - Road transport		29736.4				
8 - Other transport		1715.1				
9 - Waste treatment and disposal		2731.8				
10 - Agriculture		518.7				
11 - Nature		1325.3				
TOTAL		46148.8				

Finland	1985	1990	1991	1992	1993	2000
1 - Public power, cogeneration, district heating		8.0				
2 - Commercial, institutional, residential combustion		61.0				
3 - Industrial combustion and processes		35.0				
4 - Non combustion processes		3.0				
5 - Extraction and distribution of fossil fuels						
6 - Solvent use						
7 - Road transport		397.6				
8 - Other transport		41.4				
9 - Waste treatment and disposal		10.0				
10 - Agriculture						
11 - Nature						
TOTAL		556.0				

France	1985	1990	1991	1992	1993	2000
1 - Public power, cogeneration, district heating		21.0	36.6	34.6		
2 - Commercial, institutional, residential combustion		1892.0	1896.4	1888.5		
3 - Industrial combustion and processes		598.1	557.3	555.0		
4 - Non combustion processes		668.3	640.5	876.2		
5 - Extraction and distribution of fossil fuels		0.0	0.0	0.0		
6 - Solvent use		0.0	0.0	0.0		
7 - Road transport		6812.2	6722.7	6369.7		
8 - Other transport		512.2	511.7	511.5		
9 - Waste treatment and disposal		232.2	232.4	232.6		
10 - Agriculture						
11 - Nature		193.9	27.0	48.8		
TOTAL		10930.1	10624.8	10316.9		

TABLE 9.6 (*continued*)

Germany	1985	1990	1991	1992	1993	2000
1 - Public power, cogeneration, district heating		774.0	648.0	629.0		
2 - Commercial, institutional, residential combustion		2052.0	1532.0	1390.0		
3 - Industrial combustion and processes		1738.0	1505.0	1476.0		
4 - Non combustion processes						
5 - Extraction and distribution of fossil fuels		0.0	0.0	0.0		
6 - Solvent use						
7 - Road transport		6013.0	5620.0	5634.0		
8 - Other transport		332.0	299.0	276.0		
9 - Waste treatment and disposal						
10 - Agriculture						
11 - Nature						
TOTAL		10909.0	9604.0	9135.0		

Hungary	1985	1990	1991	1992	1993	2000
1 - Public power, cogeneration, district heating			140.2	78.7		
2 - Commercial, institutional, residential combustion			18.4	18.0		
3 - Industrial combustion and processes			9.9	8.2		
4 - Non combustion processes			258.2	250.0		
5 - Extraction and distribution of fossil fuels						
6 - Solvent use						
7 - Road transport			487.0	480.0		
8 - Other transport						
9 - Waste treatment and disposal						
10 - Agriculture			1.3	0.9		
11 - Nature						
TOTAL			915.0	835.7		

Ireland	1985	1990	1991	1992	1993	2000
1 - Public power, cogeneration, district heating		3.3				
2 - Commercial, institutional, residential combustion		79.6				
3 - Industrial combustion and processes		0.9				
4 - Non combustion processes		0.0				
5 - Extraction and distribution of fossil fuels		0.0				
6 - Solvent use		0.0				
7 - Road transport		304.6				
8 - Other transport		3.8				
9 - Waste treatment and disposal		38.9				
10 - Agriculture		0.0				
11 - Nature		0.0				
TOTAL		431.1				

Italy	1985	1990	1991	1992	1993	2000
1 - Public power, cogeneration, district heating	25.1	23.1				
2 - Commercial, institutional, residential combustion	420.9	259.6				
3 - Industrial combustion and processes	4.8	620.2				
4 - Non combustion processes	837.8	379.7				
5 - Extraction and distribution of fossil fuels	0.0	0.0				
6 - Solvent use						
7 - Road transport	5231.6	5534.4				
8 - Other transport	73.2	719.3				
9 - Waste treatment and disposal	136.0	1705.0				
10 - Agriculture	28.8	27.2				
11 - Nature	160.8	1078.8				
TOTAL	6919.0	10347.3				

TABLE 9.6 (*continued*)

Netherlands	1985	1990	1991	1992	1993	2000
1 - Public power, cogeneration, district heating	1.0	5.0	2.0	4.0		
2 - Commercial, institutional, residential combustion	39.0	100.8	33.0	12.0		
3 - Industrial combustion and processes	125.0	11.7	115.0	120.0		
4 - Non combustion processes	188.0	254.1	159.0	102.0		
5 - Extraction and distribution of fossil fuels		1.5				
6 - Solvent use		1.0				
7 - Road transport	923.0	675.0	599.0	584.0		
8 - Other transport	28.0	21.0	38.0	38.0		
9 - Waste treatment and disposal	2.0	2.3	2.0	2.0		
10 - Agriculture		7.8				
11 - Nature		26.0				
TOTAL	1307.0	1106.2	947.0	863.0		

Norway	1985	1990	1991	1992	1993	2000
1 - Public power, cogeneration, district heating	0.2	0.3	0.3	0.3	0.3	0.0
2 - Commercial, institutional, residential combustion	115.5	126.1	112.0	111.6	111.6	113.0
3 - Industrial combustion and processes	4.5	10.6	11.1	11.4	11.8	12.0
4 - Non combustion processes	36.1	60.0	48.6	46.3	51.1	56.0
5 - Extraction and distribution of fossil fuels		0.8	0.5	0.5	0.5	1.0
6 - Solvent use						
7 - Road transport	407.1	713.0	678.3	652.1	631.1	372.0
8 - Other transport	24.6	29.8	29.2	29.3	29.7	47.0
9 - Waste treatment and disposal						
10 - Agriculture						
11 - Nature						
TOTAL	588.0	940.5	880.1	851.0	836.0	602.0

Poland	1985	1990	1991	1992	1993	2000
1 - Public power, cogeneration, district heating					20.0	
2 - Commercial, institutional, residential combustion					6130.0	
3 - Industrial combustion and processes					100.0	
4 - Non combustion processes					25.0	
5 - Extraction and distribution of fossil fuels					0.0	
6 - Solvent use					0.0	
7 - Road transport					1590.0	
8 - Other transport						
9 - Waste treatment and disposal					790.0	
10 - Agriculture					0.0	
11 - Nature						
TOTAL					8655.0	

Portugal	1985	1990	1991	1992	1993	2000
1 - Public power, cogeneration, district heating		2.0	2.1	2.7	2.1	
2 - Commercial, institutional, residential combustion		117.0	120.0	120.0	120.0	
3 - Industrial combustion and processes		330.3	316.3	316.6	316.6	
4 - Non combustion processes		10.7	9.9	7.6	7.6	
5 - Extraction and distribution of fossil fuels		0.0	0.0	0.0	0.0	
6 - Solvent use		0.0	0.0	0.0	0.0	
7 - Road transport		614.1	648.4	687.9	709.6	
8 - Other transport		12.0	11.9	12.0	12.2	
9 - Waste treatment and disposal		0.0	0.0	0.0	0.0	
10 - Agriculture		0.0	0.0	0.0	0.0	
11 - Nature		0.4	0.4	0.1	0.1	
TOTAL		1086.4	1109.0	1146.9	1168.2	

TABLE 9.6 *(continued))*

Romania	1985	1990	1991	1992	1993	2000
1 - Public power, cogeneration, district heating				47.8		
2 - Commercial, institutional, residential combustion				9.0		
3 - Industrial combustion and processes				2.2		
4 - Non combustion processes				108.4		
5 - Extraction and distribution of fossil fuels						
6 - Solvent use						
7 - Road transport				329.2		
8 - Other transport						
9 - Waste treatment and disposal						
10 - Agriculture						
11 - Nature						
TOTAL				497.7		

Russian Federation	1985	1990	1991	1992	1993	2000
1 - Public power, cogeneration, district heating						
2 - Commercial, institutional, residential combustion						
3 - Industrial combustion and processes						
4 - Non combustion processes						
5 - Extraction and distribution of fossil fuels						
6 - Solvent use						
7 - Road transport	9370.0	8871.0	8979.0	8199.0		
8 - Other transport						
9 - Waste treatment and disposal						
10 - Agriculture						
11 - Nature						
TOTAL	14122.0	13174.0	12869.0	11574.0		

Slovakia	1985	1990	1991	1992	1993	2000
1 - Public power, cogeneration, district heating				110.0		
2 - Commercial, institutional, residential combustion				101.0		
3 - Industrial combustion and processes						
4 - Non combustion processes				2.0		
5 - Extraction and distribution of fossil fuels				2.0		
6 - Solvent use						
7 - Road transport				123.0		
8 - Other transport				4.0		
9 - Waste treatment and disposal						
10 - Agriculture						
11 - Nature						
TOTAL				342.0		

Spain	1985	1990	1991	1992	1993	2000
1 - Public power, cogeneration, district heating		15.6				
2 - Commercial, institutional, residential combustion		889.8				
3 - Industrial combustion and processes		405.4				
4 - Non combustion processes		248.4				
5 - Extraction and distribution of fossil fuels						
6 - Solvent use						
7 - Road transport		2610.4				
8 - Other transport		110.8				
9 - Waste treatment and disposal		526.6				
10 - Agriculture		142.6				
11 - Nature		26.2				
TOTAL		4975.5				

Strategies and Policies for Air Pollution Abatement

TABLE 9.6 (*continued*)

Sweden	1985	1990	1991	1992	1993	2000
1 - Public power, cogeneration, district heating		8.0	7.0	7.0	10.0	10.0
2 - Commercial, institutional, residential combustion		69.0	72.0	71.0	71.0	44.0
3 - Industrial combustion and processes		25.0	25.0	26.0	26.0	29.0
4 - Non combustion processes		6.0	6.0	6.0	6.0	6.0
5 - Extraction and distribution of fossil fuels		0.0	0.0	0.0	0.0	0.0
6 - Solvent use						
7 - Road transport		1118.0	1086.0	1054.0	1017.0	534.0
8 - Other transport		107.0	102.0	97.0	92.0	123.0
9 - Waste treatment and disposal		14.0	14.0	14.0	14.0	14.0
10 - Agriculture		0.0	0.0	0.0	0.0	0.0
11 - Nature		2.0				
TOTAL		1349.0	1312.0	1275.0	1236.0	760.0

Switzerland	1985	1990	1991	1992	1993	2000
1 - Public power, cogeneration, district heating		0.0	0.0	0.0	0.0	
2 - Commercial, institutional, residential combustion		98.3	98.3	98.3	98.3	
3 - Industrial combustion and processes		19.7	19.4	19.4	19.2	
4 - Non combustion processes		29.4	29.3	29.3	29.3	
5 - Extraction and distribution of fossil fuels						
6 - Solvent use						
7 - Road transport		254.0	230.0	203.3	182.0	
8 - Other transport		25.0	25.0	25.0	25.0	
9 - Waste treatment and disposal		4.0	4.0	4.0	4.0	
10 - Agriculture						
11 - Nature						
TOTAL		430.4	406.0	379.3	357.8	

United Kingdom	1985	1990	1991	1992	1993	2000
1 - Public power, cogeneration, district heating	49.0	50.0	47.0	45.0	40.0	
2 - Commercial, institutional, residential combustion	502.0	296.0	301.0	265.0	294.0	
3 - Industrial combustion and processes	71.0	70.0	69.0	69.0	56.0	
4 - Non combustion processes					0.0	
5 - Extraction and distribution of fossil fuels	27.0	33.0	35.0	36.0	36.0	
6 - Solvent use						
7 - Road transport	4887.0	6309.0	6304.0	6029.0	6018.0	2481.0
8 - Other transport	40.0	41.0	41.0	43.0	43.0	
9 - Waste treatment and disposal	220.0	220.0	220.0	220.0	220.0	
10 - Agriculture	1.0	1.0	1.0	1.0	1.0	
11 - Nature						
TOTAL	5797.0	7020.0	7021.0	6708.0	6708.0	3324.0

United States	1985	1990	1991	1992	1993	2000
1 - Public power, cogeneration, district heating	294.0	285.0	285.0	283.0		
2 - Commercial, institutional, residential combustion	6363.0	5195.0	5065.0	4676.0		
3 - Industrial combustion and processes	628.0	649.0	656.0	647.0		
4 - Non combustion processes	4088.0	4743.0	4674.0	4608.0		
5 - Extraction and distribution of fossil fuels						
6 - Solvent use						
7 - Road transport	66693.0	54251.0	53366.0	50157.0		
8 - Other transport	14332.0	13283.0	12916.0	13317.0		
9 - Waste treatment and disposal	1744.0	1517.0	1480.0	1517.0		
10 - Agriculture						
11 - Nature						
TOTAL	97885.0	83807.0	82266.0	79092.0		

TABLE 9.6 (*concluded*)

Comments :

Denmark. 1985 : source category 7 based on sales.

European Community : not including emissions from the former GDR.

Finland. 1990 : preliminary data.

Germany. 1990, 1991, 1992 : source category 3 includes source category 4.
　　　　　　　1992 : preliminary data.

Hungary. 1991, 1992 : source category 7 includes source category 8.

Netherlands. 1992 : provisional data.

Norway. Source category 1 includes waste combustion with energy generation.
　　　　　Source category 3 includes gas turbines in the North Sea.
　　　　　Source category 5 includes gas flaring and VOC from leakage from petrol handling.
　　　　　Source category 7 includes cars and motor cycles.
　　　　　Source category 8 includes mobile oil platforms.

Poland. 1993 : source category 7 includes source category 8.

Slovakia. 1992 : source category 1 includes source category 3.
　　　　　　1992 : source category 7 and source category 8 according to the COPERT method.

Sweden. 1991, 1992 , 1993 : estimate.

United States. 1985 : miscellaneous = 3743 kt.
　　　　　　　　1990 : miscellaneous = 3884 kt.
　　　　　　　　1991 : miscellaneous = 3824 kt.
　　　　　　　　1992 : miscellaneous = 3887 kt.

GROSS CONSUMPTION OF PRIMARY ENERGY

Explanatory notes

Gross consumption of primary energy: data related to gross consumption of primary energy are computed as the algebraic sum of production of primary energy + net trade.

Production of primary energy: production of primary energy refers to the quantities of energy extracted, calculated after any operation for removal of inert matter contained in fuels.

Net trade: net trade is computed as the algebraic sum of imports + exports + change in stocks + marine bunkers.

Changes in stocks: are measured at the beginning and at the end of the year.

Marine bunkers: quantities of fuels delivered to sea-going ships of all flags.

SUMMARY DESCRIPTION OF COMMODITIES

Solid fuels and derivatives: hard coal and derivatives such as patent fuel, hard coal coke, gas coke, coke-oven coke. Brown coal lignite and derivatives such as brown-coal coke, brown-coal briquettes.

Liquid fuels: crude petroleum as well as crude oils extracted from bituminous minerals, other inputs to petroleum refineries, natural gas liquids. Liquefied petroleum gas and other petroleum gases.

Gaseous fuels: natural gas. Derived gases.

Nuclear energy: nuclear energy is the thermal energy production from nuclear fuels, released as a result of fission inside reactors.

Hydro- and geothermal energy: hydrothermal and geothermal energy is the electric energy produced in hydrothermal and geothermal power plants.

Electricity: electricity includes energy production from hydro-electric, geothermal, nuclear and conventional thermal power plants assessed at the heat value of electricity (3.6 TJ.GWh).

Steam and hot water: steam and hot water obtained from geothermal sources and distributed as such for final consumption. Steam and hot water produced by public thermal power plants and thermal power plants equipped for the combined generation of electricity energy and heat. Steam purchased and recovered.

Other forms of energy: energy derived from non-conventional sources of energy not mentioned previously, e.g. solar energy, wind energy, wave-tidal energy and temperature gradients (excluding renewables derived from biomass and hydropower).

TABLE 10

Gross consumption of primary energy

(Millions of tonnes of oil equivalent)

Country	Energy category	1980	1985	1990	2000	2005	2010
Austria							
	1- Solid fuels	3.685	4.334	4.146	3.15	2.65	
	2- Liquid fuels	12.114	9.903	10.533	8.87	8.04	
	3- Gaseous fuels	4.193	4.699	4.234	4.58	4.25	
	4- Nuclear energy						
	5- Electricity			0.043			
	6- Hydro- and geothermal energy	2.787	3.25	3.453	3.69	3.81	
	7- Steam and hot water						
	8- Other forms of energy	1.137	1.755	2.417	2.62	2.72	
	TOTAL	23.894	23.851	25.786	22.91	21.46	
Belgium							
	1- Solid fuels	10.6		10.6	9.5		12.3
	2- Liquid fuels	23.2		18.7	22.5		23.5
	3- Gaseous fuels	9.1		8.1	12.2		12.4
	4- Nuclear energy	2.8		10.7	11.2		10.5
	5- Electricity			0.3			
	6- Hydro- and geothermal energy						
	7- Steam and hot water						
	8- Other forms of energy			0.2			
	TOTAL	45.7		48.1	55.4		58.7
Bulgaria							
	1- Solid fuels	10.025	10.588	9.544	9.974	10.349	10.422
	2- Liquid fuels	12.133	13.061	9.937	8.17	9.041	9.907
	3- Gaseous fuels	3.423	4.439	5.369	3.708	4.652	6.058
	4- Nuclear energy	1.593	3.391	3.869	2.327	3.333	3.898
	5- Electricity	0.33	0.37	0.326	0.151	0.16	0.168
	6- Hydro- and geothermal energy	0.32	0.192	0.159	0.314	0.348	0.382
	7- Steam and hot water						
	8- Other forms of energy	0.028	0.028	0.028	0.029	0.03	0.034
	TOTAL	27.852	32.069	29.232	24.673	27.913	30.869
Canada							
	1- Solid fuels	21.7	26.5	25.1	23.1	26	29.2
	2- Liquid fuels	94.8	74.4	76.3	81	90.1	97.3
	3- Gaseous fuels	40.6	46.4	55.7	73.2	79	84.6
	4- Nuclear energy	9.7	15.5	18.7	31	31.2	30.5
	5- Electricity						
	6- Hydro- and geothermal energy	18.7	21.8	24.5	25.3	26.8	30.4
	7- Steam and hot water	1	0.8	0.5	0.6	0.6	0.7
	8- Other forms of energy	9.1	11	11	15.9	17.1	18.6
	TOTAL	195.6	196.4	211.8	250.1	270.2	290.6
Croatia							
	1- Solid fuels	1.52	1.41	1.32			
	2- Liquid fuels	4.32	3.95	4.48			
	3- Gaseous fuels	1.24	1.69	2.28			
	4- Nuclear energy	0	0.49	0.41			
	5- Electricity	0.26	0.42	0.55			
	6- Hydro- and geothermal energy	1.49	1.16	0.9			
	7- Steam and hot water	0	0	0			
	8- Other forms of energy	0	0	0			
	TOTAL	8.83	9.12	9.93			

TABLE 10 (*continued*)

Country	Energy category	1980	1985	1990	2000	2005	2010
Cyprus							
	1- Solid fuels		0.04	0.065	0.072	0.075	0.079
	2- Liquid fuels		0.91	1.469	2.276	2.629	2.883
	3- Gaseous fuels		0.01	0.024	0.046	0.055	0.067
	4- Nuclear energy						
	5- Electricity						
	6- Hydro- and geothermal energy						
	7- Steam and hot water						
	8- Other forms of energy		0.04	0.098	0.143	0.165	0.187
	TOTAL		1	1.656	2.537	2.924	3.216
Denmark							
	1- Solid fuels	6.32	8.24	8.65	6.92	5.75	
	2- Liquid fuels	12.79	10.07	7.95	7.82	8.12	
	3- Gaseous fuels	0.01	0.58	1.86	4.31	5.29	
	4- Nuclear energy						
	5- Electricity						
	6- Hydro- and geothermal energy						
	7- Steam and hot water						
	8- Other forms of energy	0.02	0.03	0.16	0.38	0.49	
	TOTAL	19.65	19.14	18.92	18.61	19.65	
Finland							
	1- Solid fuels	5.96	6.317	6.462	12.8		13
	2- Liquid fuels	11.336	9.489	9.244	7.5		6.9
	3- Gaseous fuels	1.056	1.068	2.653	3.7		6.1
	4- Nuclear energy	1.656	4.495	4.532	4.4		4.4
	5- Electricity	0.303	1.182	2.686	0		0
	6- Hydro- and geothermal energy	2.529	3.053	2.688	3.2		3.3
	7- Steam and hot water	0.113	0.17	0.176			
	8- Other forms of energy	1.66	1.86	2.119	1.9		2.1
	TOTAL	24.64	27.638	30.559	33.5		35.8
Germany							
	1- Solid fuels	138	145	129	74	71	69
	2- Liquid fuels	142	120	123	122	110	105
	3- Gaseous fuels	51	49	54	55	62	63
	4- Nuclear energy	13	32	34	32	31	30
	5- Electricity				1	3	6
	6- Hydro- and geothermal energy	6	4	4	4	5	5
	7- Steam and hot water						
	8- Other forms of energy	1	3	3	3	5	5
	TOTAL	351	353	347	291	287	283
Greece							
	1- Solid fuels	3.2	6.1	7.6			
	2- Liquid fuels	11.6	11	13			
	3- Gaseous fuels	0	0.1	0.1			
	4- Nuclear energy	0	0	0			
	5- Electricity	0.1	0.2	0.1			
	6- Hydro- and geothermal energy	0.8	0.6	0.4			
	7- Steam and hot water						
	8- Other forms of energy						
	TOTAL	15.6	18	21.2			

TABLE 10 (*continued*)

Country	Energy category	1980	1985	1990	2000	2005	2010
Hungary							
	1- Solid fuels			6.614	5.895	7	7.569
	2- Liquid fuels			8.213	9.1	9.24	9.555
	3- Gaseous fuels			8.914	10.171	10.839	11.623
	4- Nuclear energy			4.163	3.753	3.753	3.753
	5- Electricity			0.957	0.541	0.541	0.541
	6- Hydro- and geothermal energy			0.006	0.015	0.015	0.015
	7- Steam and hot water						
	8- Other forms of energy						
	TOTAL			28.867	29.474	31.387	33.055
Italy							
	1- Solid fuels	12.61	16.25	15.717	16.7	17	
	2- Liquid fuels	96.58	83.49	91.452	86.3	86.6	
	3- Gaseous fuels	22.63	27.19	39.005	60.4	67	
	4- Nuclear energy	0.58	1.83				
	5- Electricity	0.52	2.04	2.98	2.3	1.95	
	6- Hydro- and geothermal energy	6.19	5.84	5.491	5.2	5.5	
	7- Steam and hot water						
	8- Other forms of energy						
	TOTAL	139.11	136.64	154.74	170.9	178.05	
Netherlands							
	1- Solid fuels	4.44	6.69	9.1	6.84		9.75
	2- Liquid fuels	29.33	20.26	23.69	21.9		27.1
	3- Gaseous fuels	30.42	32.35	30.8	36.27		42.5
	4- Nuclear energy	1.09	1.02	0.91	2.41		2.2
	5- Electricity	0	0.44	0.79			
	6- Hydro- and geothermal energy	0	0	0.01			
	7- Steam and hot water	0	0	0			
	8- Other forms of energy	0	0	0			
	TOTAL	65.28	60.76	65.3	68.42		81.55
Norway							
	1- Solid fuels		2.2	2.1	2.1	2.1	2.2
	2- Liquid fuels		6.2	5.8	7.7	8.9	8.8
	3- Gaseous fuels		1.2	1.2	1.2	1.2	1.2
	4- Nuclear energy						
	5- Electricity		7.8	8.3	10	10.4	10.6
	6- Hydro- and geothermal energy						
	7- Steam and hot water		0	0.1			
	8- Other forms of energy						
	TOTAL		17.4	17.5			
Poland							
	1- Solid fuels	137			112.8	115.1	115.6
	2- Liquid fuels	26.4			33.1	35.5	38.6
	3- Gaseous fuels	12.5			19	22.8	25
	4- Nuclear energy	0			0	0	0
	5- Electricity						
	6- Hydro- and geothermal energy						
	7- Steam and hot water						
	8- Other forms of energy	2.3			4.5	6.7	8.8
	TOTAL	178.2			169.3	180	188.1

TABLE 10 (*continued*)

Country	Energy category	1980	1985	1990	2000	2005	2010
Romania							
	1- Solid fuels	11.728	12.605	10.122			
	2- Liquid fuels	20.991	19.955	16.421			
	3- Gaseous fuels	31.9	35.959	28.907			
	4- Nuclear energy						
	5- Electricity	24.393	30.243	30.208			
	6- Hydro- and geothermal energy	5.572	5.695	5.282			
	7- Steam and hot water	33.718	35.642	39.816			
	8- Other forms of energy	0.47	0.394	0.336			
	TOTAL	128.77	140.49	134.09			
Slovenia							
	1- Solid fuels	2.041	2.283	1.769	1.791	1.547	1.302
	2- Liquid fuels	1.985	1.7	1.973	1.575	1.6	1.625
	3- Gaseous fuels	0.436	0.698	0.744	1.202	1.33	1.457
	4- Nuclear energy	0	1.102	1.257	1.135	1.138	1.141
	5- Electricity	0.985	0.02	0.103	0.002	0.001	0
	6- Hydro- and geothermal energy	0.319	0.296	0.282	0.371	0.404	0.436
	7- Steam and hot water						
	8- Other forms of energy	0	0	0.009	0.017	0.022	0.028
	TOTAL	4.866	6.1	6.137	6.092	6.041	5.99
Spain							
	1- Solid fuels	13.338		18.762	21.498		
	2- Liquid fuels	50.05		47.175	56.255		
	3- Gaseous fuels	1.581		5	13.482		
	4- Nuclear energy	1.375		14.138	12.512		
	5- Electricity	0.137		0.037	0.491		
	6- Hydro- and geothermal energy	2.544		2.203	3.142		
	7- Steam and hot water						
	8- Other forms of energy			2.46	3.518		
	TOTAL	68.751		89.701	110.9		
Sweden							
	1- Solid fuels	5.8	8.2	8.3	9.7	10.2	
	2- Liquid fuels	24.5	18.3	16.1	17.2	18.2	
	3- Gaseous fuels	0.2	0.3	0.6	1	1.1	
	4- Nuclear energy	6.7	15.5	17.6	18.8	18.8	
	5- Electricity						
	6- Hydro- and geothermal energy	5.1	6.1	6.3	5.5	5.5	
	7- Steam and hot water						
	8- Other forms of energy	0.1	0.4	0.7	1.5	1.5	
	TOTAL	42.4	48.8	49.6	53.7	55.3	
Switzerland							
	1- Solid fuels	0.81	1.26	1.2			
	2- Liquid fuels	12.45	11.92	12.34			
	3- Gaseous fuels	0.96	1.41	1.81			
	4- Nuclear energy	9.52	14.43	15.12			
	5- Electricity	0.7	0.74	0.18			
	6- Hydro- and geothermal energy	9.38	9.14	8.58			
	7- Steam and hot water						
	8- Other forms of energy						
	TOTAL	32.42	37.42	38.87			

TABLE 10 (*concluded*)

Country	Energy category	1980	1985	1990	2000	2005	2010
United Kingdom							
	1- Solid fuels	71	61	65	47	45	44
	2- Liquid fuels	71	67	73	84	90	98
	3- Gaseous fuels	42	48	52	62	73	84
	4- Nuclear energy	8	13	14	13	8	2
	5- Electricity	0	0	3	4	4	6
	6- Hydro- and geothermal energy	1	1	2	1	1	2
	7- Steam and hot water						
	8- Other forms of energy	0	0	0	2	4	4
	TOTAL	193	190	209	214	226	241

Notes :

Germany : Electricity included in hydro- and geothermal energy (1980, 1985, 1990).

Greece : 1990 = data for 1989.

Netherlands : Nuclear energy includes hydroelectricity, hot water and other forms of energy (2000, 2010).

Poland : For 2000, 2005 and 2010, mean value of the "low" and "high" scenario.

Sweden : Liquid fuels include foreign shipping (1 Mtoe).

TABLE 11.1

Ambient air quality standards (related to health effects)
(mg/Nm^3)

Country	Sulphur dioxide						Nitrogen dioxide						Ozone					
	Short term		Medium term		Long term		Short term		Medium term		Long term		Short term		Medium term		Long term	
	Standard	(Average time)	Standard	(Average time)	Standard	(Average time)	Standard	(Average time)	Standard	(Average time)	Standard	(Average time)	Standard	(Average time)	Standard	(Average time)	Standard	(Average time)
Austria	0.5 Smog alarm: 0.4/0.6/0.8 for the 3-hour average value	(30 min)	0.2	(24 h)	-	-	0.2 Smog alarm: 0.35/0.6/0.8 for the 3 hours average value.	(30 min)	-	-	-	-	Smog alarm: 0.2/0.3/0.4 for the 3-hour value.		-	-	-	-
Belgium	-		0.4	(24 h)	0.12/0.25/0.35 For 50th/98th/98th percentile value (EEC directive on SO2/black smoke).	(24 h)	-		0.15/0.45 For NO2/NOx.	(24 h)	0.2 98th percentile.	(1 h)	0.18/0.36 Information/Alarm value (EEC Directive on Ozone 92/72). Value for Benelux: 0.24.	(1 h)	0.11 As in EEC Directive on Ozone 92/72.	(8 h)	-	
Bulgaria	0.5 By June 1994.	(30 min)	0.15	(24 h)	0.05	(1 yr)	0.2	(30 min)	0.1	(24 h)	0.05	(1 yr)	0.16	(1 h)	0.05	(24 h)	0.03	(1 yr)
Canada	0.9	(1 h)	0.3	(24 h)	0.06	(1 yr)	0.4 For NOx.	(1 h)	0.2 For NOx.	(24 h)	0.1 For NOx.	(1 yr)	0.16	(1 h)	0.05	(24 h)	0.03	(1 yr)
Croatia	-		0.125	(24 h)	0.05 Sampling: 24 h.	(1 yr)	0.135	(1 h)	0.08	(24 h)	0.05 Sampling: 1 h.	(1 yr)	-		-		0.11 Sampling: 1 h.	(1 yr)
Cyprus	0.25 98th percentile.	(1 h)	-		0.08	(1 yr)	0.4 98th percentile.	(1 h)	0.15 98th percentile.	(24 h)	-		0.175 95th percentile.	(1 h)	0.1	(24 h)	-	
Czech Republic	0.5	(30 min)	0.15	(24 h)	0.06 Based on daily average values.	(1 yr)	0.2	(30 min)	0.1	(24 h)	0.08 Based on daily average values.	(1 yr)	-		0.16	(8 h)	-	
Denmark	-		0.25 98th percentile. All year.	(24 h)	0.08 50th percentile. All year. Winter: 0.13 (50th percentile).	(24 h)	0.2 98th percentile. All year.	(1 h)	-		-		0.18 Warning. Alarm: 0.36 (1h).	(1 h)	0.11 Threshold value.	(8 h)	-	
Finland	0.5 99th percentile.	(1 h)	0.2 98th percentile.	(24 h)	0.04	(1 yr)	0.3 98th percentile.	(1 h)	0.15 98th percentile.	(24 h)	-		-		-		-	
Germany	As in EEC Directive 89/427.		As in EEC Directive 89/427.		As in EEC Directive 89/427.		As in EEC Directive 85/203.		-		0.08	(1 yr)	As in EEC Directive 92/72.		As in EEC Directive 92/72.		As in EEC Directive 92/72.	
Greece	-		0.25 98th percentile.	(24 h)	0.08 Median.	(24 h)	-		-		0.2 98th percentile.	(1 h)	-		-		-	
Hungary	0.25	(1 h)	0.15	(24 h)	0.07	(1 yr)	0.1	(1 h)	0.085	(24 h)	0.07	(1 yr)	0.11	(1 h)	0.1	(24 h)	-	
Italy	0.125 Warning jointly with Particulates, NOx and O3 (Alarm: 0.25).	(24 h)	0.13 Median value (between Oct. and March).	(24 h)	0.08 Median value (0.25 for the 98th percentile).	(24 h)	-		0.2 Warning value (Alarm: 0.4).	(1 h)	0.2 98th percentile.	(1 h)	0.18 Warning jointly with particulates, NOx and SO2 (Alarm: 0.36).	(1 h)	-		-	(1 h)
Netherlands	0.83 Alarm value for summer and winter smog.	(1 h)	0.5	(24 h)	0.075/0.2/0.25 For 50th/95th/98th percentile value.	(24 h)	0.15 Limit value for busy traffic.	(1 h)	-		0.135/0.175 For the 98th/99.5th percentile value.	(1 h)	0.24 Alarm value for summer and winter smog. Maximum 2 days per year exceedance allowed in the year 2000.	(1 h)	0.16 Maximum 5 days per year exceedance allowed in the year 2000; in the longer term no exceedances allowed.	(8 h)	0.1 Seasonal average.	

TABLE 11.1 (*continued*)

Country	SO₂ (1)	SO₂ (2)	SO₂ (3)	Susp. part. (4)	Susp. part. (5)	Susp. part. (6)	NO₂ (7)	NO₂ (8)	NO₂ (9)	O₃ (10)	O₃ (11)
Norway	0.4 (15 min) Where SO2 is the overall dominating pollution.	0.09 (24 h) Combined with suspended particulates and other pollution.	0.1 (6 m) Combined with suspended particulates and other pollution.					0.05 (24 h)	0.1 (6 m)	0.08 (1 h)	- (8 h)
Poland	0.6/0.44 (30 min) (until 1998/from 1999): For special areas: 0.25/0.15.	0.2/0.15 (24 h) (until 1998/from 1999). For special areas: 0.075/0.075.	0.032/0.032 (1 yr) (until 1998/from 1999). For special areas: 0.011/0.011.	0.15 (30 min) For special areas: 0.15.	0.05 (24 h) For special areas: 0.05.		0.5 (30 min) For special areas: 0.15.	0.15 (24 h) For special areas: 0.05.	0.05 (1 yr) For special areas: 0.03.	0.1 (1 h) For special areas: 0.05.	0.03 (24 h) For special areas: 0.02.
Portugal	-	0.1/0.15 (24 h) Guide value.	0.1/0.25 (6 m) Limit value for the 50th/98th percentile value.					0.05/0.135 (24 h) Guide value for the 50th/98th percentile (Limit value: 0.2 for the 98th percentile).		0.11/0.18 (1 h) Guide value for the 8 h/1h average value.	0.065 (24 h) Guide value.
Romania	0.75 (30 min)	0.25 (24 h)	0.06 (1 yr)	0.3 (30 min)	0.1 (24 h)	0.06 (1 yr)	0.1 (30 min)	0.1 (24 h)	0.04 (1 yr)	0.1 (30 min)	0.03 (24 h)
Slovakia	0.5 (30 min)	0.15 (24 h)	0.06 (1 yr) Based on daily average values.	0.2 (30 min)	0.1 (24 h) Based on daily average values.		0.1 (30 min)		0.08 (1 yr) Based on daily average values.	-	0.16 (8 h)
Slovenia	0.35 (1 h)	0.125 (24 h)	0.05 (1 yr) For average concentrations. For the 98th percentile: 0.25/0.2/0.1 for 30min/1h/24h average time.				0.2 (1 h)	0.04 (24 h) For average concentrations. For the 98th percentile: 0.15/0.12/0.08 for 30 min/1h/24h average time.	0.15 (1 yr)	0.1 (1 h)	0.1 (8 h); 0.12 (1 yr)
Spain	-	0.25/0.35 (24 h) If particulates > 0.35/If particulates < 0.35. Maximum 7 days per year and no more 3 consecutive days.	0.08/0.12 (6 m) If particulates > 0.04/If particulates < 0.04.	0.957	0.2 Maximum 1 hour.	0.2 Maximum 7 days.	0.05 Guide value.	0.18 Information value (Alert: 0.36).		0.11 (8 h) Mean value.	
Sweden	0.2 (1 h) 98th percentile.	0.1 (24 h) To be exceeded only once a year.	0.05 (6 m)	0.11 (1 h) 98th percentile.	0.05 (24 h)		0.075 (1 h)	0.075 (24 h)	0.05	0.12 (1 h) For the 99.9th percentile (ceiling value: 0.2).	-
Switzerland	0.1 (1 h) 95th percentile value of 1/2 hour values.	0.1 (24 h) To be exceeded only once a year.	0.03 (1 yr)	0.1 (1 h) 95th percentile value of 1/2 hour values.	0.03 (24 h)		0.08 To be exceeded only once a year.	0.08 (24 h) To be exceeded only once a year.	0.03	0.1 (1 h) 98th percentile of 1/2 hour during one month (maximum 1 hour average: 0.12 to be exceeded only once a year).	-
Ukraine	-	0.05 (24 h)		0.05 (24 h)	0.04 (24 h)		0.04 (24 h)	-		0.03 (24 h)	0.03 (24 h)
United Kingdom	-		As in EEC Directives on smoke/SO2 80/779, 81/857 and 89/427.						As in EEC Directive on NOx 85/203.		As in EEC Directive on Ozone 92/72.
United States	-	0.365 (24 h)	0.08 (1 yr)		0.15 (24 h)	0.05 (1 yr)		0.1 (24 h)	0.1 (1 yr)	0.235 (1 h)	-
Yugoslavia	0.35/0.15 (1 h) Mean value for urban/rural areas.	0.15/0.1 (24 h) Mean value for urban/rural areas.	0.05/0.03 (1 yr) Mean value for urban/rural areas.	0.15/0.085 (1 h) Mean value for urban/rural areas.	0.085/0.07 (24 h) Mean value for urban/rural areas.	0.06/0.05 (1 yr) Mean value for urban/rural areas.					-

TABLE 11.1 (continued)

Country	Particulates						Lead				Comments
	Short term		Medium term		Long term		Short or Med. term		Long term		
	Standard	(Average time)	Standard	(Average time)	Standard	(Average time)	Standard	(Average time)	Standard	(Average time)	
Austria	-		0.2 PM 10.	(24 h)	-		-		-		-
Belgium	-		-		0.08/0.25 For the 50th/98th percentile.	(24 h)	-		0.002 Yearly average value.	(24 h)	Other guidelines for NMVOCs, CO, fluorine, HMs, suspended dust, dust falls and others.
Bulgaria	0.5	(30 min)	0.25	(24 h)	0.15	(1 yr)	0.001	(24 h)	0.001	(1 yr)	-
Canada	-		0.12	(24 h)	0.07	(1 yr)	-		-		-
Croatia	-		0.12	(24 h)	0.06 Sampling: 24 h.	(1 yr)	-		0.001 Sampling: 24 h.	(1 yr)	Values set out in the draft of the act on ambient air quality standards.
Cyprus	0.25 For inhalable particulates (PM10).	(1 h)	0.25 98th percentile for total suspended particulates. 0.15 for inhalable particulates (PM10).	(24 h)	0.15 For total suspended particulates. 0.1 for inhalable particulates (PM10).	(1 yr)	0.002 98th percentile.	(24 h)	0.001	(1 yr)	-
Czech Republic	0.5	(30 min)	0.15	(24 h)	0.06 Based on daily average values.	(1 yr)	-		0.0005	(1 yr)	Other guidelines for cadmium and CO.
Denmark	-		0.3 95th percentile. All year.	(24 h)	0.15 Mean value. All year.	(1 yr)	-		0.002 Mean value. All year.		-
Finland	-		0.15 98th percentile.	(24 h)	0.06	(1 yr)	-		-		-
Germany	As in EEC Directive 80/779.		As in EEC Directive 80/779.		As in EEC Directive 80/779.		-		0.002 As in EEC Directive 82/884.	(1 yr)	-
Greece	-		0.25 98th percentile (for black smoke).	(24 h)	0.08 Median.	(1 yr)	-		0.002 Mean value.	(24 h)	-
Hungary	0.2		0.1		0.05		0.0003		-		-
Italy	-		0.09 Warning jointly with SO2, NOx and O3 (Alarm: 0.18).	(24 h)	0.15 Mean value (0.3 for the 95th percentile).	(24 h)	-		0.002 Mean value.	(24 h)	Other guidelines for NMVOCs, CO and fluorine.
Netherlands	-		0.15	(24 h)	0.03/0.075/0.09 For the 50th/95th/98th percentile value.	(24 h)	0.002 For the 98th percentile value.	(1 h)	0.0005	(1 yr)	Other guidelines for CO, benzene and other VOCs.
Norway	-		0.07 PM 10.	(24 h)	0.04 PM 10 (0.03 for PM 2.5).	(6 m)	-		-		-

TABLE 11.1 (concluded)

Country						
Poland	-	**0.120** (24 h) PM 10. For special areas: 0.08.	**0.05** (1 yr) PM 10. For special areas: 0.04.	**0.0001** For special areas: 0.00005	**0.0002** (1 yr) For special areas: 0.00001	Values set out for 44 different pollutants including CO, benzene, other VOCs, HMs, ….
Portugal	-	**0.1/0.15** (24 h) Guide value for black smoke.	**0.08/0.25** Limit value for the 50th/98th percentile for black smoke (0.15/0.3 for the limit values for annual average/95th percentile for the gravimetric method).	-	**0.002** (1 yr) Limit value.	Other guidelines for CO.
Romania	**0.5** (30 min)	**0.15** (24 h)	**0.075** (1 yr)	**0.0007** (24 h)	-	
Slovakia	**0.5** (30 min)	**0.15** (24 h)	**0.06** (1 yr) Based on daily average values.	-	**0.0005** (1 yr)	Other guidelines for cadmium and CO.
Slovenia	-	**0.175** (24 h) For total suspende particulates. 0.125 for black smoke	**0.07** (1 yr) For total suspended particulates. 0.05 for black smoke	-	**0.001** (1 yr)	
Spain	-	**0.35** (24 h) Maximum 18 days.	**0.15**	-	**0.002**	
Sweden	-	**0.09** (24 h) 98th percentile. For black smoke.	**0.04** For black smoke.	Recommendations from WHO.	Recommendations from WHO.	
Switzerland	-	**0.15** (24 h) For total suspended particulates. 95th percentile of the daily means of the year.	**0.07** For total suspended particulates. Yearly average value.	-	**0.001** (1 yr)	Other guidelines for CO. Deposition values for cadmium, zinc and thallium.
Ukraine	-	**0.15** (24 h)	-	**0.0003** (24 h)	-	
United Kingdom	-	-	As in EEC Directives on Smoke/SO2 80/779, 81/857 and 89/427.	-	As in EEC Directive on Lead 82/884	
United States	-	**0.150** (24 h) PM 10.	**0.05** (1 yr) PM 10.	**0.0015** Quarterly.	-	
Yugoslavia	**0.15** (1 h) For black smoke.	**0.05/0.04** (24 h) Mean value for urban/rural areas for black smoke.	**0.05/0.03** (1 yr) Mean value for urban/rural areas for black smoke.			

TABLE 11.2

Ambient air quality standards (related to ecological effects)

(mg/Nm^3)

Country	Sulphur dioxide Short term Standard (Average time)	Medium term Standard (Average time)	Long term Standard (Average time)	Ozone Short term Standard (Average time)	Medium term Standard (Average time)	Long term Standard (Average time)
Austria	0.14/0.30 (30 min) April-Oct./Nov.-March for conifers. 0.3 for deciduous trees between April and Oct.	0.05/0.1 (24 h) April-Oct./Nov.-March for conifers. 0.1 for deciduous trees between April and Oct.	-	-	-	-
Belgium	-	0.1/0.15 (24 h)	0.04/0.06 (24 h) Yearly average value.	0.2 (1 h) EEC Directive on Ozone.	0.065 (24 h) EEC Directive on Ozone.	-
Croatia	-	0.1 (24 h)	0.03 (1 yr) Sampling : 24 h.	0.2 (1 h)	0.065 (24 h)	0.06 (1 yr) Sampling : 24 h.
Denmark	-	-	-	0.2 (1 h) Threshold value.	0.065 (24 h) Threshold value.	-
Finland	-	-	0.025 (1 yr)	-	-	-
Germany	-	-	0.06 (1 yr) Mean value.	As in EEC Directive 92/72. (1 h)	As in EEC Directive 92/72. (24 h)	As in EEC Directive 92/72.
Italy	-	0.1-0.15 (24 h) Implementation of the EEC Directives 80/779, 82/884, 84/360 and 85/203 (guidelines also for NOx and black smoke).	0.04-0.06 (24 h) Implementation of the EEC Directives 80/779, 82/884, 84/360 and 85/203 (guidelines also for NOx and black smoke).	-	-	-
Netherlands	-	-	0.03/0.08/0.1 (24 h) For the 50th/95th/98th percentile value.	0.24 (1 h) Target value : 0.12.	0.16 (8 h)	0.1 (8 m) Seasonal average. Target value : 0.05.
Norway	0.15 (1 h) For vegetation.	0.05 (24 h) For vegetation.	0.02 (1 yr) For vegetation.	0.15 (1 h) For vegetation.	0.06 (8 h) For vegetation.	0.05 (6 m) For vegetation. 7-hour mean value (0900-1600 hours) for the growing season.
Portugal	-	0.1/0.15 (24 h) Guide values.	0.04/0.06 (1 yr) Guide values.	-	0.065 (24 h) Guide value.	-
Slovenia	-	0.1 (24 h) For rural sites.	0.03 (1 yr) For rural sites.	0.2 (1 h) For rural sites.	0.065 (24 h) For rural sites.	0.06 (1 yr) For rural sites. During the growing season.
Spain	-	-	0.08/0.12 (24 h) If particulates > 0.04/If particulates < 0.04.	0.2 (1 h)	0.065 (24 h)	-

TABLE 11.2 (concluded)

					(1 h)		
Sweden	-	0.1 95th percentile value of the year.	-	0.15 Ceiling value.	-	-	0.05 From April to Sept. (9 am to 4 pm).
Switzerland	0.03 Yearly average value.	0.1 24-hour average : to be exceeded only once a year.	0.1 98th percentile of 1/2 hour during one month (maximum 1-hour average : 0.12 to be exceeded only once a year).	-	-		

TABLE 12

Fuel quality standards

Country	Fuel oil light (% S)	Fuel oil medium (% S)	Fuel oil heavy (% S)	Solid fuel. Hard coal. (% S)	Solid fuel. Lignite. (% S)	Leaded petrol (g Pb/l)	Unleaded petrol (g Pb/l)
Austria	0.2 Extra-light : 0.1	0.6	1.0	0.4/0.5/0.6 Expressed in g S/MJ. For steam boilers 0-2 MWth/2-5 MWth/5-10 MWth.	1.0 Expressed in % S. For steam boilers < 10 MWth.	banned Leaded petrol completely banned by Nov. 1993.	0.01 Diesel : 0.1 % S (from Oct. 1995: 0.05 % S).
Belgium	0.2	1.0	1.0-3.0	–		0.15	0.013
Bulgaria	0.2-0.3	1.25 1.35 for ships.	3.5	2.7	2.5-3.5	0.15 0.05 % S.	0.01
Canada	0.7	–	1.0-1.25	No standard	No standard	– Not legal for on-road vehicles.	–
Croatia	<2.0 Extra-light : <1.0	<3.0	<4.0	–	–	<0.6 Lead content defined by INA-refinery standards.	<0.013
Cyprus	1.0	4.0	4.0	Not applicable	Not applicable	0.15 0.4 for super leaded.	
Czech Republic	1.0 For households.	3.0 For business use.	–	0.78/0.78/1.90 Expressed in g S/MJ. For households/business/energy installations.	1.07/1.20/1.90 Expressed in g S/MJ. For households/business/energy installations.	–	
Denmark	0.2 Diesel : 0.05	–	1.0	0.9 Not for power plants > 25 MWth.	Not used	Not used	0.013
European Community	Diesel : 0.2/0.05 (by 1.10.1994/1.10.1996).	Gas oil : 0.2 (by 1.10.1994)				0.15-0.4 Directive 85/210/EEC.	0.013 Directive 85/210/EEC.
Finland	0.2	0.2	1.0	1.0	1.0	0.15	0.013
Germany	0.2 Diesel : 0.05	Almost exclusively used in plants with FGD or in fluidized bed combustion.	Almost exclusively used in plants with FGD or in fluidized bed combustion.	Almost exclusively used in plants with FGD or in fluidized bed combustion.	Almost exclusively used in plants with FGD or in fluidized bed combustion.	0.15 Only super is available leaded (DIN 51600).	0.013 EN 228.
Hungary	0.3	1.2 Maximum.	3.0	–	–	0.15	0.013
Italy	0.3 0.2 in urban areas.	0.3	3.0 4.0 only with major permit.	1.0	–	0.15 Maximum 5 % benzene.	0.013
Netherlands	0.2 Gas oil for diesel vehicles : 0.05 (by 1996).	0.7	1.0	1.2	1.2	0.15	0.013 Lead-free "Eurosuper" on voluntary basis.

TABLE 12 (*concluded*)

Norway	0.25	0.25	0.25	-	0.15 — Maximum content of benzene : 50 ml/l.	0.013
Poland	<0.3	<3.0			<0.15 — <0.1 % S	0.013 — <0.1 % S
Portugal	1.0	2.0	3.0	3.0	0.4 — 0.15 from Jan. 1995).	0.013
Romania	0.10 or 0.25 — Depending on trademark.	2.0	1.0 or 3.0 — Depending on trademark.	3.0	0.3-0.6 — Depending on octane content.	-
Slovakia	2.0 — Diesel fuel : 0.3	0.5-3.5	0.5-3.0	Under preparation	0.15	0.005
Slovenia	2.0 — Extra-light :1.0. Diesel : 0.2	3.0	-	No standard	0.6	0.02 — < 0.013
Spain	1.0	2.7	3.5	1.15 — Import : 1.0	0.15	0
Sweden	0.2	-	0.8	No standard	0.15 — 0.10 % S	0.013 — 0.05 % S
Switzerland	0.2 — Diesel : 0.05	1.0 — With FGD : 2.8	1.0 — With FGD : 2.8	1.0 — With FGD : 3.0	0.15	0.013
United Kingdom	No single standard — Gas oil : Directive 93/12/EEC.	No single standard — Gas oil : Directive 93/12/EEC.	No single standard — Gas oil : Directive 93/12/EEC.	No single statutory standard.	0.15 — Directive 85/210/EEC.	0.013 — Directive 85/210/EEC.
Yugoslavia	2.0 — Extra-light : 1.0. Diesel : 1.0 (Extra-light : 0.5).	3.0 — Low sulphur content . 1.0	4.0 — Low sulphur content . 1.0	-	0.4-0.6	0.013

FGD : flue gas desulphurization.

TABLE 13.1

Emission standards for sulphur

Country	Power generation (unit : g/Nm3)			Industrial processes (unit : g/Nm3)					
	Small plants	Medium-sized plants	Large plants	Smelters	Refineries	Iron and steel plants	Cement plants	Pulp mills	Gas plants
Austria	**0.4/0.4/1.7** For new plants. 10 MWth < power < 50 MWth (for brown coal / other solid / liquid fuel).	**0.4/0.2/0.35** For new plants. 50 MWth < power < 300 MWth (for brown coal/ other solid/ liquid fuel).	**0.4/0.2/0.2** For new plants. Power > 300 MWth (for brown coal/ other solid / liquid fuel).	**0.3/0.5** For gas or liquid / solid fuel.			**0.2** Max. : 0.4 if sulphide-containing material is used.	**0.3/0.4/0.7** Depending on process. For new plants (0.45 / 0.8 / 1.0 for existing plants).	-
Bulgaria	**2.0/2.0** Power < 5 MWth (until 1996 / from 1996).	**2.0/2.0** 5 MWth < power < 50 MWth (until 1996 / from 1996).	**3.5/0.65** Power > 50 MWth (until 1996 / from 1996).	-	-	**1.0/0.5** (until 1996 / from 1996).	**0.75/0.75** (until 1996 / from 1996).	**1.0/0.5** (until 1996 / from 1996).	-
Canada	**0.9** Power > 5 MWth (7 % O2 vol.).	-	-	Value set case by case.	Value set case by case.	Value set case by case.	Value set case by case.	Value set case by case.	Value set case by case.
Czech Republic	**2.5** For solid/liquid fuels and 0.2 MWth < power < 50/5 MWth (6 %/3 % O2 vol.). For gaseous fuels : 0.035 (power > 0.2 MWth, 3% O2 vol.).	**1.7** For solid/liquid fuels and 50/5 MWth < power < 300 MWth (6 %/3 % O2 vol.).	**0.5** For solid /liquid fuels and power > 300 MWth (6 %/3 % O2 vol.).	-	-	-	-	-	-
Denmark	**2.0** 50 MWth < power < 100 MWth and for solid fuels. For liquid fuels : 1.7 (50 < P < 300 MWth).	**0.4-2.0** 100 MWth < power < 500 MWth and for solid fuels. For liquid fuels : 0.3-0.4 (300 < P < 500 MWth).	**0.4** Power > 500 MWth.	**2.0**	**1.0**	**2.0**	**2.0**	**2.0**	-
Finland	**0.4** Power > 50 MWth.	-	-	-	-	-	-	-	-
Germany	**1.0/0.85/0.035** 10 MWth < power < 100 MWth (for solid / liquid / gaseous fuel).	**0.8/0.68/0.035** 100 MWth < power < 300 MWth (for solid / liquid / gaseous fuel).	**0.4/0.4/0.035** Power > 300 MWth (for solid / liquid / gaseous fuel).	**0.5**	As power generation.	**0.5/0.4**	**0.4**	As power generation.	-
Italy	**2.0/0.4-1.7/0.035** 50 MWth < power < 100 MWth (for solid/ liquid/ gaseous fuel).	**0.4-2.0/0.4-1.7/0.03** 100 MWth < power < 500 MWth (for solid/ liquid / gaseous fuel). In the range 200-500 MWth a stricter standard may be set (not lower than 0.4).	**0.4/0.4/0.035** Power > 500 MWth (for solid / liquid / gaseous fuel).	-	-	-	-	-	-

TABLE 13.1 (*concluded*)

Country									
Netherlands	**0.7/1.7** After May 1987. Power < 300 MWth (for solid / liquid fuel).	**0.7/1.7** After May 1987. Power < 300 MWth (for solid / liquid fuel).	**0.2/0.2** After May 1987. Power > 300 MWth (for solid / liquid fuel). For gas, between 0.005 and 0.8 depending on the plant.	**2.0/1.5/1.0** After 1990/after 1995/after 1999.	Permit.	Permit.	Permit.	Permit.	Permit.
Norway	Permit.	Permit.	Permit.	Permit.	Permit.	Permit.	Permit.	Permit.	Permit.
Portugal	5.3	5.3	As in Directive 88/609/EEC.	As in Directive 88/609/EEC.	0.75	0.75	0.4	0.5	0.25
Romania	1.7 Power < 300 MWth.	0.4 300 MWth < power < 500 MWth.	0.4 Power > 500 MWth.	0.5	0.5	0.5	0.5	0.5	0.5
Slovakia	2.5/1.7/0.035 0.2 MWth < power < 50 MWth (for solid / liquid / gaseous fuel).	1.7/1.7/0.035 50 MWth < power < 300 MWth (for solid / liquid / gaseous fuel).	0.5/0.5/0.035 Power > 300 MWth (for solid / liquid / gaseous fuel).	General rule : 2.5 (if discharge > 20 kg/h). Specific limit by process.	General rule : 2.5 (if discharge > 20 kg/h). Specific limit by process.	General rule : 2.5 (if discharge > 20 kg/h). Specific limit by process.	General rule : 2.5 (if discharge > 20 kg/h). Specific limit by process.	General rule : 2.5 (if discharge > 20 kg/h). Specific limit by process.	General rule : 2.5 (if discharge > 20 kg/h). Specific limit by process.
Slovenia	2.0 For solid fuels. Power < 50 MWth.	0.4 For solid fuels. 50 MWth < power < 300 MWth.	0.4 For solid fuels. Power > 300 MWth.	1.7	0.5	0.5	0.4	0.5	0.5
Spain	2.0 Power < 100 MWth. For new installations (after July 1987).	0.4-2.0 100 MWth < power < 500 MWth. For new installations (after July 1987).	0.4 Power > 100 MWth (exceptionally 0.8). For new installations (after July 1987).	5.9	2.4	2.4	-	(5 kg/ton).	-
Sweden	0.1/0.19 (yearly average/max. value). Plants emitting < 400 ton of S per year/> 400 ton of S.	0.1/0.19 (yearly average/max. value). Plants emitting < 400 ton of S per year/> 400 ton of S.	0.05 New coal-fired plants > 500 MW.	Since 1993 general rule: 50 or 100 mg S/MJ for individual installations.	Since 1993, general rule: 50 or 100 mg S/MJ for individual installations.	Since 1993, general rule: 50 or 100 mg S/MJ for individual installations.	Since 1993, general rule: 50 or 100 mg S/MJ for individual installations.	Since 1993, general rule: 50 or 100 mg S/MJ for individual installations.	Since 1993, general rule: 50 or 100 mg S/MJ for individual installations.
Switzerland	1.7 (3 % O_2 vol.), 5 MWth < power < 50 MWth.	1.7 (3 % O_2 vol.), 50 MWth < power < 100 MWth.	0.4 (3 % O_2 vol.). Power > 100 MWth.	0.35/0.10 < 300 MW/>300 MW.	0.25 Mass flow > 2500 g/h.	0.25 Mass flow > 2500 g/h.	0.5	4 kg/t (for incineration of sulphite liquid).	0.12 (15 % O_2 vol.).
United Kingdom			For power > 50 MWth as in directive 88/609/EEC.	For power > 50 MWth as in Directive 88/609/EEC.					
Yugoslavia	2.5 50 MWth < power < 100 MWth. Standards to be adopted for new plants.	1.45 100 MWth < power < 1000 MWth. Standards to be adopted for new plants.	0.65 Power > 1000 MWth. Standards to be adopted for new plants.						

TABLE 13.2

Emission standards for nitrogen oxides

Country	Power generation (unit: g/Nm3)			Industrial processes (unit: g/Nm3)		Vehicles (unit: g/km)			
	Small plants	Medium-sized plants	Large plants	Nitric acid plants	Fertilizer plants	Petrol-fuelled light-duty vehicles	Petrol-fuelled heavy-duty vehicles	Diesel-fuelled light-duty vehicles	Diesel-fuelled heavy-duty vehicles
Austria	**0.4/0.3/0.15** For new plants and 50 MWth < power < 150 MWth (for coal / liquid / gaseous fuel).	**0.3/0.2/0.1** For new plants and 150 MWth < power < 300 MWth (for coal / liquid / gaseous fuel).	**0.25/0.15/0.1** For new plants and power > 300 MWth (for coal / liquid / gaseous fuel).			**0.62** US 83 standards.		**0.62** US 83 standards.	**9.0** In g/kWh.
Bulgaria	**0.5/0.5** Power < 5 MWth (until 1996 / from 1996).	**0.5/0.5** 5 MWth < power < 50 MWth (until 1996 / from 1996).	**1.0/0.6** Power > 50 MWth (until 1996 / from 1996).	**1.0/0.5** until 1996 / from 1996.	**0.1/0.03** until 1996 / from 1996.				
Canada	**0.5** Power > 25 MWth.					**0.6**			
Czech Republic	**0.65/0.2** For solid/gaseous fuels and power>0.2 MWth (6 %/3 % O2 vol.). For liquid fuels and 0.2 MWth < power < 5 MWth : 0.5.	**0.45** For liquid fuels and power > 5 MWth (3% O2 vol.).							
Denmark	**0.2/0.25** Power < 50 MWth (special emission limits for small gas motors and gas turbines).	**0.2/0.25**	**0.2/0.25**	**0.5**	**0.5**	**1.13** HC + NOx. EEC Directive 91/441.		As petrol-fuelled.	**9.0** In g/kWh (EEC Directive 91/542).
Finland	**0.18** Gas plants with power > 50 MWth.	**0.42** 50 MWth < power < 150 MWth.	**0.14** Power > 50 MWth.			**0.62** Since 1990.		**1.1** Since 1992.	**8.0** Since 1993.
Germany	**0.5/0.45/0.2** 1 MWth < power < 50 MWth (for solid / liquid / gaseous fuel).	**0.4/0.3/0.2** 50 MWth < power < 300 MWth (for solid / liquid / gaseous fuel).	**0.2/0.15/0.1** Power > 300 MWth (for solid / liquid / gaseous fuel).	**0.45**		**0.97/1.13** HC + NOx. EEC Directive 91/441.		As petrol-fuelled.	**8.0/9.0** In g/kWh (EEC Directive 91/542).
Greece			EEC Directive 88/609.	5 kg NO2/ton HNO3 (after 1981).					
Italy	**0.65/0.45/0.35** 50 MWth < power < 500 MWth (for solid / liquid / gaseous fuel).	In the range 300-500 MWth a stricter standard may be set (not lower than 200 mg/Nm3).	**0.2/0.2/0.2** Power > 500 MWth (for solid / liquid / gaseous fuel).						

TABLE 13.2 (concluded)

Country								
Netherlands	0.65/0.5 Power < 300 MWth (for solid / gaseous fuel).	1.0/0.7/0.5 Power > 300 MWth (for solid / liquid / gaseous fuel).	0.31/1.13 For new / existing plants.	0.31/1.13 For new / existing plants.	EEC regulations.	EEC regulations.	EEC regulations.	EEC regulations.
Norway	Permit.	Permit.	Permit.	Permit.	0.62 US 83 standards.	EEC regulations.	0.62 US 87 standards.	8.0 In g/kWh (EEC Directive 91/542).
Portugal	1.5	EEC Directive 88/609.	0.45	.2	EEC regulations.	EEC regulations.	EEC regulations.	EEC regulations.
Romania	0.45 Power < 300 MWth.	0.45 Power > 300 MWth.	0.5	0.5	EEC regulations.	EEC regulations.	EEC regulations.	
Slovakia	0.65/0.5/0.2 0.2 MWth < power < 5 MWth (for solid / liquid / gaseous fuel).	0.55/0.45/0.2 5 MWth < power < 50 MWth (for solid / liquid / gaseous fuel).	0.3	0.5				8.0 In g/kWh.
Slovenia	0.5 1 MWth < power < 50 MWth. 0.4 50 MWth < power < 300 MWth.	0.3 Power > 300 MWth.	0.45	0.5				
Spain	0.65-0.13/0.45/0.35 For new plants (for solid/ liquid / gaseous fuel).		0.205					
Sweden			0.25 Mass flow > 2500 g/h.	0.25 Mass flow > 2500 g/h.	0.62 1.1 for light-duty trucks.	0.62 1.1 for light-duty trucks.	0.62	9.0 In g/kWh.
Switzerland	0.45 5 MWth < power < 50 MWth.	0.3 50 MWth < power < 100 MWth.	0.15 Power > 100 MWth	0.25 Mass flow > 2500 g/h.	0.25 Mass flow > 2500 g/h.	0.62 1.1 for light-duty trucks.	0.62 1.1 for light-duty trucks.	9.0 In g/kWh.
United Kingdom	Standards for individual processes.	Standards for individual processes.	Standards for individual processes.	Standards for individual processes.	EEC Directive 91/441.	EEC Directive 91/441.		EEC Directive 91/542.
Yugoslavia	0.4 50 MWth < power < 100 MWth. Standards to be adopted for new plants. 0.4 100 MWth < power < 1000 MWth. Standards to be adopted for new plants.	0.4 Power > 1000 MWth. Standards to be adopted for new plants.	0.4 Power > 1000 MWth. Standards to be adopted for new plants.	0.4				

TABLE 13.3

Emission standards for volatile organic compounds

Country	Stationary source (unit : g/Nm3)	Mobile source (unit : g/km)	Fuel volatility (unit : g/test, % RVP)	Evaporation from organic substances
Austria	0.02-0.15 Depending on the plant.	0.25/1.2 Light-duty/heavy-duty vehicles.		
Bulgaria	0.02-0.2			
Canada		0.25		Process dependent.
Cyprus	0.05-0.15			
Denmark	0.005-0.3	1.13 HC + NOx (EEC Directive 91/441).	Summer : max 80 kPa ; winter : 95 kPa.	2.0 g/test For petrol-fuelled vehicles (EEC Directive 91/441).
Finland		0.25 Light-duty vehicles.		
Germany	0.02/0.1/0.15 For non-carcinogenic VOC, according to 3 classes of risk.	1.1/1.23 In g/kWh. For light-duty trucks (EEC Directive 93/59).	Summer : 35-70 kPa ; winter : 55-90 kWh (EN 228).	10-15 weight/% For organic solvents in paints (environmental label).
Netherlands	Permit.	According to EU legislation.		Permit.
Norway		0.25/0.5 For petrol- and diesel-fuelled passenger cars (US-83 emission standard) / light-duty trucks.	45-90 kPa / 70-105 kPa (for 98 octan, summer/winter). 55-90 kPa / 65-100 kPa (for 95 octan, summer/winter).	
Portugal	0.05	EEC regulations.		
Romania	< 0.15			< 0.15
Slovakia	Depending on the plant.	1.1 In g/kWh. For heavy-duty vehicles.		
Slovenia	0.02-0.15			
Sweden	No standard.	No standard.	80 kPa / 95 kPa (summer/winter).	No standard.
Switzerland	0.02/0.1/0.15 For non-carcinogenic VOCs, according to 3 classes of risk.	0.25/0.5 Petrol-fuelled light-duty vehicles/ trucks. 1.23 g/KWh for heavy-duty vehicles.		
United Kingdom		EEC Directives 91/441 and 91/452.		

TABLE 14.1

Monitoring of air quality. General description

Country	Ambient air quality					Wet deposition	Precipitation measurements	Notes
	Total number of monitoring sites	Percentage of rural sites	Percentage of urban or industrial sites (%)	Percentage of stations managed at a national level (%)	Percentage of stations managed at a regional or local level (%)	Total number of measuring sites	Total number of measuring sites	
Austria	232	14	86	4	96	33	1200	
Belgium	265	20	80	0	100	11	48	
Bulgaria	105		100	100		1	1	
Canada	199	30	70	2	98	120		
Croatia	190	13	87	13	87	13	80	
Cyprus	6	2	4	2	4			
Czech Republic	93	40	60			8	800	Automatic monitoring stations only.
Denmark	16	38	62	69	31	2	17	
European Community	3307							
Finland	112	12	88	7	93	58	470	
France	930	100			100			DOAS measurements.
Germany	31	100		100		25	8	UBA stations only. Over 500 stations at local level.
Greece	22	4	96	54	46		2	
Hungary	41	5	95	100	0	9	700	
Italy	584		100		100	172	76	
Netherlands	46	56	44	100			15	
Norway	56	79	21	100	0	28	28	
Poland	210							National sites only.
Portugal	74	12	88	30	70	7	5	
Romania	166	9	91		100	76	226	
Slovakia	40	18	82	100		8	8	
Slovenia	20	45	55	35	65	39	27	
Spain	1108	1	99	1	99	5	5	
Sweden	225	80	20	15	85		32	DOAS measurements.
Switzerland	120	37	63	13	87	50	2	DOAS measurements.
Ukraine	171					59	34	
United Kingdom	48	31	69	100		32	32	National sites only.
United States	4200							
Yugoslavia	29						12	

TABLE 14.2

Ambient air quality monitoring. Description

Country	Total number of SO2 monitors	Total number of NOx monitors	Total number of O3 monitors	Total number of particulates monitors	Total number of black smoke monitors	Total number of CO monitors	Total number of NH3 monitors	Total number of hydrocarbons monitors	Other
Austria	204	182	135	144		77		7	Hydrogen sulphide
Belgium	95	22	10	19	80	1	10	25	Heavy metals ; fluorides ; chlorides ; hydrogen sulphide.
Bulgaria	103	101	7	95		10	25	7	
Canada	78	88	126	94	39	58		40	
Croatia	68	22		4	54	4	20	4	Hydrogen sulphide ; phenols ; chlorides ; fluorides ; heavy metals.
Cyprus	6	6	6	6		6		2	Hydrogen sulphide ; lead ; cadmium.
Czech Republic	93	93	25	93		30	2	2	Heavy metals.
Denmark	16	11	9	16	5	6	6	2	
European Community	2208	979	459	1000	1050	524		174	
Finland	71	29	10	63		6	4	4	
France	420	135	55	120	80	45		40	Lead.
Germany	31	31	31	31		18			
Greece	22	22	21		21	20			
Hungary	47	47	26	37		40	1	21	
Italy	512	435	202	452		340	3	200	
Netherlands	39	45	38	18	14	21	8	10	
Norway	25	23	14	0	8	0	13	0	
Poland									
Portugal	50	27	15	40		14		1	
Romania	143	143	3	35		3	119	3	
Slovakia	33	33	17	28		10		5	Hydrogen sulphide.
Slovenia	20	8	7	2		2	0	1	
Spain	571	78	25	109	455	38	10	7	
Sweden	45	45	20	5	45	10	4	25	
Switzerland	90	99	116	56		40	2	25	Heavy metals ; benzene ; toluene ; xylene.
Ukraine									
United Kingdom	23	26	31	14		21		8	Heavy metals ; speciated hydrocarbons ; PCBs ; PAHs ; dioxins ; furans.
United States									
Yugoslavia	29	3			29				

TABLE 15

Status of the Convention and its related Protocols (as of 31 May 1995)

	1979 Convention (a)		1984 EMEP Protocol (b)		1985 Sulphur Protocol (c)		1988 NOx Protocol (d)		1991 VOC Protocol (e)		1994 Sulphur Protocol (f)	
	Signature	Ratification*	Signature	Ratification*	Signature	Ratification*	Signature	Ratification	Signature (1)	Ratification* (2)	Signature	Ratification*
Austria	13.11.1979	16.12.1982 (R)		04.06.1987 (Ac)	9.7.1985	04.06.1987 (R)	1.11.1988	15.01.1990 (R)	19.11.1991	23.08.1994 (R)	14.06.1994	
Belarus	14.11.1979	13.06.1980 (R)	28.09.1984	04.10.1985 (Al)	9.7.1985	10.09.1986 (Al)	1.11.1988	08.06.1989 (Al)				
Belgium	13.11.1979	15.07.1982 (R)	25.02.1985	05.08.1987 (R)	9.7.1985	09.06.1989 (R)	1.11.1988		19.11.1991		14.06.1994 (1)	
Bosnia and Herzegovina		06.03.1992 (Sc)		06.03.1992 (Sc)								
Bulgaria	14.11.1979	09.06.1981 (R)	04.04.1985	26.09.1986 (Ap)	9.7.1985	26.09.1986 (Ap)	1.11.1988	30.03.1989 (R)	19.11.1991		14.06.1994	
Canada	13.11.1979	15.12.1981 (R)	03.10.1984	04.12.1985 (R)	9.7.1985	04.12.1985 (R)	1.11.1988	25.01.1991 (R)	19.11.1991		14.06.1994	
Croatia		08.10.1992(Sc)		08.10.1992(Sc)							14.06.1994	
Cyprus		20.11.1991 (Ac)		20.11.1991 (Ac)								
Czech Republic	14.11.1979	01.01.1993 (Sc)		01.01.1993 (Sc)		01.01.1993 (Sc)		01.01.1993 (Al)(2)	19.11.1991		14.06.1994	
Denmark	14.11.1979	18.06.1982 (R)	28.09.1984	29.04.1986 (R)	9.7.1985	29.04.1986 (R)	1.11.1988	01.03.1993 (Al)(2)	19.11.1991		14.06.1994	
Finland	13.11.1979	15.04.1981 (R)	07.12.1984	24.06.1986 (R)	9.7.1985	24.06.1986 (R)	1.11.1988	01.02.1990 (R)	19.11.1991	11.01.1994 (Al)	14.06.1994	
France	13.11.1979	03.11.1981 (Ap)	22.02.1985	30.10.1987 (R)	9.7.1985	13.03.1986 (Ap)	1.11.1988	20.07.1989 (Ap)	19.11.1991		14.06.1994	
Germany	13.11.1979	15.07.1982 (R)(2)	26.02.1985	07.10.1986 (R)(2)	9.7.1985	03.03.1987 (R)(2)	1.11.1988	16.11.1990 (R)	19.11.1991	08.12.1994 (R)	14.06.1994	
Greece	14.11.1979	30.08.1983 (R)		24.06.1988 (Ac)			1.11.1988		19.11.1991		14.06.1994	
Holy See	14.11.1979											
Hungary	13.11.1979	22.09.1980 (R)	27.03.1985	08.05.1985 (Ap)	9.7.1985	11.09.1986 (R)	3.05.1989	12.11.1991 (Ap)	19.11.1991		09.12.1994	
Iceland	13.11.1979	05.05.1983 (R)										
Ireland	13.11.1979	15.07.1982 (R)	04.04.1985	26.06.1987 (R)	9.7.1985	26.06.1987 (R)	1.05.1989	17.10.1994 (R)			17.10.1994	
Italy	14.11.1979	15.07.1982 (R)	28.09.1984	12.01.1989 (R)	9.7.1985	05.02.1990 (R)	1.11.1988	19.05.1992 (R)	19.11.1991		14.06.1994	
Latvia		15.07.1994 (Ac)										
Liechtenstein	14.11.1979	22.11.1983 (R)		01.05.1985 (Ac)	9.7.1985	13.02.1986 (R)	1.11.1988	24.03.1994 (R)	19.11.1991	24.03.1994 (R)	14.06.1994	
Lithuania		25.01.1994 (Ac)										
Luxembourg	13.11.1979	15.07.1982 (R)	21.11.1984	24.08.1987 (R)	9.7.1985	24.08.1987 (R)	1.11.1988	04.10.1990 (R)	19.11.1991	11.11.1993 (R)	14.06.1994	
Netherlands	13.11.1979	15.07.1982 (Al)(3)	28.09.1984	22.10.1985 (Al)(3)	9.7.1985	30.04.1986 (Al)(3)	1.11.1988	11.10.1989 (Al)(3)	19.11.1991	29.09.1993 (Al)	14.06.1994	30.05.1995 (Al)(2)
Norway	13.11.1979	13.02.1981 (R)	28.09.1984	12.03.1985 (Al)	9.7.1985	04.11.1986 (R)	1.11.1988	11.10.1989 (R)	19.11.1991	07.01.1993 (R)	14.06.1994	
Poland	13.11.1979	19.07.1985 (R)(2)		14.09.1988 (Ac)								
Portugal	14.11.1979	29.09.1980 (R)		10.01.1989 (Ac)					02.04.1992			
Romania	14.11.1979 (1)	27.02.1991 (R)										
Russian Federation	13.11.1979	22.05.1980 (R)	28.09.1984	21.08.1985 (Al)	9.7.1985	10.09.1986 (Al)	1.11.1988	21.06.1989 (Al)				
San Marino	14.11.1979											
Slovakia		28.05.1993 (Sc)		28.05.1993 (Sc)		28.05.1993 (Sc)		28.05.1993 (Sc)				
Slovenia		06.07.1992 (Sc)		06.07.1992 (Sc)								
Spain	14.11.1979	15.06.1982 (R)		11.08.1987 (Ac)			1.11.1988	04.12.1990 (R)	19.11.1991	01.02.1994 (R)	14.06.1994	
Sweden	13.11.1979	12.02.1981 (R)	28.09.1984	12.08.1985 (R)	9.7.1985	31.03.1986 (R)	1.11.1988	27.07.1990 (R)	19.11.1991	08.01.1993 (R)	14.06.1994	
Switzerland	13.11.1979	06.05.1983 (R)	03.10.1984	26.07.1985 (R)	9.7.1985	21.09.1987 (R)	1.11.1988	18.09.1990 (R)	19.11.1991	21.03.1994 (R)	14.06.1994	
Turkey	13.11.1979	18.04.1983 (R)	03.10.1984	20.12.1985 (R)								
Ukraine	14.11.1979	05.06.1980 (R)	28.09.1984	30.08.1985 (Al)	9.7.1985	02.10.1986 (Al)	1.11.1988	24.07.1989 (Al)	19.11.1991		14.06.1994	
United Kingdom	13.11.1979	15.07.1982 (R)(4)	20.11.1984	12.08.1985 (R)			1.11.1988	15.10.1990 (R)(4)	19.11.1991	14.06.1994 (R)(5)	14.06.1994	
United States	13.11.1979	30.11.1981 (Al)	28.09.1984	29.10.1984 (Al)			1.11.1988 (1)	13.07.1989 (Al)	19.11.1991		14.06.1994	
Yugoslavia	13.11.1979	18.03.1987 (R)		28.10.1987 (Ac)								
European Community	14.11.1979	15.07.1982 (Ap)	28.09.1984	17.07.1986 (Ap)				17.12.1993 (Ac)	02.04.1992		14.06.1994	
Total:	33	39	22	35	19	21	25	25	23	11	28	1

(a) Convention on Long-range Transboundary Air Pollution, adopted 13.11.1979 in Geneva, entry into force 16.3.1983.
(b) Protocol to the 1979 Convention on Long-range Transboundary Air Pollution on Long-term Financing of the Cooperative Programme for Monitoring and Evaluation of the Long-range Transmission of Air Pollutants in Europe (EMEP), adopted 28.9.1984 in Geneva, entry into force 28.1.1988.
(c) Protocol to the 1979 Convention on Long-range Transboundary Air Pollution on the Reduction of Sulphur Emissions or their Transboundary Fluxes by at least 30 per cent, adopted 8.7.1985 in Helsinki, entry into force 2.9.1987.
(d) Protocol to the 1979 Convention on Long-range Transboundary Air Pollution concerning the Control of Emissions of Nitrogen Oxides or their Transboundary Fluxes, adopted 31.10.1988 in Sofia, entry into force 14.2.1991.
(e) Protocol to the 1979 Convention on Long-range Transboundary Air Pollution concerning the Control of Emissions of Volatile Organic Compounds or their Transboundary Fluxes, adopted 18.11.1991 in Geneva.
(f) Protocol to the 1979 Convention on Long-range Transboundary Air Pollution on further Reduction of Sulphur Emissions, adopted 14.6.1994 in Oslo.

Notes: * R = Ratification, Ac = Accession, Ap = Approval, Al = Acceptance, Sc = Succession
(1) With declaration upon signature.   (3) For the Kingdom in Europe.   (5) Including the Bailiwicks of Jersey and Guernsey, the Isle of Man.
(2) With declaration upon ratification.   (4) Including the Bailiwicks of Jersey and Guernsey, the Isle of Man, Gibraltar, the United Kingdom Sovereign Base Areas of Akrotiri and Dhekelia on the Island of Cyprus.

TABLE 16

Participation in International Cooperative Programmes under the Convention

Participant	Party to EMEP (a) Protocol	EMEP data delivery in 1993	ICP Forests Task Force (b)	ICP Freshwaters Task Force (c)	ICP Materials Task Force (d)	ICP Crops Task Force (e)	ICP Integrated Monitoring Task Force (f)	TF on Mapping (g) Task Force	TF on Mapping (g) data delivery
Austria	x	x	x		x	x	x	x	x
Belarus	x	x	x				x		
Belgium	x	x	x	x		x			
Bosnia and Herzegovina	x	x							
Bulgaria	x		x	x				x	x
Canada	x		x	x	x		x		
Croatia	x	x	x						
Cyprus	x								
Czech Republic	x	x	PCC-E	x	SC		x	x	x
Denmark	x	x	x	x		x	x	x	x
Estonia			x		x	x	x	x	
Finland	x	x	x	x	x	x	PCC	x	x
France	x	x	x	x		x		x	
Germany	x	x	PCC-W	x	SC	x	x	x	x
Greece	x	x	x			x			
Hungary	x	x	x	x		x	x	x	
Iceland		x							
Ireland	x	x	x	x		x			
Italy	x	x	x		x	x			
Latvia		x	x			x	x	x	
Liechtenstein	x		x						
Lithuania		x	x				x	x	
Luxembourg	x		x						
Netherlands	x	x	x	x	x	x	x	x	x
Norway	x	x	x	PCC	SC		x	x	x
Poland	x	x	x			x	x	x	x
Portugal	x	x	x		x		x		
Republic of Moldova		x	x						
Romania			x	x					
Russian Federation	x	x	x	x	x	x	x	x	x
Slovakia	x	x	x						
Slovenia	x	x	x					x	
Spain	x	x	x		x	x	x	x	x
Sweden	x	x	x	x	PCC	x	x	x	x
Switzerland	x	x	x	x		x	x	x	x
Turkey	x	x	x						
Ukraine	x	x	x				x		
United Kingdom	x	x	x	x	SC	PCC	x	x	x
United States	x		x	x	x				
European Community	x	x	x		x				
Total:	34	32	37	18	16	19	21	20	14

PCC : Programme Coordinating Centre.
SC   : Sub-centre.

(a) - Cooperative Programme for Monitoring and Evaluation of the Long-range Transmission of Air Pollutants (EMEP), established in 1977.
(b) - ICP for Assessment and Monitoring of Air Pollution Effects on Forests, established in 1985.
(c) - ICP for Assessment and Monitoring of Acidification of Rivers and Lakes, established in 1986.
(d) - ICP for Effects on Materials, including Historic and Cultural Monuments, established in 1986.
(e) - ICP for Research on Evaluating Effects of Air Pollutants and Other Stresses on Agricultural Crops, established in 1987.
(f) - ICP on Integrated Monitoring of Air Pollution Effects on Ecosystems, established in 1987 as a pilot programme.
(g) - Task Force on Mapping of Critical Levels and Loads, established in 1988 ; assistance provided by the Coordination Center for Effects, Bilthoven (Netherlands).

TABLE 17

Sulphur emissions (1980-2010) in the ECE region as a percentage of 1980 levels

Country	1980	1981	1982	1983	1984	1985	1986	1987	1988	1989	1990	1991	1992	1993	1995	2000	2005	2010
Austria	100	-	-	61	-	49	-	38	31	23	23	21	19	18	20	20	-	-
Belarus	100	99	96	96	93	93	93	110	105	97	96	98	69	59	80	75	66	-
Belgium	100	86	84	68	60	48	46	44	43	39	38	39	37	-	-	30	28	26
Bulgaria	100	-	-	-	-	-	-	118	109	106	99	81	55	69	67	67	60	55
Canada	100	92	78	79	86	80	79	82	83	80	71	68	66	66	61	64	67	68
Croatia	100	-	-	-	-	-	-	-	-	-	120	-	-	-	-	89	83	78
Cyprus	-	-	-	-	-	-	-	-	-	-	-	-	-	-	-	-	-	-
Czech Republic	100	104	106	104	102	101	96	96	92	89	83	79	68	63	50	24	-	-
Denmark	100	80	82	70	66	75	63	56	54	43	40	54	42	35	37	20	20	20
Finland	100	91	83	64	63	66	57	56	52	42	45	33	24	21	-	20	20	20
France	100	78	75	63	56	44	40	39	37	40	39	41	37	34	-	26	23	22
Germany	100	99	100	98	102	104	102	98	86	83	75	59	52	-	-	17	13	-
Greece	100	-	-	-	-	125	-	-	-	-	128	-	-	-	-	149	145	143
Hungary	100	-	-	-	-	86	83	79	75	67	62	56	51	-	-	55	50	40
Iceland	100	-	-	-	100	100	-	-	-	-	-	-	-	-	-	-	-	-
Ireland	100	86	71	64	64	63	73	78	68	73	80	81	72	-	70	-	-	-
Italy	100	-	-	83	70	59	59	60	58	53	59	-	-	-	40	32	27	-
Liechtenstein	100	-	-	58	25	67	-	-	-	-	25	-	-	-	-	25	-	-
Luxembourg	100	-	-	-	-	-	-	-	-	-	-	-	-	-	-	42	-	-
Netherlands	100	95	82	66	61	53	54	54	51	42	41	36	34	34	-	19	-	11
Norway	100	89	77	73	67	69	64	52	47	42	38	32	26	26	-	24	-	-
Poland	100	-	-	-	-	105	102	102	102	95	78	73	69	66	-	63	53	34
Portugal	100	-	-	115	-	74	88	82	77	-	106	109	130	109	-	114	111	-
Romania	-	-	-	-	-	-	-	-	-	-	-	-	-	-	-	-	-	-
Russian Federation	100	97	99	97	91	86	80	79	72	65	62	61	54	48	-	62	60	60
Slovakia	100	-	-	-	-	79	77	79	76	73	70	57	49	42	-	43	38	31
Slovenia	100	108	109	115	106	102	104	93	89	90	83	77	80	77	-	39	19	16
Spain	100	-	-	77	-	66	59	57	48	59	70	-	-	-	-	65	-	-
Sweden	100	85	73	60	58	53	54	45	44	32	26	22	20	20	20	20	-	-
Switzerland	100	-	-	-	75	69	-	63	58	54	49	49	47	46	44	45	46	48
Turkey	100	-	-	-	32	37	41	-	-	-	-	-	-	-	-	-	-	-
Ukraine	100	91	89	91	90	90	88	85	83	80	72	66	62	57	54	54	54	54
United Kingdom	100	91	86	75	76	76	80	80	78	76	77	73	71	63	60	47	30	20
United States	100	95	89	87	90	89	86	86	88	88	87	87	87	-	-	63	-	60
Yugoslavia	100	100	101	108	112	118	116	119	124	125	125	110	98	99	125	167	219	280
European Community	100	-	-	-	-	53	-	-	-	-	-	-	-	-	-	35	-	-

Notes : See footnotes to table 1.

Parties to the Sulphur Protocol.

TABLE 18

Nitrogen oxides emissions (1980-2010) in the ECE region as a percentage of 1987 levels

Country	1980	1981	1982	1983	1984	1985	1986	1987	1988	1989	1990	1991	1992	1993	1995	2000	2005	2010
Austria	105			103		105		100	97	94	95	92	86	78	73	66		
Belarus	89	89	89	90	91	90	98	100	100	100	108	107	85	78	95	83	70	
Belgium	138					98	96	100	104	108	107	108	109					70
Bulgaria								100	100	99	90	66	63	57	72	91	84	70
Canada	96	94	93	92	92	97	96	100	104	104	98	97	95	98	97	98	101	106
Croatia																		
Cyprus						90	90	100	100	110	110	130	130	140	150	180	200	200
Czech Republic	115	100	100	102	103	102	101	100	105	113	91	89	86	70	70	49		
Denmark	91	79	86	84	88	97	103	100	97	90	89	106	91	87	84	67	64	
Finland	98	92	91	87	86	93	95	100	102	105	105	106	95	94		83	83	83
France	112	104	104	101	100	99	99	100	99	109	97	99	98	93				
Germany	100	97	96	98	101	101	102	100	98	93	88	85	84					
Greece																		
Hungary	103					99	100	100	97	93	90	77	69		106	105		
Iceland																		
Ireland	63	75	75	74	73	79	87	100	106	110	100	103	109		113	112	105	
Italy	78				82	91	95	100	104	107	108				112	110	108	
Liechtenstein																		
Luxembourg																		
Netherlands	97	96	94	93	96	96	98	100	100	98	95	94	92	95		42		20
Norway	78	75	77	80	86	91	97	100	97	98	97	93	93	95		68		
Poland	98					98	104	100	101	97	84	79	74	75		88		
Portugal	143			166		83	95	100	105	475	191	200	214	211				
Romania								100	69		239	218	120					
Russian Federation	65	72	75	74	71	72	71	100	89	96	101	97	87	86				
Slovakia								100		115	115	108	97	93				
Slovenia	91	92	92	91	92	94	102	100	104	102	100	94	96	108				
Spain	107			105		94	96	100	100	111	141					100		
Sweden	98	96	95	92	95	98	100	100	95	93	92	91	90	90	87	72	70	72
Switzerland	98	75	83	80	107	81		100	97	95	92	88	81	75	64	50	49	50
Turkey																		
Ukraine	105	105	105	105	101	97	102	100	100	97	100	90	76	64	64	64	64	64
United Kingdom	90	88	87	88	88	92	96	100	104	107	108	107	104	104	93	76	70	70
United States *	86	85	83	80	82	81	81	83	86	85	85	85	83			83	83	92
Yugoslavia	78	83	84	89	96	97	97	100	105	103	110	95	82	90	110	147	192	246
European Community																		

Notes : See footnotes to table 2.

* : Reference year for the United States is 1978 (21 830 kt).

Parties to the NOx Protocol.

CHARTS AND MAPS

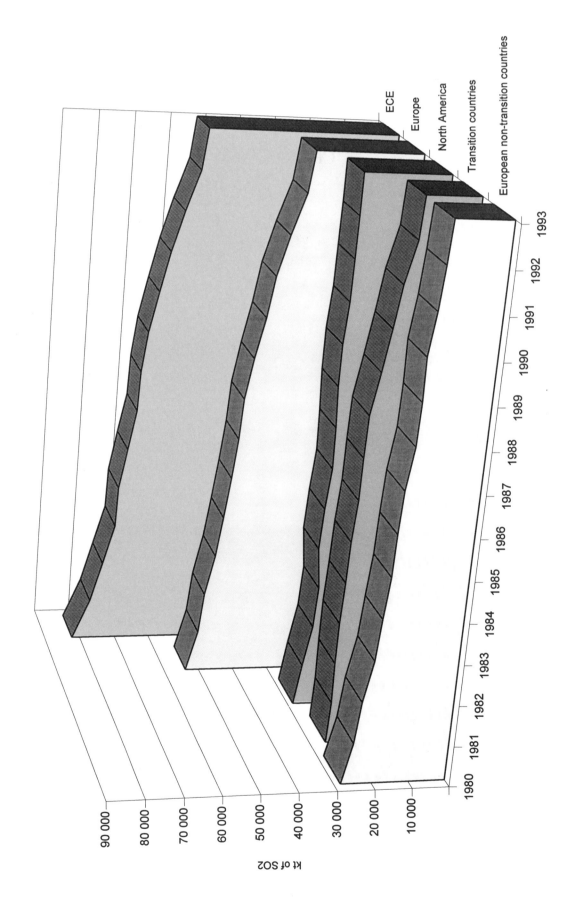

Figure I.1. Emissions of sulphur (1980-1993) in the ECE region

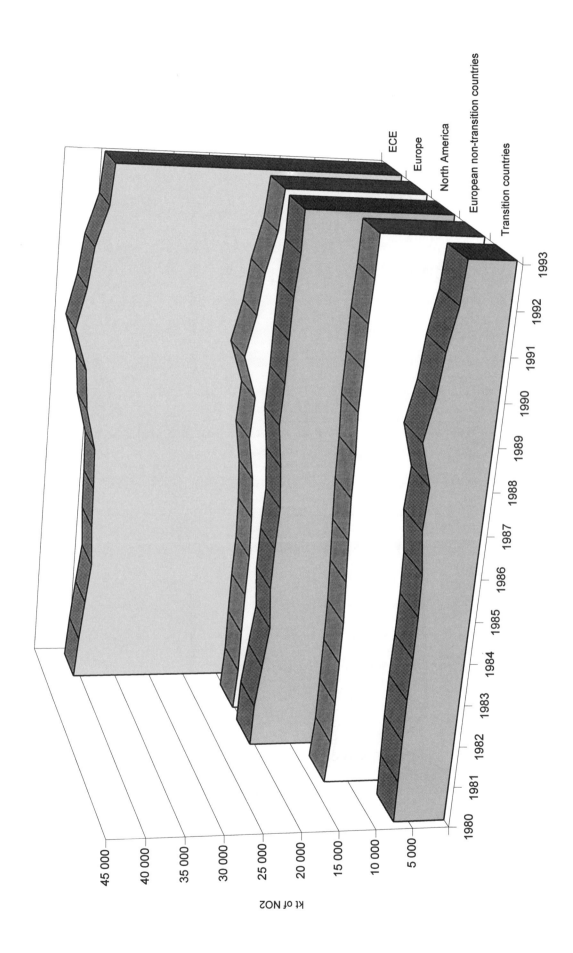

Figure I.2. Emissions of nitrogen oxides (1980-1993) in the ECE region

Figure II.1. Emissions of air pollutants by source category

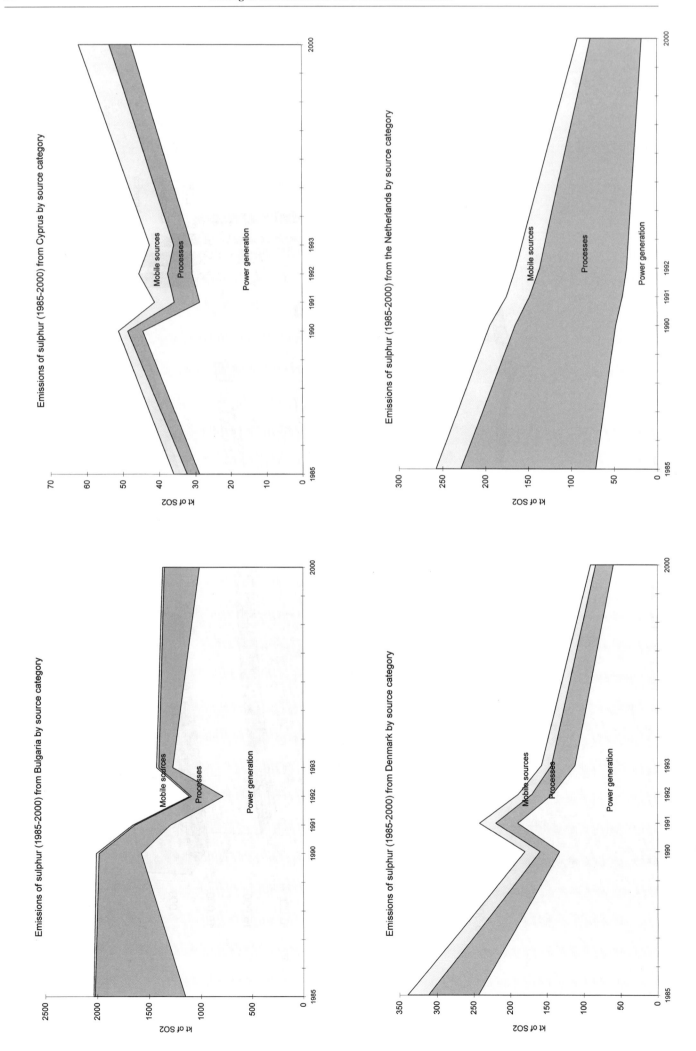

Figure II.1.   Emissions of air pollutants by source category (*continued*)

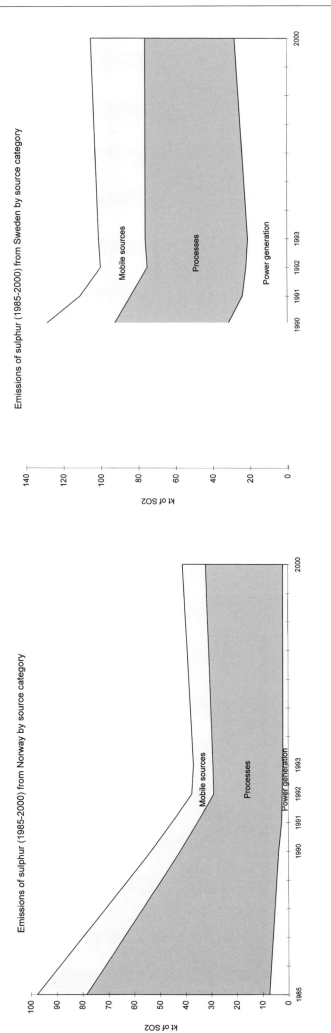

Emissions of sulphur (1985-2000) from Sweden by source category

Emissions of sulphur (1985-2000) from Norway by source category

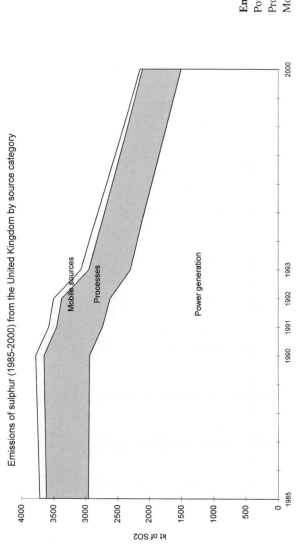

Emissions of sulphur (1985-2000) from the United Kingdom by source category

Emissions of sulphur:

Power generation:	EMEP source category 1 and 2
Processes:	EMEP source category 3 and 4
Mobile sources:	EMEP source category 7 and 8

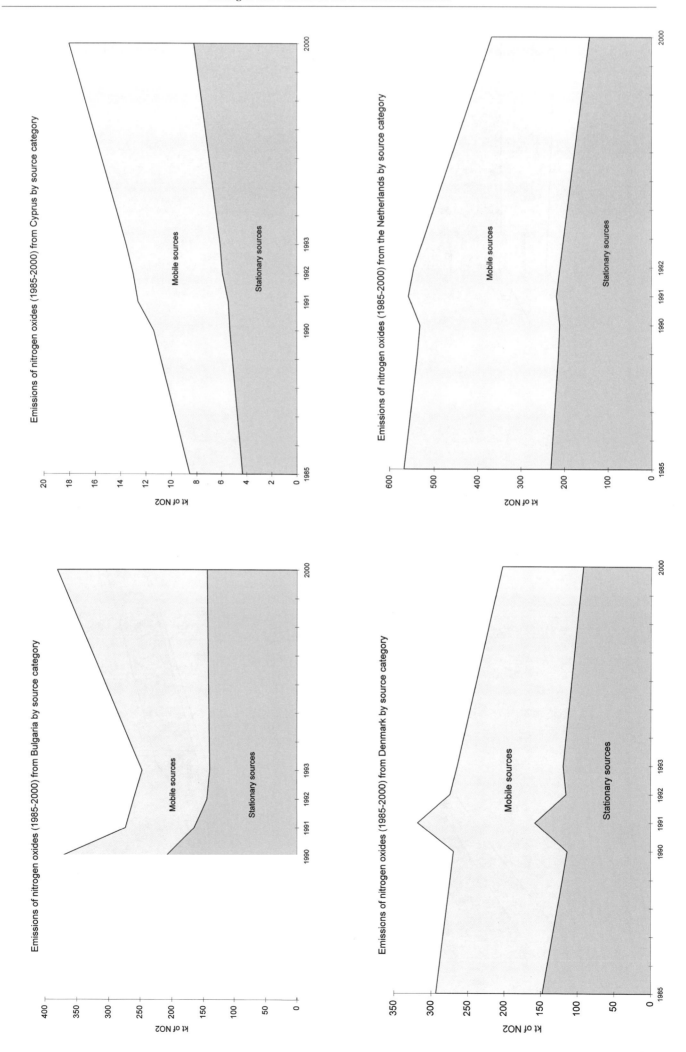

Figure II.2. Emissions of air pollutants by source category

Figure II.2. Emissions of air pollutants by source category (*continued*)

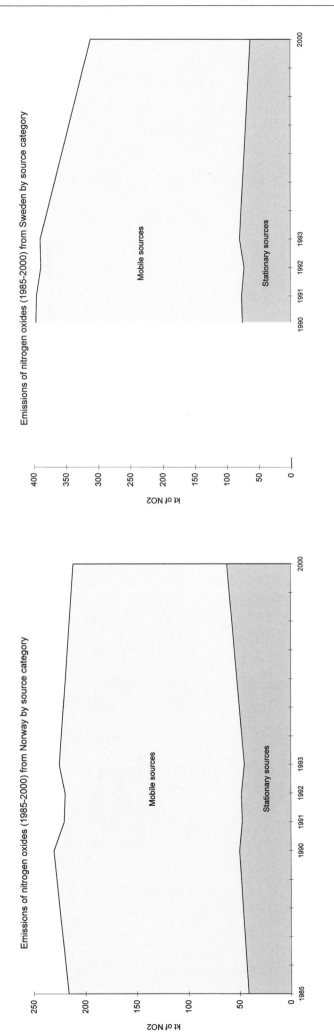

Emissions of nitrogen oxides (1985-2000) from Norway by source category

Emissions of nitrogen oxides (1985-2000) from Sweden by source category

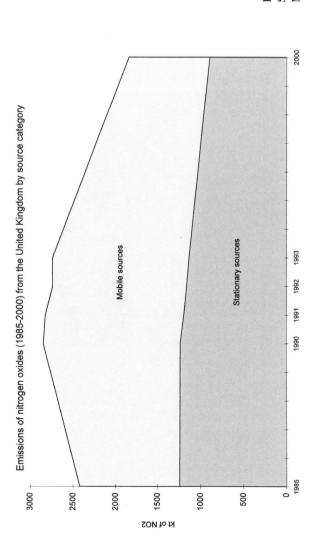

Emissions of nitrogen oxides (1985-2000) from the United Kingdom by source category

Emissions of nitrogen oxides:
Stationary sources: EMEP source category 1 to 5
Mobile sources: EMEP source category 7 and 8

Figure II.3.   Emissions of air pollutants by source category

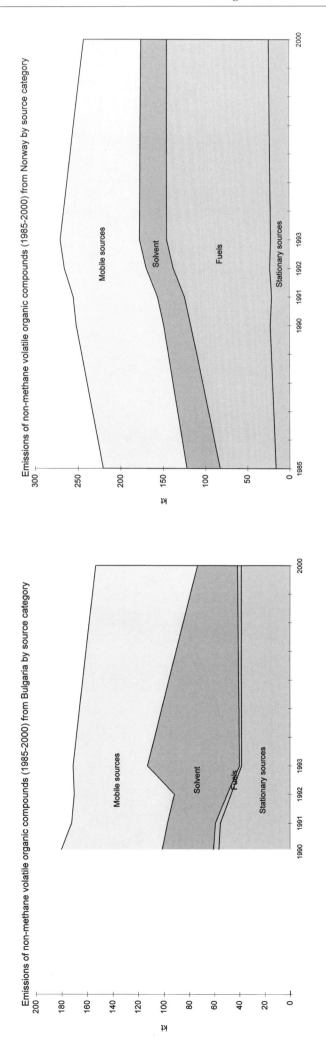

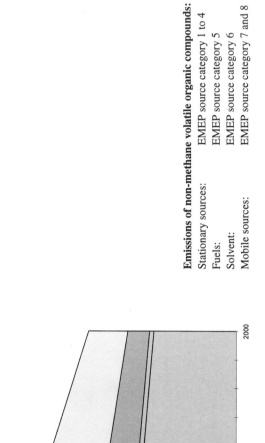

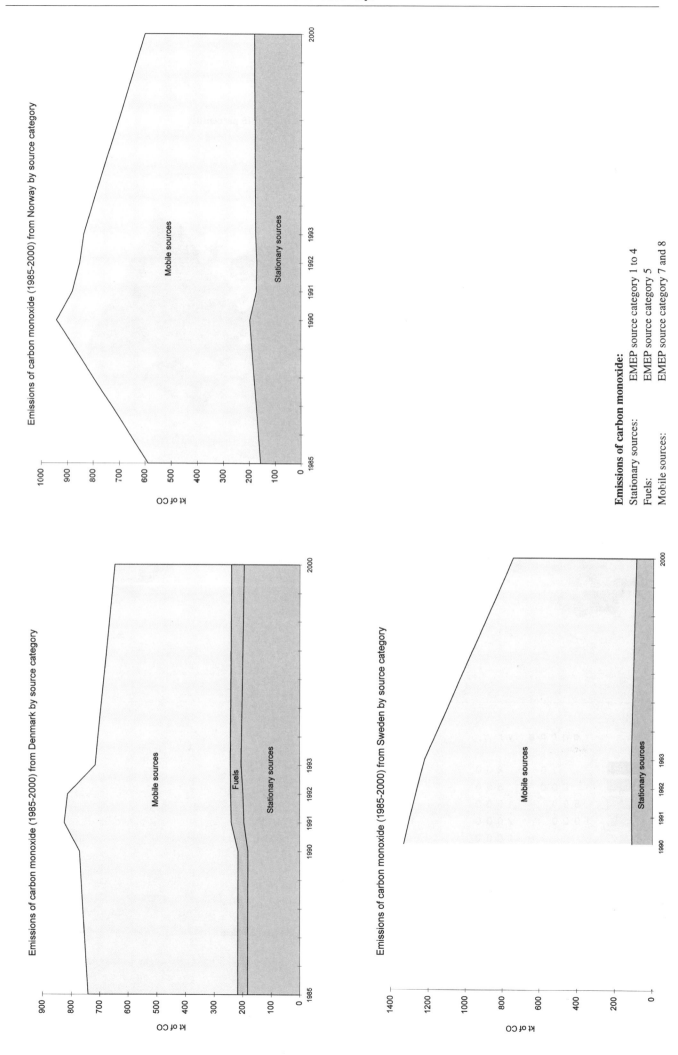

Figure II.4.   Emissions of air pollutants by source category

Emissions of carbon monoxide (1985-2000) from Denmark by source category

Emissions of carbon monoxide (1985-2000) from Norway by source category

Emissions of carbon monoxide (1985-2000) from Sweden by source category

kt of CO

Mobile sources

Fuels

Stationary sources

Emissions of carbon monoxide:
Stationary sources: EMEP source category 1 to 4
Fuels: EMEP source category 5
Mobile sources: EMEP source category 7 and 8

Figure III.1.   Map of critical loads of sulphur (5 percentile)

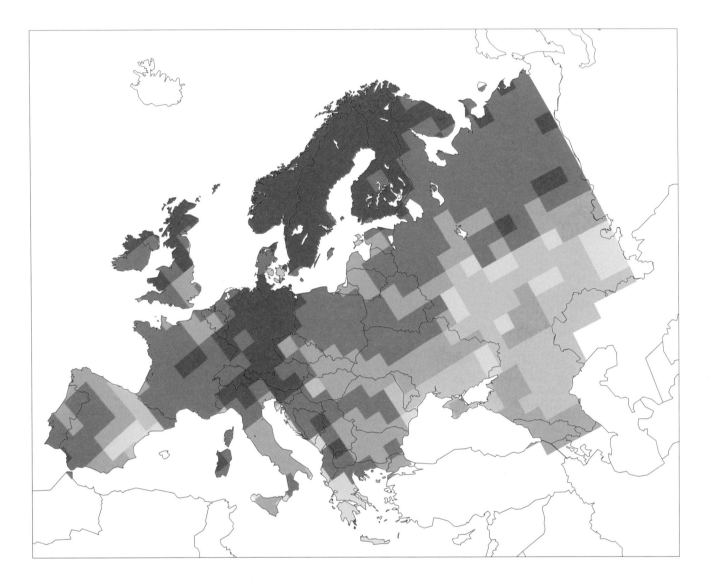

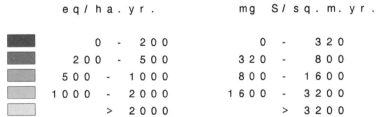

eq / ha . yr .	mg S/ sq . m . yr .
0 - 200	0 - 320
200 - 500	320 - 800
500 - 1000	800 - 1600
1000 - 2000	1600 - 3200
> 2000	> 3200

Source: RIVM-Coordination Center for Effects

The boundaries shown on this map do not imply official endorsement or acceptance by the United Nations.

Figure III.2. Map of critical loads of acidity (5 percentile)

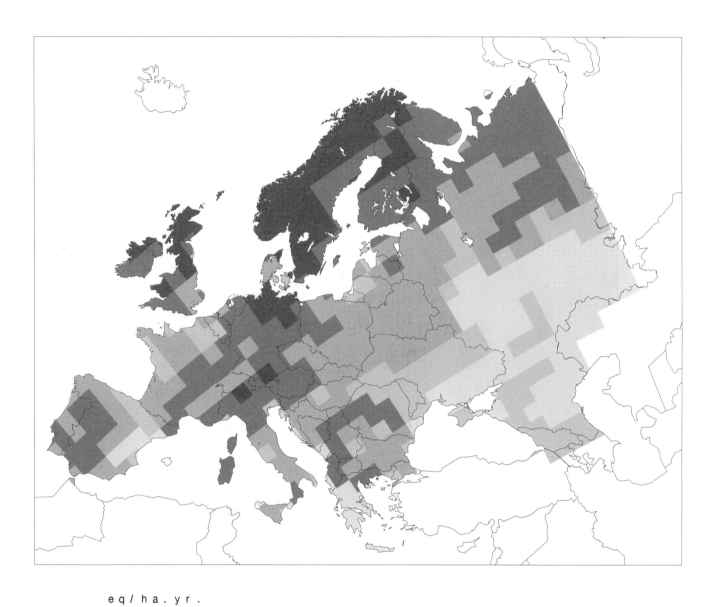

eq/ha.yr.

▓	0 - 200
▓	200 - 500
▓	500 - 1000
▓	1000 - 2000
▓	> 2000

Source: RIVM-Coordination Center for Effects

The boundaries shown on this map do not imply official endorsement or acceptance by the United Nations.

Figure IV.1.   Map of the emissions of sulphur in 1990
in the 50 km x 50 km EMEP grid system

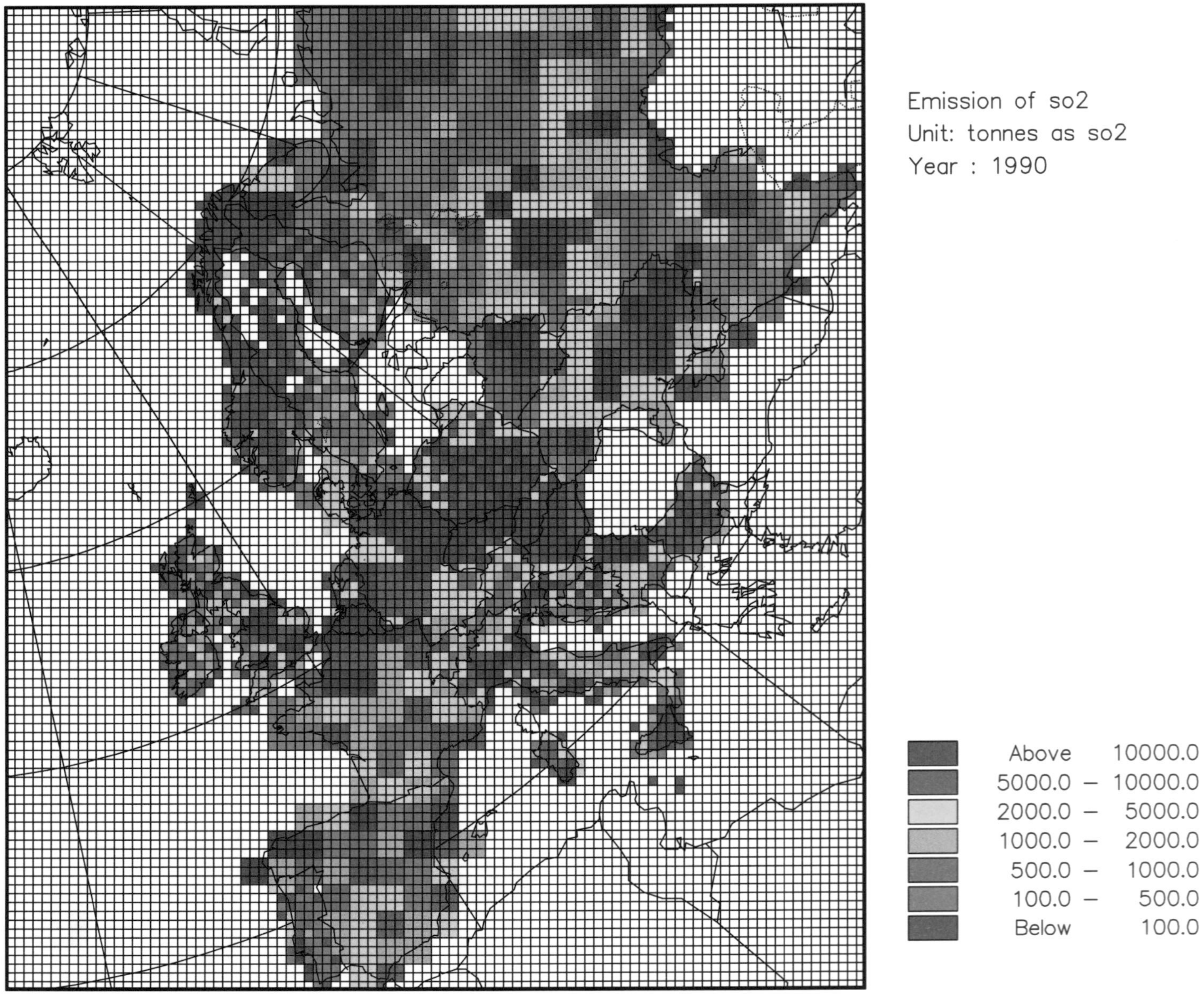

Emission of so2
Unit: tonnes as so2
Year : 1990

Above	10000.0
5000.0 —	10000.0
2000.0 —	5000.0
1000.0 —	2000.0
500.0 —	1000.0
100.0 —	500.0
Below	100.0

Source: Meteorological   Synthesizing
Centre-West. The Norwegian Meteorological Institute.

*The boundaries shown on this map do not imply
official endorsement or acceptance by the United
Nations.*

**Figure IV.2.   Map of the emissions of nitrogen oxides in 1990
in the 50 km x 50 km EMEP grid system**

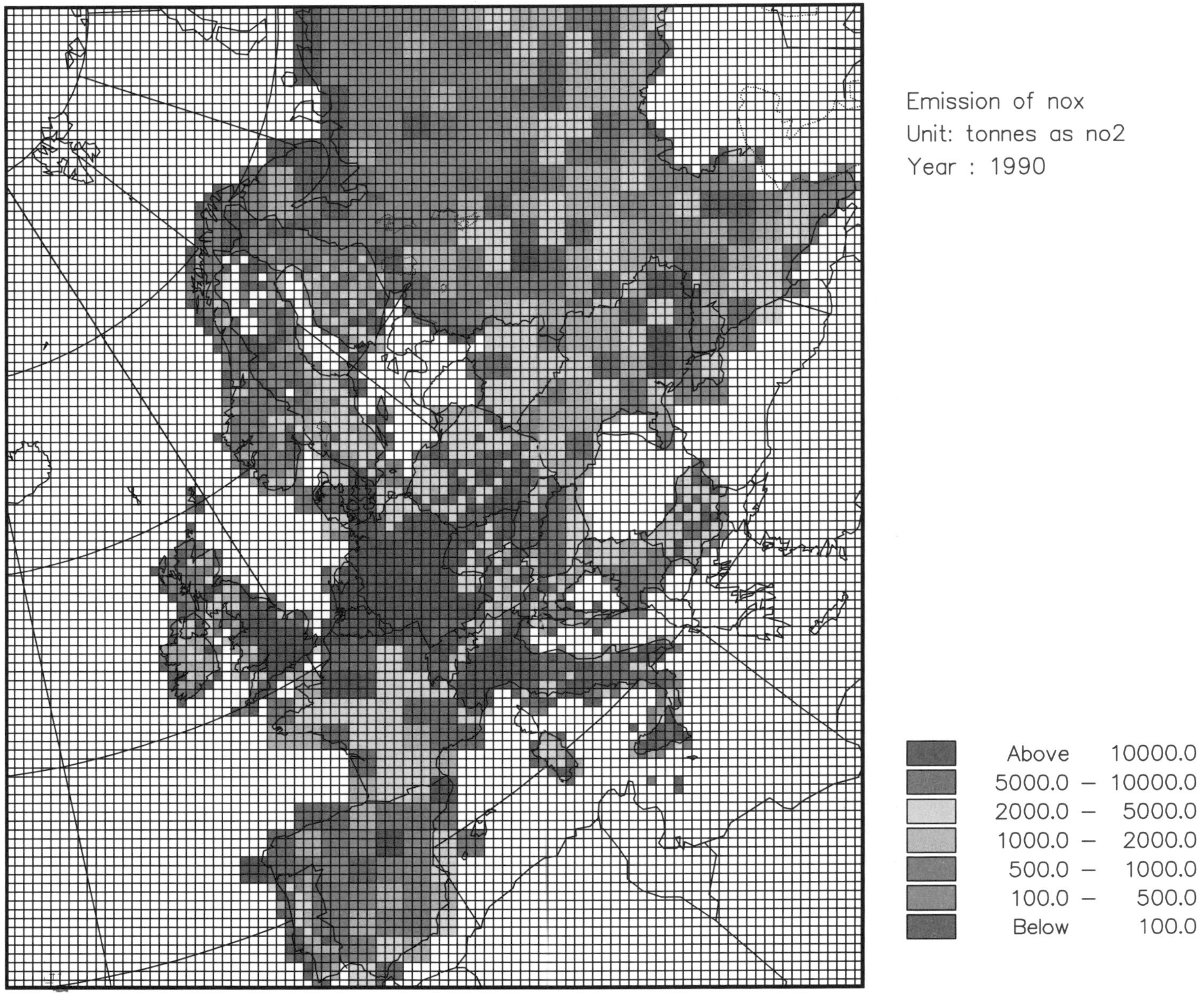

Emission of nox
Unit: tonnes as no2
Year : 1990

Above	10000.0
5000.0 —	10000.0
2000.0 —	5000.0
1000.0 —	2000.0
500.0 —	1000.0
100.0 —	500.0
Below	100.0

Source: Meteorological   Synthesizing
Centre-West. The Norwegian Meteorological Institute.

*The boundaries shown on this map do not imply
official endorsement or acceptance by the United
Nations.*

Figure IV.3.   Map of the emissions of ammonia in 1990 in the 50 km x 50 km EMEP grid system

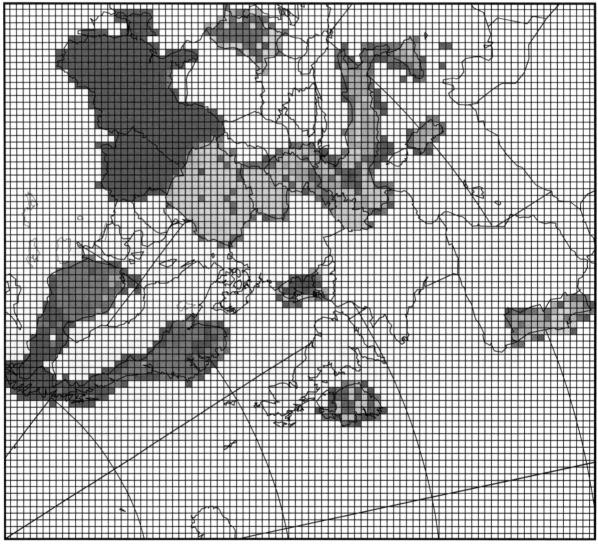

Emission of nh3
Unit: tonnes as nh3
Year : 1990

Above		10000.0
5000.0	—	10000.0
2000.0	—	5000.0
1000.0	—	2000.0
500.0	—	1000.0
100.0	—	500.0
Below		100.0

Source: Meteorological   Synthesizing
Centre-West. The Norwegian Meteorological Institute.

*The boundaries shown on this map do not imply
official endorsement or acceptance by the United
Nations.*

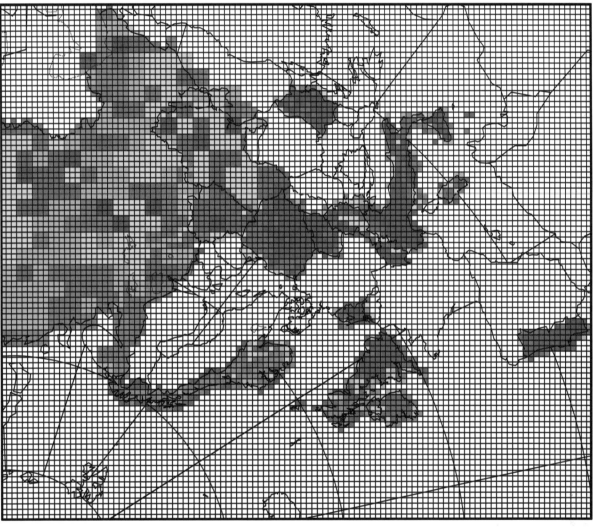

Figure IV.4. Map of the emissions of nmvocs in 1990 in the 50 km x 50 km EMEP grid system

Emission of nmvoc
Unit: tonnes
Year : 1990

Above	10000.0
5000.0 —	10000.0
2000.0 —	5000.0
1000.0 —	2000.0
500.0 —	1000.0
100.0 —	500.0
Below	100.0

Source: Meteorological Synthesizing Centre-West. The Norwegian Meteorological Institute.

The boundaries shown on this map do not imply official endorsement or acceptance by the United Nations.

Figure V. Sulphur emissions in the ECE region as a percentage of 1980 levels
(based on the latest data available, see table 1)

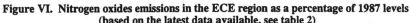

Figure VI. Nitrogen oxides emissions in the ECE region as a percentage of 1987 levels
(based on the latest data available, see table 2)

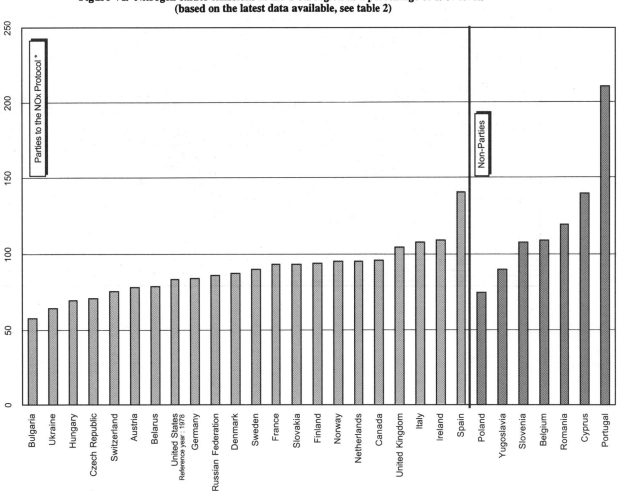

*For Liechtenstein, Luxembourg and the European Community no emission data have been received for the reference year.